MW00466327

"As the storm clouds of secularism threaten tod[ ]
is a growing need for young believers to know[ ]
as they do. In *12 Crucial Truths of the Christi*[ ]
addressed that need with clarity, completeness, and conviction. What is most impressive
about this magnificent work is that it addresses crucial doctrinal and apologetic issues
within a single volume. That alone is worth the price of the book."

—**J.P. Moreland**, distinguished professor of philosophy, Talbot
School of Theology; author of *The God Question*

"Truth has never been more aggressively denied and resisted than it is today, not only
in the world but also in the church. And there has never been a father-son team more
skillful at defending the truth in a spirit of grace than Josh and Sean McDowell. This
book is a godsend that will help young and old. I'm already planning on buying multiple copies to give away."

—**Randy Alcorn**, author of more than 60 books, including
Heaven, Truth, and *The Grace and Truth Paradox*

"With all the chaos in today's culture, it's easy for Christians to lose sight of the essentials
of the faith, but those foundational truths could not be more important. This book is
an indispensable resource for anyone who wants to get back to the basics of what Christians believe and why. It's accessible, practical, and full of valuable theological insights
for believers young and old."

—**Natasha Crain**, speaker, podcaster, and author of
four books, including *Faithfully Different*

"More than ever, followers of Jesus Christ must lovingly and boldly engage an increasingly deteriorating culture with a biblical worldview. Dynamic father-son duo Josh and
Sean McDowell have provided to the church of our Lord Jesus Christ a compelling, credible, and accessible answer to this urgent need. I fully recommend *12 Crucial Truths of
the Christian Faith*."

—**Dr. Mark Yarbrough**, president, Dallas Theological Seminary

"In *12 Crucial Truths of the Christian Faith*, my friends Josh and Sean McDowell explore
the core foundational tenets of Christianity, delivering 12 easily digestible 'theology 101'
teachings that reaffirm our faith and give us firm footing for knowing what we believe
and why. This much-needed resource shares the framework of our faith that should be
ingrained in every believer and lived out in relationship with others."

—**Dr. Tony Evans**, president, The Urban Alternative, and
senior pastor, Oak Cliff Bible Fellowship

"Josh and Sean have created a great apologetics primer for our modern society. Their book *12 Crucial Truths of the Christian Faith* explains the eternal truths of Christianity from an apologetics perspective (i.e., giving reasons why we should believe each truth). However, it also goes beyond traditional theology/apologetic books by highlighting why these truths are important for today's biggest questions. The existence of God, the reliability of Scripture, and the humanity of Jesus are not just important concepts for understanding Christianity. Each of these truths ground other cultural issues—such as our identities as humans, sexuality, marriage, and our understanding of love—all hotly contested issues in our modern world. Essentially, this book gets beneath the theological and evidential questions and emphasizes what these truths mean for our *existential* questions. The pages are filled with stories from Josh's and Sean's childhood and parenting journeys, showing caregivers and mentors how to make these truths relevant to the needs of today's generation."

—**Hillary Morgan Ferrer**, president,
Mama Bear Apologetics

"Josh and Sean McDowell have done an incredible job of creating a definitive work on developing a biblical worldview while at the same time making it personal. Just like other resources written by them, this will be a classic and the go-to book to help us understand how these 12 essential truths are keys to our faith. What I like so much about the McDowells is this doesn't read like a stodgy theology book, but rather a book filled with life-changing information presented in a very practical and readable manner."

—**Jim Burns**, PhD, president, HomeWord,
author of *Doing Life with Your Adult Children: Keep
Your Mouth Shut and the Welcome Mat Out*

"Wow! Josh and Sean have written a book that has it all: theology and apologetics marinated in heartfelt devotions that will help you apply *12 Crucial Truths of the Christian Faith* to your life. Highly recommended in this age of skepticism and confusion!"

—**Dr. Frank Turek**, author and president
of CrossExamined.org

"In many ways this book is Josh and Sean McDowell's crowning work! I have long been a fan of both authors (Josh has been one of the greatest influences in my life!), but *12 Crucial Truths of the Christian Faith* is the embodiment of their lives' effort. This book is apologetics made practical, but it is far more. It is apologetics made relational. I was challenged and encouraged on every page."

—**Skip Heitzig**, author of *The Bible from 30,000 Feet*,
pastor of Calvary Church, Albuquerque

"Josh and Sean McDowell are a big reason books on apologetics and worldview are said to represent the fastest-growing segments of Christian publishing. These authors are to be commended for serving the needs of a public more spiritually hungry than ever and who are seeking solid answers for their questions about God.

Their newest book, *12 Crucial Truths of the Christian Faith*, is a must read for many reasons. This work amply covers topics that are core to what Christianity *is*, but which are rarely addressed by apologetics writers. From the nature of truth to explanations of the Trinity, and from inspiring insights about Christ's coming to His ascension, *12 Crucial Truths of the Christian Faith* will benefit all who open its pages. For decades, apologetics books bearing the name 'McDowell' have truly represented the best in compelling scholarship and trustworthy content—and this volume is no exception."

—**Dr. Alex McFarland**, director, Biblical Worldview and Apologetics, Charis Bible College, Woodland Park, Colorado

"People are looking for meaning and purpose in life like never before in my lifetime. How does one find hope for the future in a world that believes there is no such thing as truth? Josh and Sean McDowell know that the only thing that gives us true purpose in life is found in the Christian faith. Josh and Sean uncover the beauty of the Christian faith by stating and clearly explaining 12 truths of Christianity. These truths will lead believers to develop an authentic biblical worldview and cause them to live their lives with purpose and hope. This book is a must read for every believer, both young and old."

—**Dr. Glen Schultz**, founder and director, Kingdom Education Ministries

"The apologetics works of father/son writing duo Josh and Sean McDowell have a special place in my heart and on my bookshelf. They communicate biblical truth in a way that makes sense to non-theologians like me. Among their works, *12 Crucial Truths of the Christian Faith* will now have a special place. Josh and Sean let us into their lives through vulnerable stories of joy and pain, all while making the biblical and logical case for 12 central truths of the Christian faith. This book is a key to unlocking the secret of how to communicate truth in a relational way. I believe it will inspire believers and nonbelievers alike."

—**Jeff Myers**, PhD, president Summit Ministries

"Josh McDowell's ministry has changed my family and my life. Witnessing the legacy carried on by his son, Sean, shows that Josh has practiced what he's preached. Many people say that the next generation is our future—but they won't be our future unless we make them our present. My friends Josh and Sean McDowell understand this and teach us how to prioritize faith and the next generation in *12 Crucial Truths of the Christian Faith*. Go get your copy now!"

—**Nick Hall**, evangelist, founder and president of Pulse

"If you want to know why you believe what you believe and how it matters for your life and relationships, you need to read *12 Crucial Truths of the Christian Faith* by Josh and Sean McDowell. This book will show you how to experience the essentials of a relevant faith based on the story of God's creation, incarnation, and re-creation. You will discover how these 12 truths can transform your perspective, your purpose, and your passion for God and others."

—Reverend Samuel Rodriguez, author of
From Survive to Thrive: Live a Holy, Healed, Healthy, Happy, Humble, Hungry, and Honoring Life

JOSH McDOWELL
& SEAN McDOWELL

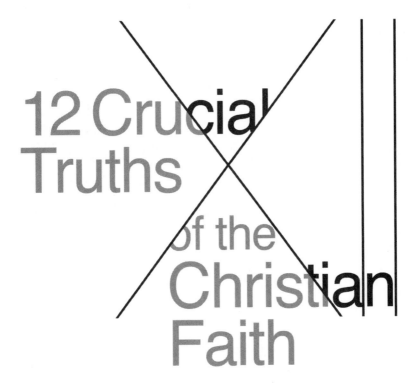

12 Crucial Truths of the Christian Faith

HARVEST HOUSE PUBLISHERS
EUGENE. OREGON

Cover design by Studio Gearbox
Interior design by KUHN Design Group

The material in this book has been abridged and updated from *The Unshakable Truth* ®, copyright © 2010 by Josh McDowell Ministry and Sean McDowell.

Every effort was made to correctly attribute authorship to sources quoted. If any further acknowledgment needs to be made, please contact us, and we will provide the correct attribution in the next printing.

For bulk, special sales, or ministry purchases, please call 1-800-547-8979. Email: Customerservice@hhpbooks.com

This logo is a federally registered trademark of the Hawkins Children's LLC. Harvest House Publishers, Inc., is the exclusive licensee of this trademark.

12 Crucial Truths of the Christian Faith
Copyright © 2010, 2023 by Josh McDowell Ministry and Sean McDowell
Published by Harvest House Publishers
Eugene, Oregon 97408
www.harvesthousepublishers.com

ISBN 978-0-7369-8702-8 (pbk)
ISBN 978-0-7369-8703-5 (eBook)

Library of Congress Control Number: 2023938658

Printed in the United States of America

23 24 25 26 27 28 29 30 31 / LB / 10 9 8 7 6 5 4 3 2 1

ACKNOWLEDGMENTS

A work of this magnitude is not completed without long hours and extensive collaboration with many people. We wish to recognize the following individuals for their valuable contribution to this book.

Dave Bellis, my (Josh's) longtime friend and colleague, for laying the foundation for this book via *The Unshakable Truth*. In many respects, Dave could be considered a "third author," and we are deeply grateful for his original contribution.

Jason Carlson and Mark Fitter for their insightful analysis regarding the theological perspective presented in the book. Our thanks to Casey Luskin for his help on the chapter on God's existence.

We are grateful for the staff at Josh McDowell Ministry: Matthew Tingblad for his tireless work in shoring up the section on the reliability of the Bible. Duane Zook for seeing *The Unshakable Truth* as "a diamond in the rough" and pushing this revision forward. Dave Bottorff for his dedication to the project and doing all the things necessary to bring this book to completion.

Thanks to the incredible people at Harvest House: Bob Hawkins Jr. and LaRae Weikert for their vision for this work and for all the patience and encouragement they gave us. Kim Moore, who provided invaluable overall leadership to the publishing process. This book, *12 Crucial Truths of the Christian Faith*, is a slight abridgment and update from our 2010 book *The Unshakable Truth*. Our appreciation to Kris Bearss for her extensive editorial help and guidance in making this happen. And to the team at Harvest House who have been involved in the many details required to bring a book to press—we thank you.

Josh McDowell
Sean McDowell

CONTENTS

Introduction

The Real Meaning of Truth

Nearly 20 centuries ago, a high government official, trained in politics and the law, asked a question that has echoed all the way into the twenty-first century.

Imagine Pontius Pilate, then the Roman governor of Judea, standing in his elaborate palace, magisterially bedecked. He posed a set of serious questions to the man who stood shackled between two soldiers.

"Are you the King of the Jews?" Pilate asked. The prisoner was accused of sedition.

This prisoner, unlike most, stood straight in the presence of the governor and looked him in the eyes as he spoke. "I am not an earthly king...My kingdom is not of this world."

"You *are* a king then?" the governor said.

"*You* say that I am a king," the prisoner answered, aware his interrogator was in a prickly political position, "and you are right." He looked at the politician with eyes that seemed to read not only his face but his soul. "I was born for that purpose," he continued, "and I came to bring truth to the world. All who love the truth recognize what I say is true."

Pilate responded, "What *is* truth?"

Imagine for a moment you are in that hall with Pilate and his prisoner. Imagine the words of the governor's question echoing off the marbled walls. Imagine the expression on Pilate's face as he posed the question, scornful at first, then turning serious when the answer did not come quickly.

Imagine the governor's thoughts: *Who is this man? Why does he gaze at me so?* And the prisoner's thoughts: *Have I not just told you? I came to bring truth to the world. Pilate, you are looking at the answer to your own question: I am the truth.*[1]

TRUTH IN RELATIONSHIP

On that day in his Jerusalem palace when he met Jesus, Pilate was not merely discussing the truth; he was literally looking at it. Truth was standing before him, clothed in human flesh! Just days earlier, Jesus had told his disciple Philip, "I am the way, the truth, and the life" (John 14:6). He was saying truth is a person to relate to, "the way" is a person to interact with and follow, and he is the only true source of life. Truth, a way of living, and life itself is embodied in the person of God. And the means to obtain the truth, the way, and the life is through a relationship with Jesus.

To explain or present a biblical worldview and the truths of the faith outside of relationship is to distort and invite error into Christianity. Jesus wasn't simply trying to correct the theology of the Jewish leaders with his teachings. Neither was he launching a new philosophy of the Jewish religion. He was offering a way to restore God's original design for a world gone mad. He was offering the means to restore the God-human relationship that had been broken by sin. Relationship was key. And it still is.

A number of years ago Dartmouth Medical School commissioned a scientific study of young people. The project, which was called "Hardwired to Connect," analyzed the results of more than 260 studies of youth. The report stated that 100 percent of all the studies they analyzed showed that from the moment a baby is born, his or her brain is physically, biologically, and chemically hardwired to connect with others in relationships.[2] That shouldn't surprise us, since we were created in the image of a relational God for the purpose of relationships. In fact, the healthier we are relationally, the more receptive we will be to God's relational truth.

Author and speaker Mark Matlock made this observation about the students with whom he was ministering:

> Some of my students were incredibly intelligent and even showed an interest in Christ, but they never seemed to make a breakthrough.

I was trying to convince them of the evidence of Christ, and they just couldn't get it. Looking back, I realize many of these students were emotionally wounded (or even abandoned) individuals who simply could not connect to what I was saying.[3]

It stands to reason that if truth is intrinsically relational in nature and we experience struggles or dysfunctions in our relational life, it will be more difficult to receive the truth. But the other side of this coin is that receiving the truth in all its relational meaning can overcome the problems in our relationships. Truth not only points out our wrong and corrects us; it brings relational healing as well, because truth is a person who lovingly cares for us.

As relational beings we think *and* we feel. We have both a mind and a heart. Truth was meant to be proclaimed in the context of relationships so it would reach both our intellect and our emotions. This is the kind of proclamation Paul referred to when he depicted the process that brought the Thessalonians to a vibrant faith: "We loved you so much that we were delighted to share with you *not only* the gospel of God but our lives as well, because you had become so dear to us" (1 Thessalonians 2:8 NIV).

Paul was passing on the faith relationally just as Christ had modeled it. The truth he proclaims to us appeals to our minds by pointing out our dilemma (sin and death). But it goes on to demonstrate a love that ultimately provides a solution—a way to regain a relationship with God. We live in a broken and relationally disconnected culture. Each of us has relational and emotional struggles. "Truth only"—a set of facts that appeal solely to the intellect—will not solve our emotional and relational issues. Rather, it is truth within the context of relationships that we can believe with our minds and experience with our emotions. It is God's penetrating truth that reveals our true condition, loves and accepts us for who we are, and makes provision to freely forgive us. Relational truth is what each of us needs and craves.

TRUTH IN CONTEXT

As a teenager, I (Josh) sincerely wanted the answers to *Who am I? Why am I here? Where am I going?* I certainly didn't find answers at home. My father was the town drunk. I grew up watching in fear and horror as my father beat my mother and wreaked havoc at home. I experienced sexual abuse from a man named Wayne, whom my parents hired as a part-time cook and house-keeper. I eventually told my mother about what Wayne was doing, but she didn't believe me. I can't describe to you the pain of abandonment I felt when my mother refused to believe me. Also, growing up I never remember my father saying that he loved me. The only love I ever felt was from a struggling, abused mother who died suddenly when I was a teenager. So my home was not a place to find answers.

In the small Michigan community where I grew up, everyone seemed to be into religion, so my search started there. I really got into the church scene. But I must have picked the wrong church because I felt worse inside the church than I did outside. So I gave up on the church to provide me any answers.

Then I thought that education might have the answers, so I enrolled in a university. I soon became unpopular with my professors because I hounded them with so many questions. But I learned that my professors had just as many problems, frustrations, and unanswered questions as I did.

Next, I tried prestige. I thought I could find a noble cause, commit to it, and in the process become well known. So I ran for various student offices. It was great at first. People got to know me, and I enjoyed spending the university's money getting the speakers to campus that I wanted. I also liked the idea of spending the students' money for throwing parties. But the prestige thing soon wore off. I would wake up on Monday morning, usually with a headache from the night before, dreading the next five days. I endured Monday through Friday just to experience the party nights on the weekend. But every Monday brought the meaningless cycle all over again.

About that time I noticed a small group of people who seemed different from the others. They appeared to know who they were and where they were going. They had a clear set of convictions about what they believed. And what really stood out was that they appeared to be genuinely happy. Their happiness and joy weren't like mine. I was happy only when things were going great—when I was having "fun." But they seemed to possess an inner source of joy that I longed for.

I befriended these people and tried to figure out what they knew that I didn't. One day I asked one of the women in the group what made her so different. She had told me before that she hadn't always been this way, but she had changed. So I asked her, "What changed your life?"

Her answer shocked me. She used two words as a solution, two words I never thought I'd hear at the university. She simply said, "Jesus Christ." I immediately told her I was fed up with religion and the church and was certain it wasn't a solution. This woman shot back, "I didn't say *religion,* I said *Jesus Christ.*"

She and her friends went on to explain that a relationship with God through Jesus Christ offered what I would come to know as a biblical truth. They told me it was Christ and his worldview—seeing everything from a biblical perspective—that would answer all the questions I had. They didn't offer to walk me through a shallow prayer or get me to go to church. What they did was challenge me to intellectually examine the claims of Jesus and to determine, in essence, whether God's worldview written in Scripture was credible. I accepted their challenge out of pride. I wanted to prove Christianity was a farce.

What I discovered was that I was the farce. My quest for happiness and meaning was found in Christ.

Most people who know my testimony assume I came to Christ through the intellectual route. They think my examination of the evidence of Christ's deity, his resurrection, and the reliability of Scripture convinced me that God had spoken—and therefore I trusted in Christ. The convincing evidence certainly got my attention, but it was God's love that drew me to him. I saw love between a group of Jesus-followers who devoted themselves to God and one another. God demonstrated his love to me through them. By the power of the Holy Spirit, my life was transformed through a relationship with God. I discovered a whole new way of thinking and living that empowered me to live out truth from his perspective.

WE HAVE A MODEL IN FORMING
OUR BIBLICAL WORLDVIEW

For us as humans, that relational context is key. The early church provides the ideal model for how the relational truth of God was imparted so effectively to others. Christianity was birthed from Judaism. Jesus' immediate followers were Jewish men and women who had been raised in a Hebraic model of education. Today practically all modern education in North America, including that of most churches and Christian schools, employs a form of teaching based on a Hellenistic model. Essentially, this Hellenistic approach is to present a student with rational and logical constructs of information that he or she is required to absorb intellectually. To determine if the subject matter has in fact been absorbed, students are asked to regurgitate the information back to the teacher. This is called testing. If the student can accurately repeat the information, he or she passes the course, and the pupil is said to have been "taught."

The Hebraic model of education is quite different. Its goal is not mere memorization of repeatable facts; the goal is for the truth to become one with the pupil to the point that it is lived out. Under this approach, truth is to be learned by practicing it in relationship with others. This means we have not necessarily "learned" a truth simply because we can repeat it to a mentor. It is learned only when it is reflected in our lives in relationship to God, to others, or to our environment. In this educational model, the testing isn't in whether we have the information correctly stuffed into our heads, but rather how the truth has transformed our attitude and behavior.

If we see Christianity simply as a worldview to be discussed, debated, and proven on a rational basis rather than demonstrated on a relational and transformational basis, we will undoubtedly not see Christianity as God intended. Nor will we be passing on the faith effectively to the next generation.

Early in the second century the church firmly established a relational model enabling individuals to embrace the faith and pass it on to others. By AD 130 Justin Martyr declared the Christian faith revolved around a continuing cycle of believing, belonging, and behaving. These three components were not compartmentalized into three disciplines; they were seen as a whole—integrated and continuous.

Believing or knowing the truth is a process of understanding who God is and how we relate to him and others. This truth we believe leads naturally to a transformation of our lives in relationship with God. This is where belonging comes in. Entering into a relationship with God bonds us with others who share that relationship, enabling us to experience a sense of belonging.

The apostle talked about the "unity in our faith" by which "the whole body is fitted together perfectly. As each part does its own special work, it helps the other parts grow, so that the whole body is healthy and growing and full of love" (Ephesians 4:13, 16). We know the truth, and then we become that truth in relationship with God and others in the body of Christ.

The truth process does not stop with believing and belonging. It continues on and affects our behavior. When we become intimate with the truth, it transforms our very being and how we relate to others in community with them. The result is godly living. Truth is to be lived out.

The early church saw this as an organic cycle of bringing new converts to spiritual maturity and equipping them to pass on the faith to others. They modeled before their children and a needy world what it meant to be in relationship with God, both as individuals and as a community of believers. A sense of belonging was established. They would walk their children and new converts through an intentional, life-changing process by instructing them to know and believe the truth handed down by the apostles. They taught them to live out that truth like devoted followers of Jesus and initiated them into an active engagement of the world around them.

This process naturally embedded within each follower of Christ a biblical worldview. The Christian faith was then and still is *an integrated and organic cycle of intimately knowing the truth, being the truth in relationship with God and others, and living the truth before the world around us, starting in our own families.*

This process of forming a biblical worldview and passing on our faith can still work in the twenty-first century. But we do face some challenges, both in dealing with influences in our own lives and influences in the society we're part of. In order to address those challenges, let's look individually at each of the three elements that make up this cycle we've just outlined and consider how to make them work in the present day.

KNOW THE TRUTH

Picture a small-group Bible study. The group leader, who has just finished reading a Scripture passage, turns to a group member and asks, "Pam, what does this verse mean?"

Pam, a professed Christian, pauses to reflect on the passage. "Well," she begins after a few moments of careful consideration, "what this verse means to me is…"

Chances are, most of us wouldn't even detect the subtle shift in meaning reflected in Pam's use of the words *to me*. But the importance of those two tiny words must not be underestimated. They are indicative of a condition that exists among most Christians today. Most Christians are not looking to the biblical text in order to know *the* truth; they are actually looking for "their truth." The vast majority in our culture, including many professed Christians, say there is no objective moral truth. In a world with no objective moral truth, one cannot claim any specific truth is to be found in a given Bible verse. Therefore, the best we can do with the Bible is use it as a foil to determine a personal "truth" that meshes with our own way of thinking and thus has meaning only "to me."

Many pastors and church small-group leaders have become group facilitators rather than teachers of scriptural truth. It's not so much because these leaders are not intending to share the meaning of scriptural truth—many are. The problem is many people simply hear the truth through their own filter, which, strongly influenced by a postmodern culture, tells them all truth is subjectively and personally determined.

Awhile back, I (Sean) was speaking at a youth rally on the topic of sexuality. In the middle of my talk a girl interrupted and echoed the five words I've so often heard from young people: "Who are you to judge?" She was saying I had no right to make moral judgments, because truth is subjective—that is, it was "my truth," which makes all views equal. This girl, like most of us, has grown up in a culture of moral relativism that prides itself on accepting many truths. We have been told we need to be tolerant of all beliefs and to think that no one way is better than another. In fact, the moment anyone claims to have *the truth,* he or she is labeled as arrogant, bigoted, and judgmental.

Truth, however, is not personal and subjective, as so many people believe. It is based on objective reality.

Greg Koukl, president of Stand to Reason, has pointed out that a person could believe with great conviction that ice cream controls diabetes. But it doesn't change the objective fact that insulin is the controlling factor. The same is true for morality. Even if someone believed rape was right, it would still be wrong.

Moral truth isn't something you or I create or decide for ourselves. In fact, it isn't even something God decides. It is something he *is*. The basis of everything we call moral and right springs from the truth that resides in the character of the eternal God who is outside us, above us, and beyond us.

One of the appealing aspects of deciding your own truth is that you can embrace it as something that is personally and experientially yours. But discovering a truth outside yourself is even more personal and experiential when you understand that Jesus is the truth—he is the exact representation of his Father God. And when the person of truth—Jesus—enters our lives, he is there to transform us into a representation of himself.

I realize, of course, Christians can talk all day about how we know the truth because we have experienced Jesus personally. Yet we cannot expect that claim to convince others that what we proclaim as truth is actually true. They can simply claim it might be true for us, but that doesn't make it true for everyone.

Unless that truth can be proven or demonstrated to be true, we cannot expect others to get on board with belief. And that is where knowing why we believe something is true comes into play.

Jesus wanted his followers to believe in him for who he claimed to be, but he didn't want them to believe in him blindly. He wanted them to be confident that what he was asking them to believe was true. So he appealed to the evidence. "Don't you believe that I am in the Father and the Father is in me?" he asked. Then he urged them to "at least believe because of what you have seen me do" (John 14:10-11).

As we said above, truth is more than just a set of facts; it is relational and emotional. It brings joy. But it is impossible for our hearts to rejoice in what our minds reject. That is why we need to know not only *what we believe* but *why we believe it.*

The Bible repeatedly invites us to examine why a truth is true so we can form our convictions. The apostle John, who had firsthand knowledge of the truth, wrote, "Jesus' disciples saw him do many other miraculous signs besides the ones recorded in this book. But these are written so that you may believe that Jesus is the Messiah, the Son of God, and that by believing in him you will have life" (John 20:30-31). In other words, John recorded evidence that confirmed Jesus to be the one true God so we could know the truth with confidence and deep conviction.

So as you explore each essential truth of the faith in this book, you will equally examine both the truth you are to believe as well as the evidence for why you can believe it with confidence. Of course, no matter how convincing the evidence is, you still must exercise faith. For example, I (Sean) didn't have exhaustive knowledge about Stephanie before I married her. I couldn't know 100 percent she was the person of integrity I firmly believed her to be. But I did have sufficient evidence to make a wise, informed decision on the moral character of the person I was dating. And now that we have been happily married for more than two decades, I thank God we each took that step of reasonable faith.

You will seldom, if ever, have exhaustive evidence, but you can find sufficient evidence to establish that what you believe is credible and objectively true. That is what knowledgeable faith does—it rests its case on sufficient evidence. Noted author and apologist J.P. Moreland aptly defines faith as "a trust in what we have reason to believe is true."[4] A faith rooted in truth that we have reason to believe is objectively true will ground us both intellectually and experientially. We can then offer to others a faith that appeals both to the heart and the mind.

BE THE TRUTH

Simply knowing what we believe and why we believe it is not, in itself, sufficient. The truth we believe must also become the very core of who we are. Buying into the Christian faith involves *being a living representation of the truth.*

We McDowells had a friend named Frank; his son was called Frankie. Frank was a man of few words; so was his son. Frank appeared most comfortable when his hands were thrust into his pants pockets; Frankie was no different. Frank was a skilled mechanic; Frankie was fascinated by mechanical things. Not once did Frankie's father ever sit down with him to teach him these behaviors or interests. The son was a representation of his father due to sheer genetics and by simply being in relationship with his dad.

Being a representation of the truth is about allowing the truth of God to penetrate us so intimately that it transforms our very lives. "As the Spirit of the Lord works within us," Paul states, "we become more and more like him and reflect his glory even more" (2 Corinthians 3:18). The purpose of Christ's Spirit—the truth—coming into our lives is to become like the truth-giver. Frankie had the DNA of his father, so it was natural for him to become like his father. When we receive the Holy Spirit of truth, the apostle Peter says we "share in his divine nature" (2 Peter 1:4). Metaphorically speaking, God's very DNA is implanted in us, and a process of transformation begins as we "become conformed to the image of His Son" (Romans 8:29 NASB).

There was a college student years ago, we'll call him Chad, who registered for all his classes and moved into a dorm room. Chad was working himself through school and was on a tight budget. So for breakfast, lunch, and supper all he could afford to eat was cheese and crackers in his dorm room. Day in and day out, his meals consisted of nothing but mouse food. After a couple of weeks he grew extremely tired of cheese and crackers, so he decided to splurge for one meal and eat at the college cafeteria. He loaded up his tray with meat and potatoes, salad, vegetables, and a couple desserts. When he came to the cashier he asked, "How much for all this?" The cashier responded, "Do you have your student ID?" "Yes," Chad answered. "Well, it won't cost you anything. All your meals were included in your registration."

From the first day of school Chad had had full access to all the food he could eat. Yet he failed to understand how the college meal program was applicable to him. There are many believers who have knowledge of God's truth and may even know why they believe it, but for some reason they fail to understand how that truth is relevant to their lives. Consequently, the power of that truth isn't appropriated to their life. So in the chapters that follow, as we discover step-by-step what we believe and why we believe it, we will also uncover the relevant and transforming nature of each truth when it is applied to our specific needs. That application leads to our "brand-new nature...continually being renewed as [we] learn more and more about Christ, who created this new nature within [us]" (Colossians 3:10).

When we know the truth and become a representation of the truth, we are not only beginning to embrace a biblical worldview, but we are in a position to effectively pass it on to others. Someone has said, "We teach what we know, we impart who we are." And if we become a living representation of God's truth, we will demonstrate it in our lives—we will live it.

LIVE THE TRUTH

John the disciple of Jesus said, "Let us stop just saying we love each other; let us really show it by our actions. It is by our actions that we know we are living in the truth" (1 John 3:18-19). Truth is to be lived, and when it is lived, it also becomes an example to others.

Lest you give up hope before you even begin, let us be quick to say that being a representation of the truth doesn't mean we must live perfect lives. I (Sean) remember a time when I was still living with my parents, and my dad was in a heated argument with Mom. To be honest, Dad was being pretty awful. At one point he threw a folder down on the table and said, "I'm out of here." He stormed out the door and drove off. I remember thinking, *Man, is he ever ticked.*

I, along with my sisters, went back to doing whatever we had been doing prior to the "Josh explosion." But it wasn't long before Dad was back and called us all in for a meeting. In front of us all he told my mom how wrong he had been and how sorry he was that he had hurt her, and he sought her forgiveness. He turned to each of us kids and told us how disrespectful he had been to our mother, and he sought our forgiveness too. Now, my dad's earlier actions were far from a perfect model of Christlikeness, but he was, nonetheless, a great model of one who was truly following Christ. How? When he realized his offense and sought forgiveness, he was being sensitive to the convicting Spirit of God. My dad was a model of a person who sincerely desires to be conformed to the image of Christ.

Believe it or not, those around us need to see us fail and humbly seek forgiveness. The Spirit of truth through his Word is there "to make us realize what is wrong in our lives. It straightens us out and teaches us to do what is right" (2 Timothy 3:16). Being a living reflection of the truth in a fallen world means we sometimes mess up, but when we do, we must realize it and make amends. The great apostle Paul said, "I don't mean to say that I have already achieved these things or that I have already reached perfection! But I keep working toward that day when I will finally be all that Christ Jesus saved me for and wants me to be" (Philippians 3:12).

So as we cover 12 truths of the faith in the pages that follow, we will not only discover: 1) what it is we believe, but 2) why we believe it; then 3) how these truths are relevant to life and how they transform us internally; and finally, 4) how we can live truth out so that it can be imparted to those we love. As these truths take root in our innermost being, we will be reflecting Christ's way, his truth, his life—living out biblical truth.

GOD EXISTS

As a young teenager, I (Josh) didn't like who I was—the son of the town drunk. I hated my father and everything he stood for, and that impacted what I thought about myself in a significant way. As I grew older and left home, I took with me the puzzling question of "Who am I really?"

As a skeptic, I questioned the existence of a personal God. So I didn't have a definitive answer of who I was meant to be as God's creation. Yet as I would stare up at the stars at night I wondered how everything got here. Planet Earth orbited the sun in just one galaxy among billions that filled deep space. I felt so small and alone in such a vast universe. And to be honest I secretly hoped there was some Intelligent Being out there who could help me understand who I was and what my life was all about.

DOES GOD EXIST?

We do live on a planet in a vast universe. Our home on earth seems so insignificant and small, suspended as it is in the vastness of space. Is God out there somewhere in the vastness? Think about space for a moment. It seems to stretch on and on without any possibility of ending. When we try to imagine the size even of the known universe, it's impossible to truly comprehend. But let's try.

Why Does Anything Exist?

The expanses of the universe are so immense that we measure them using the light-year, which is the distance light travels in 365 days. Light travels at the speed of 186,282 miles per second. In a year, that distance, multiplied out and rounded off, increases to almost 6 trillion miles. To put that in a perspective we can almost grasp, it takes a sunbeam just over 8 minutes to travel the 93 million miles from the sun to earth. So what is the size of the observable universe in terms of light-years?

Scientists say matter is spread over a space at least 93 billion light-years across. Our galaxy is one of an estimated 2 trillion galaxies in the observable universe, has somewhere between 100 and 400 million stars, and is roughly 100,000 light-years across. Our Milky Way's largest galactic neighbor, the Andromeda Galaxy, is approximately 2.5 million light-years away.[1] As finite beings we simply cannot grasp such distances, such magnitude.

Thinking about time presents a similar dilemma. It's impossible to conceive of a beginning or an ending of time because the only thing we can imagine before or after time is just more time. Since everything we experience has a starting and an ending, the concept of eternity is incomprehensible to us.

Time and the vastness of space are for the most part mysteries to us. Could it all be here just by chance? Where did it all come from?

Another great mystery is the three-pound wonderment inside your skull. Your eyes blink and follow the words on this page. The words are symbols with specific meaning that string together thoughts, which you can understand as you read. Meanwhile, your heart pumps; you inhale and exhale; your body is digesting and processing food.

All these involuntary muscle movements are controlled by the miracle organ called the brain. Your ability to walk, run, sit, sleep, touch, see, hear, smell, taste, and feel every type of emotion is being processed right now through over 100 billion nerve cells called neurons.

Your neurons gather and transmit electrochemical signals that tell your muscles to move the parts of your body so they will accomplish what you want them to do. These neurons are like the gates and wires in a computer—only immeasurably more complex. And they are tiny. How small? Medical doctors Joe McIlhaney and Freda McKissic Bush explain, "About 30,000 fit on the head of a pin. Yet if the neurons in just one human brain (about 100 billion) were placed end to end, they would circle the earth four times." And the brain also has more than 100,000 trillion synaptic connections. This is why they conclude, "The human brain is, without question, the most complicated three-pound mass of matter in the known universe."[2]

If the brain is so complex, then how did it come to be? Where did you and your brain, the Milky Way Galaxy, and all that is in the universe come from? Why is there *something* in existence instead of nothing? What or who brought everything into being? And for what purpose?

An Impersonal Power?

Some would say all that exists was created by the universe itself and will one day be reabsorbed by the universe. In this view, an entity or being called God does not actually exist. God, they say, is a cosmic life force that includes all the substance of the universe. Nature and the idea of God are the same. This is called *pantheism*. Further, from this cosmic life force we are all empowered to be god and to be one with the universe. The classic phrase used to describe this belief is "God is all and all is God." This is the view of God that was propagated so effectively in the movie *Avatar*.

Some who disagree with pantheistic doctrine say that a supreme being who is not a part of the universe created everything that exists, but essentially this being is uninvolved in any further way with creation. This is the view of Deists, who typically reject most supernatural events (prophecy, miracles) and assert that God, "the Supreme Architect," has a plan for the universe that is not altered either by his intervention in the affairs of human life or by suspension of the natural laws of the universe.[3]

Those who hold to this Deist philosophy believe there is a God, but he is like a master clockmaker who designed the world, wound it up, and since then has let it run on its own. Someone with this view would not bother to pray to God for help in time of need or for strength to resist temptation. In this view, God is an impersonal being who has left us to make it on our own.

WHAT WE BELIEVE ABOUT GOD

Christians, however, believe a personal being existed before time and space as we know it. This being spoke the words "Let there be…" and by the power of his will all that exists came into being (Genesis 1:3). We believe those words came from the voice of a personal, infinite God who "created everything there is. Nothing exists that he didn't make" (John 1:3). We believe this God is the Intelligent Designer of all that exists.

The questions naturally arise: What is the nature of this God, is he knowable, and why did he create us? While a God with the power to create vast universes is beyond our comprehension in many ways, he is knowable to us finite creatures. How? We can know him truly, sufficiently, and with confidence because of *what he has revealed* about himself to us. For example, God is known to us by at least six characteristics.

God is eternal. "Eternal" means life without beginning or end. There was never a moment when God didn't exist, nor will he ever end. That is impossible for our minds to grasp. Moses could not understand it. He was out on the backside of the desert herding sheep when God showed up in a bush burning with flames that didn't consume it. When God sent him to tell the people of Israel he was going to deliver them out of Egypt, Moses said, "'They won't believe me. They will ask, "Which god are you talking about? What is his name?" Then what should I tell them?' God replied, 'I AM THE ONE WHO ALWAYS IS. Just tell them "I AM has sent me to you"'" (Exodus 3:13-14). The great I AM has no birthday and will have no funeral.

The prophet Isaiah said, "Don't you know that the LORD is the everlasting God, the Creator of all the earth? He never grows faint or weary. No one can measure the depths of his understanding" (Isaiah 40:28).

God is omnipotent. God is almighty and all-powerful. If he wants to do something that is not logically contradictory and consistent with his good character, he can do it.

Job said to God, "I know that you can do anything, and no one can stop you" (Job 42:2). King David said, "How great is our Lord! His power is absolute" (Psalm 147:5). The prophet Jeremiah said, "O Sovereign LORD! You have made the heavens and earth by your great power. Nothing is too hard for you" (Jeremiah 32:17). The eternal, never-ending God is also the ever-powerful God who can accomplish anything he desires.

God is omnipresent. God is ever-present. His presence encompasses all the galaxies. At the same time, he is with you right now right where you are. King David said, "I can never escape from your spirit! I can never get away from your presence! If I go up to heaven, you are there; if I go down to the place of the dead, you are there" (Psalm 139:7-8). Because we are finite beings it is hard to imagine a being who is everywhere-present, but this is a characteristic of God. "'Am I a God who is only in one place?' asks the Lord. 'Do they think I cannot see what they are doing? Can anyone hide from me? Am I not everywhere in all the heavens and earth?'" (Jeremiah 23:23-24). The ever-present God spans the reach of the universe and yet is there to hear you whisper a prayer.

God is immutable. By his very nature God can always be counted on because he will not change. The psalmist said the earth will perish, "but you [God] remain forever…you are always the same; your years never end" (Psalm 102:26-27). The writer of the book of Hebrews said, "Jesus Christ is the same yesterday, today, and forever" (Hebrews 13:8).

We can rest secure in a God who does not waver or lie. He will always do what he says he will do. "God is not a man, that he should lie. He is not a human, that he should change his mind. Has he ever spoken and failed to act? Has he ever promised and not carried it through?" (Numbers 23:19). The immutable God is worthy of our complete trust.

God is omniscient. God knows all. Everything past, present, and future, he knows. He has infinite knowledge. Speaking through the prophet Isaiah he declared, "I am God, and there is no one else like me. Only I can tell you what is going to happen even before it happens. Everything I plan will come to pass, for I do whatever I wish" (Isaiah 46:9-10). King David said, "O Lord, you have examined my heart and know everything about me" (Psalm 139:1). Such awesome knowledge is beyond us. Imagine the hard drives of a trillion computers filled with all the information known to humans…and it wouldn't even scratch the surface of God's knowledge.

God is personal. Even though he is the eternal, almighty, ever-present, unchanging, and all-knowing God, he is also a God who desires personal interaction. On one hand his power and awesome might is fearful, yet he is the "God who is passionate about his relationship with you" (Exodus 34:14).

This is actually what I (Josh) was searching for but didn't know it. To know the God of the universe in a personal way would answer so many questions as to who I was, why I was here, and where I was going. God is not an absentee

God who created the universe and then left it to its own devices. He is active and involved with his creation. He entered our world in the form of a human; at the moment of salvation he enters our lives in the form of his Holy Spirit; he answers our prayers and gives us strength through the Holy Spirit; he empowers us to resist temptation and wants to fulfill his purpose in our lives. He is a personal, interactive God who desires a relationship with his creation. Therefore:

> **We believe the truth that there is an infinite, personal God of the universe.**

The angel that spoke to Mary stated it well: "Nothing is impossible with God" (Luke 1:37). While he is infinite in his existence, power, presence, and knowledge, he wants a relationship with each of us personally. That's what is so amazing. A God who needs nothing and who can do anything and everything still wants and desires to have an intimate, personal relationship with you and me! That is the God who is and always will be, the God you and I can believe in with confidence.

EVIDENCE FOR GOD'S EXISTENCE

We may *believe* a personal God exists, but can we *know* that he exists? It's not possible to offer absolute proof of God by having him materialize before a large crowd and demonstrate his omnipotence, omnipresence, omniscience, and glory for all to see.

Even if that happened, many people would not accept it as proof. In fact, God *did* show up in human form and demonstrated his deity with miracles and prophecies. People still doubted he was God.

God has made himself known for those who want to seek him.

Yet, we are not left without sufficient evidence of God's existence. More than enough convincing data is available for anyone who wants to examine it. God has made himself known for those who want to seek him. Jesus said, "Seek and you will find" (Luke 11:9 NIV). There is evidence of him all around us. His fingerprints can be seen anywhere you look—from the vastness of the universe to the tiniest microscopic cell. Let's look at just four evidences or arguments for the existence of God.

1. THE KALAM COSMOLOGICAL ARGUMENT

The twentieth-century developments in cosmology brought renewed focus to a classic argument for the existence of God—the kalam cosmological argument. The name *kalam* may sound sophisticated, but the argument is surprisingly simple. Philosopher William Lane Craig, the most vocal defender of the argument today, states it this way:

1. Whatever begins to exist has a cause.

2. The universe began to exist.

3. Therefore, the universe has a cause.

Given the rules of logic, if the first two premises are true, then the conclusion necessarily follows.

In teaching my (Sean's) students the first premise of this argument, I challenge them to give an example of something coming into existence from nothing. My query is typically followed by silence while the absurdity of such a request sinks in. How could *some*-thing come from *no*-thing? As the ancient Greeks regularly observed, "Out of nothing, nothing comes." Even David Hume, the great Scottish skeptic, said the idea of something arising without a cause is absurd.

We may not always know the cause of a particular event (such as the breaking of a window or the explosion of a supernova), but it seems reasonable to believe things that begin to exist have a cause. There is a multitude of different scientific evidence pointing to the universe having a beginning. Let's consider one example.

According to the second law of thermodynamics, processes taking place in a closed system always move toward a state of equilibrium. In other words, unless outside energy is added to a closed system, the usable energy within the system will eventually run down. For instance, imagine a cup of hot coffee in a room completely sealed off from the outside (no energy or matter can intrude). Eventually the coffee will cool and match the temperature of its environment. If the coffee were not yet at a state of equilibrium with the room, if the coffee's temperature were still above that of the room, then you would know definitively that it had not been there forever.

In the atheistic view, the universe is a closed system, since there is nothing beyond it (like our coffee in the sealed room). Given sufficient time, the universe will eventually run out of energy and reach a state of equilibrium known as "heat death." At this stage, all the universe's useful energy will be gone. If the universe had been in existence for an infinite duration, then it would have already run out of energy. Yet since there is disequilibrium in the temperature of the universe, it must have a finite past. Therefore, the universe had a beginning.

There is also good philosophical evidence for the beginning of the universe. Imagine you went for a walk in the park and stumbled across someone proclaiming aloud, "…five, four, three, two, one—there, I finally finished! I just counted down from infinity!" What would be your initial thought? Would you wonder how long the person had been counting? Probably not. More likely, you would be in utter disbelief. Why? Because you know that such a task cannot be done. Just as it's impossible to count up to infinity from the present moment, it's equally impossible to count down from negative infinity to the present moment.

Counting to infinity is impossible because there is always (at least) one more number to count. In fact, every time you count a number, you still have an infinite more to go, and thus you get no closer to your goal. Similarly, counting down from infinity to the present moment is equally impossible. Such a task can't even get started! Any point you pick in the past to begin, no matter how remote, would always require (at least) one more number to count before you could start there. Any beginning point would require an infinite number of previous points.

Here's the bottom line: We could never get to the present moment if we had to cross an actual infinite number of moments in the past. Yet since the present moment is real, it must have been preceded by a finite past that includes a beginning or first event. Therefore, the universe had a beginning. And if the universe had a beginning, it must have a cause. And by its very nature, that cause must be timeless, spaceless, changeless, powerful, and personal.[4]

So Who Made God?

This brings us back to the question "Who made God?" It is important to clarify that Christians do not believe *everything that exists needs a cause.* Rather, everything that *begins* to exist must have a cause. Many things that necessarily exist are uncaused, such as mathematical truths and the laws of logic. Even if our world had never been created, the law of non-contradiction would still hold. The universe had a beginning, so it must have a cause. But God by definition does not need a cause—he is uncaused.

William Lane Craig comments penetratingly, "And this is not special pleading in the case of God. After all, atheists have long maintained that the universe doesn't need a cause, because it's eternal. How can they possibly maintain that the universe can be eternal and uncaused, yet God cannot be timeless and uncaused?"[5] A God who is uncaused is the most reasonable explanation.

2. THE TELEOLOGICAL ARGUMENT

This is the argument for design. The point is made that life, the laws of nature, and the whole universe demonstrate immense specified complexity, the mark of design, and therefore the universe must have come from a Personal Designer. King David made this point when he said,

> The heavens tell of the glory of God. The skies display his marvelous craftsmanship. Day after day they continue to speak; night after night they make him known. They speak without a sound or a word; their voice is silent in the skies; yet their message has gone out to all the earth, and their words to all the world (Psalm 19:1-4).

Several years ago, I (Sean) collaborated with Dr. William Dembski in writing a book titled *Understanding Intelligent Design*. In it we covered the many facets of the arguments for intelligent design. Some of the remaining portion of this section is drawn from that book.

If you have ever visited Disneyland or Disney World, you have probably noticed the bed of flowers laid out on a sloping bank. The colors, formation, and particular flowers form a clear resemblance to Mickey Mouse. No one would attribute that gardening marvel to mere chance. Why? First, flowers of that variety and color don't just grow by chance to form the shape and color of the famous Mickey Mouse. The numerous types of flowers and their multiplicity of placements clearly indicate *complexity*. Complexity in this sense is the same as saying it is highly improbable these flowers randomly grew there or were positioned so intricately.

Second, besides being complex, the floral arrangement is laid out in a very specific manner. Certain flowers make up the eyes, others the nose, and yet others the mouth and the renowned ears. The image exhibits an independently given pattern—it's therefore *specified*.

This combination of complexity (or improbability) and specificity (or independently imposed patterning) is called *specified complexity*. Specified complexity is a marker of intelligence. The huge flower bed at Disney exhibits specified complexity and leads us to believe an intelligent gardener was its cause.

What a Single Living Cell Declares

The more complex a thing is and the more its form obviously follows specific patterns, the more it points to an intelligent designer. Take, for example, the building block of human life—a single living cell. Does it have specified complexity?

Let's briefly look at a cell magnified a billion times. On its surface we find millions of openings, like portholes in a ship. But these are not mere portholes. They regulate the flow of materials in and out of the cell. Cells exhibit nano-engineering on a scale and sophistication that scientists have hardly begun to scratch. Francis Crick, one of the co-discoverers of DNA's structure, described the cell as "a minute factory, bustling with rapid, organized chemical activity." That was in the early 1980s. Scientists now think of the cell as an automated city.

Inside the cell we find a host of raw materials maneuvered back and forth by robot-like machines all working in unison. In fact, many different objects move in perfect unison through seemingly endless conduits. The level of control in these choreographed movements is truly mind-blowing.

And this is just *one* cell. In larger organisms, cells must work together for the proper function of organs such as hearts, eyes, livers, and ears, and these in turn must work together for the life of the organism.

If we peer further inside the cell, we find coils of DNA that store the information necessary to construct proteins. Proteins themselves are remarkably complex molecular systems. A typical protein is composed of a few hundred amino acids arranged in a precisely ordered sequence that then folds into a highly organized three-dimensional structure. That structure enables the protein to perform its function inside the cell.

Biologists today cannot even describe the activities inside the cell without comparing it to machines and other feats of modern engineering. The reason is that nearly every feature of our own advanced technology can be found in the cell.[6]

As we carefully observe the inner workings of the cell, one thing becomes apparent: There is complexity and sophistication that dwarfs human technological innovation today. This is why more and more scientists are concluding that the best explanation for the cell is intelligent design.

Life Requires Vast Amounts of Information

The key feature to life is information. Life, even the simplest of bacterial cells, requires vast amounts of information to function. Cellular information is stored in DNA, and the DNA in one cell in the human body holds the equivalent of roughly eight thousand books of information. A typical human body has about 30 trillion cells, each of which contains DNA strands that, when uncoiled and strung together end to end, would be about two meters in length. Thus a conservative estimate is that if all the DNA in an adult human were strung together, it would stretch from Earth to the sun and back around two hundred times![7]

Supposing there were no Intelligent Designer. How would the needed information for life be assembled? The typical answer materialist evolutionary scientists come up with is that given enough time, matter, and chance, anything can happen. But how much time, matter, and chance are actually available? As early as 1913, the French mathematician Émile Borel argued that a million monkeys typing ten hours a day would be exceedingly unlikely to reproduce the books in the world's libraries. The universe is very old and enormous, according to Borel, but it's not old enough and big enough for something that unlikely.

> Let's narrow Borel's scope. Instead of focusing on many books, let's consider the works of Shakespeare. Here is the question: How many monkeys and how much time would be required to reproduce one of the works of Shakespeare, or even just a few lines?
>
> Work has been done on this question by MIT computational quantum physicist Seth Lloyd. According to Lloyd, in the known physical universe, chance is capable of producing only 400 bits of prespecified information (this is equivalent to a string of 400 zeroes and ones). This amounts to a sequence of 82 ordinary letters and spaces. Therefore, the longest initial segment of Hamlet's soliloquy that the entire universe—given its size and purported multibillion-year history—could by chance produce is the following two lines:
>
> TO BE, OR NOT TO BE, THAT IS THE QUESTION. WHETHER 'TIS NOBLER IN THE MIND TO SUFFER...
>
> Clearly, the phenomenon of chance is limited in its ability to explain certain features of the universe. All the chance in the known

universe can't randomly type more than two lines of Shakespeare, much less an entire book.[8]

If chance over time cannot create enough information for two lines of Shakespeare, how could it ever create the complexity of even a single "primitive" cell? A single cell requires hundreds of thousands of bits of information precisely sequenced in its DNA. So those who deny an Intelligent Designer have the impossible task of explaining how the information stored in even a simple living organism could arise out of the process of chance and time. Life simply requires too much information to occur randomly.

This is why intelligent design best explains the information content of DNA. Imagine you are walking on the beach and notice the message "Sean loves Stephanie" inscribed in the sand. What would you conclude? You might think Sean, Stephanie, or some gossipy stranger wrote it, but it would never cross your mind to attribute it to chance, necessity, or some combination of the two. Wind, water, and sand simply do not generate meaningful information. The most reasonable inference is that it is a product of intelligent design. If we justifiably infer a mind behind a simple message of 15 characters, then inferring an intelligence for the origin of the cell—which requires hundreds of thousands of bits of specified information —is fully justified.[9]

3. THE MORAL LAW ARGUMENT

Every human culture known to man has had a moral law. While there is some variety regarding moral practices across cultures, there is a striking universal agreement about the validity of moral principles such as justice, courage, and fairness. Without appeal to a higher source, what could account for the moral sense that is common to the entire human race through all of history? An objective, universal, and constant standard of moral truth seems to point most convincingly to the existence of a personal and moral God.

In *The Brothers Karamazov,* Russian novelist Fyodor Dostoyevsky aptly observed, "If there is no immortality of the soul, there can be no virtue and therefore everything is permissible." In other words, if God does not exist as the foundation of morality, then *anything goes.* If God does not exist, then we lose the right to judge the Nazis and anyone else with whom we disagree morally. They believed they were right. We think they were wrong. Without a higher law above humanity, who gets to decide moral truth? If there is no greater source above human beings, then the existence of morality is an inexplicable illusion.[10]

There are, however, those who would argue that objective morality can exist independently of God. Yet this assertion presents a problem: What is the source of objective moral values and duties if there is no God? Evil, for example, is best understood as the perversion of good. Just as crookedness implies a standard of straight, evil implies a standard of good. C.S. Lewis famously said that to complain a stick is bent makes sense only in light of the concept of straight. Similarly, there can be evil only if there is first a standard of good. But if there is no God to ground such goodness, then what defines the standard of good? Without God, morality becomes subjective, and the concept of objective good disappears. Moral good becomes a meaningless term, for it is simply whatever each of us wants it to be at a given moment, or whatever evolution has blindly wired us to believe.

The universally recognized existence of objective moral values is a strong reason for believing in God. Consider this simple argument:

1. If objective moral values and duties exist, God must exist.

2. Objective moral values and duties exist.

3. Therefore, God must exist.

We know objective moral values do exist. We don't need to be persuaded that, for example, torturing babies for fun is wrong. All reasonable people know this. Therefore, since objective moral values and duties do exist, then God must exist as well.

4. A PERSONAL-EXPERIENCE-WITH-GOD ARGUMENT

People have asked me (Josh), "How do you know you became a Christian?" "How do you know God is real?" For one, he changed my life. This transformation is one way I'm assured of the validity of my conversion and the existence of a real and personal God.

I'm sure you have heard people speak of the "bolt of lightning" that hit them when they had their first religious experience. Well, it wasn't that dramatic for me. After I prayed, nothing happened. I mean *nothing*. In fact, after I made my commitment to God, I felt worse. I actually felt I was about to vomit. *Oh, no. What have I gotten sucked into now?* I really felt I had gone off the deep end (and I'm sure some people think I did!).

The change in my life was not immediate, but it was real. In six to eighteen months, I knew that I had not gone off the deep end. I had experienced God, and that changed everything.

A personal experience with God is evidence of his reality. Some might challenge this assertion, saying an experience with God could easily be an illusion or an emotional or psychological fantasy. But those who have genuinely experienced encounters similar to what Paul the apostle experienced on the Damascus road know better. They know it is real. Such experiences are one of many affirmations of Paul's statement: "Now that you belong to Christ, you are the true children of Abraham. You are his heirs, and now all the promises God gave to him belong to you" (Galatians 3:29).

It is true that we who are followers of Jesus and children of God must accept our personal relationship with God by faith. But that doesn't make the relationship any less real. As a Christ-follower you are one of "God's very own children, adopted into his family—calling him 'Father, dear Father.' For his Holy Spirit speaks to us deep in our hearts and tells us that we are God's children" (Romans 8:15-16).

---

*Apart from an infinite, personal
Creator God we have no life or meaning.*

If you have had a personal encounter with the Creator God through Jesus Christ, you know he is real. The evidence of a personal experience with God cannot necessarily be sufficient proof to others, but it can be one of many convincing arguments to the one who knows God personally.

Many philosophers have tried to exclude God from their explanations of human existence and the meaning of life. But apart from an infinite, personal Creator God we have no life or meaning. Noted British atheist Bertrand Russell made this point perfectly clear when he declared it "nearly certain"

> that man is the product of causes which had no prevision of the end they were achieving; that his origin, his growth, his hopes and fears, his loves and his beliefs, are but the outcome of accidental collocations of atoms;...that all the labors of the ages, all the devotion, all the inspiration, all the noonday brightness of human genius, are destined to extinction in the vast death of the solar system, and that the whole temple of man's achievement must inevitably be buried beneath the debris of a universe in ruins.[11]

Either God is the "first cause" of life and of all things, or there is no lasting significance to our existence or to anything we accomplish. We and everything we do, as Russell says, will die in "a universe in ruins."

To deny the existence of an infinite, personal God leaves us without hope, purpose, or meaning in life. It's as if we were all swept downstream in a swift river and must choose between climbing onto a rock or plunging over a waterfall. One option offers security and a solid grip on stable reality; the other ends with our hurtling into a void where nothing has objective meaning or purpose.[12] But the evidence surrounding our universe and life itself simply has too much specified complexity to deny the existence of our Intelligent Designer. That leaves us, as Paul said, "no excuse whatsoever for not knowing God" (Romans 1:20). And in knowing God and reflecting his image we find the joy and happiness he intended, both for this life and the one to come. Choosing to believe in God and having a relationship with him gives us a way to understand who we really are.

And that is the subject of our next section.

DISCOVERING YOUR IDENTITY

Imagine for a moment what it must have been like when the first man and woman were created. Adam, the first human, lived in the paradise called Eden. Everything was perfect. Grasses and flowers and animals of all kinds frolicking and grazing under a canopy of clouds and sky…everything painted a breathtaking canvas of beauty.

Each new morning must have brought with it an ever-varying combination of colors, textures, and movements that converged to bring pleasure to his senses. The sounds of musical birds and sparkling waterfalls filled the air. Lush tropical trees and plants grew delicious fruit whose taste and textures brought joy to the palate and satisfaction to the body.

The perfect beauty of his world must have captivated his soul with pure rapture. In harmony with his environment as Adam was, each enchanted evening must have resulted in such satisfaction and contentment that he thought nothing could ever surpass it.

While we have no record Adam complained about his condition in the pristine garden, something was in fact missing. God said, "It is not good for the man to be alone" (Genesis 2:18). Even though he had God, Adam was not yet complete. Something was yet absent—a human relationship. Even in the perfect world of Eden before sin ever disrupted relationships, God declared human aloneness was not good. So God caused Adam to sleep, and while he slept God formed another human.

Imagine Adam's reaction when he awoke. Imagine how he might have gazed through softly waving palms to see a face so captivating that he thought he'd be content never to look at anything else again. He watches in rapt fascination as she emerges from a shroud of mist, gliding toward him with majestic elegance and grace. Her shape and form excite him like nothing ever has. As he reaches out to her, he discovers she is soft to the touch, and her fragrance fills his senses. He feels his heart beat faster; his breathing becomes deeper. He is in awe of this creature called woman. He has never experienced such beauty.

But he was intrigued by more than just her glorious face and form. There was a mystery to this attraction. Adam sensed an indefinable hunger to know more of this creature than what he could physically hold and caress and enjoy. And so did she. They were both drawn to a deeper intimacy than their physical senses could experience. Each of these first humans had a longing for an emotional connection, a bonding of the inner spirit, an intimate attachment of the soul. In short, they experienced a desire for a loving relationship. *For God had planted deep within them an identifying marker or distinguishing character of his own likeness—the capacity for loving relationships.* It is this God-created reality that removes human aloneness and makes you, you. It is your capacity for relationship that provides all the meaning, happiness, and joy you could ever hope to experience.

YOUR MARK OF PERSONHOOD: GOD'S RELATIONAL DNA

"In the beginning God created the heavens and the earth" (Genesis 1:1). Then God went on to say, "Let us make people in our image, to be like ourselves... So God created people in his own image; God patterned them after himself; male and female he created them" (verses 26-27). So before there were humans, before Planet Earth or the universe or time as we know it, God existed eternally as a loving relational being.

He is a relational God by his very nature, three personalities blended in perfect harmony—Father, Son, and Holy Spirit. (More on the Trinity is covered in chapter 9.) While he is the infinite one and we as humans are finite, we bear his relational DNA. We have inherited his ability to love another being. Scripture says, "Love comes from God...for God is love" (1 John 4:7-8).

Along with the ability to be relational—to love God and other beings besides ourselves—we have also inherited a number of other traits related to God's relational nature. We have inherited his ability to communicate our thoughts, intents, and feelings to others.

We have also inherited his sense of value for human relationships and for life itself. God said, "Honor your father and mother...Do not murder...Do not commit adultery...Do not steal...Do not testify falsely...Do not covet your neighbor's wife" (Deuteronomy 5:16-21). From God's giving of the law at Mount Sinai up through the early church and beyond, it was understood and taught that life is sacred at every stage. Promoting social justice, taking care of the poor, and defending human rights find their basis in each of us by the fact that we are purposely created in God's image. In his book *The Faith*, Chuck Colson said it well: "When Christians today see life through God's eyes…we are compelled not only to care for the poor and vulnerable but to defend every human's God-given right."[13] That is because we were created in God's relational image with value, dignity, and worth.

We have inherited God's sense of satisfaction and joy in accomplishing things through relationships. After each creative act in Genesis, this relational God "saw that it was good" (1:10). The Father, Son, and Holy Spirit found joy in their collective creative acts as the Master of the universe.

We inherited from the Master of the universe the charge to "be masters over all life" (Genesis 1:26). God told the first humans that in relationship with one another they were also to live in proper relationship with their home—Planet Earth. God said to be stewards of the earth and "to tend and care for it" (2:15). So God instilled within his human creation an environmental responsibility to relate lovingly to the planet they inherited.

As you can see, God placed humans on a plateau above the rest of creation when he fashioned them in his relational image and likeness. But this relational dimension does more than just set us apart from the rest of God's creation. It also defines who we are and gives us our sense of identity.

DISCOVERING WHO YOU ARE

When you stop to think about it, you and I largely understand ourselves—our identity—in terms of relationships. We perceive ourselves and others around us as this person's son or daughter, that person's husband or wife, someone's mother or father, or as our neighbor, friend, or pastor.

While human relationships may provide insight into your identity, the basis of your true identity resides in the fact that you are uniquely fashioned in God's image. Because sin caused us to be born alienated and disconnected from God, we have lost that instilled sense of personal identity. Even after becoming a Christian, it does not automatically become easy to discover who we really are. Although I (Josh) trusted Christ and became a Christian as a university student, I had very little, if any, experiential and emotional context in which to understand the true meaning of a loving relationship. My growing-up years were fraught with relational dysfunction, emotional pain, and chaos. Consequently, I didn't readily see myself as a one-of-a-kind person created to relate lovingly to God and others.

Yet each of us is an original. Just as no two snowflakes are ever alike, no two humans ever created are alike. Parents can certainly attest no two children are alike. Each of us, as a human child and as a child of God, has an original identity. You have been given distinct and special qualities that make you relationally unique.

Scripture recognizes our originality. One subtle but powerful indication of this is found in the familiar words penned by King Solomon: "Train up a child in the way he should go, even when he is old he will not depart from it" (Proverbs 22:6 NASB). Unfortunately, this verse is often misunderstood and misapplied. Some think it means, "Have family devotions, make sure kids attend church and youth group and a Christian school, and then when they are grown up, they will not depart from the faith." The real emphasis of this verse, however, centers on the phrase "the way he [or she] should go." The writer is referring to the *child's* way, his or her leaning or bent. The root meanings of these words suggest guiding each child according to his or her own uniqueness. In other words, parents must discern exactly who their child is—his or her abilities, interests, and talents—and then draw out and develop that uniqueness. Train the child to be the unique person God relationally created him or her to be.

The same Hebrew word used in Proverbs 22 is translated "bend" in two psalms and refers to the bending of the archer's bow (see Psalm 11:2; 64:3). Today, with precision manufacturing, almost anyone can pick up a bow with a 45-pound draw weight and do a fair job of hitting the target. But in biblical days, nothing was standardized. All archers made their own bows, and each archer had to know the unique characteristics of his own bow if he hoped to hit anything with it. God's Word is telling us that you have an inborn uniqueness your parents and caregivers are to identify and train accordingly.

My (Sean's) parents understood this truth and guided me to understand my "bent." My dad saw I had an inclination toward playing basketball. I'm not a tall person; neither is my father. But as a young person he excelled at basketball, and he sensed I had the same talent. He encouraged me to pursue it, coaching me as I learned the game. And I eventually fulfilled my dream of being a point guard for Biola University.

My parents also picked up on my inquisitiveness. I wanted to know things; I enjoyed figuring out why this was true or that was true. And I enjoyed sharing what I was learning with others. Because they cultivated my natural inclinations in these directions, I ended up majoring in philosophy and theology and becoming an educator and speaker. All this resulted in my understanding of who I am—the unique person God created in his own relational image.

WHAT IS YOUR UNIQUE IDENTITY?

God intends for you to use the unique characteristics he gave you to relate not only to him but to others. "Just as our bodies have many parts," Paul said, "and each part has a special function, so it is with Christ's body. We are all parts of his one body, and each of us has different work to do. And since we are all one body in Christ, we belong to each other, and each of us needs all the others" (Romans 12:4-5).

There will never be another you. God has specially gifted you to fill a role—a purpose—no one else can fill. You and I want to know our place in this world. God has crafted us specifically for that place that only we can fill.

You have unique characteristics with which to love and live for God in a way that only you are empowered to do. And he wants to exercise his love and life in and through you in a unique and original fashion. Paul declares,

> There are different ways God works in our lives, but it is the same God who does the work through all of us. A spiritual gift is given to each of us as a means of helping the entire church...It is the one and only Holy Spirit who distributes these gifts. He alone decides which gift each person should have (1 Corinthians 12:6-7, 11).

Some aspects of your uniqueness are readily apparent. Your personal identification is distinctly yours. Your fingerprints are unique; your retina scans are distinct; your face and body are at least slightly different from those of anyone else who ever existed on the planet. But it's not always so easy to understand the distinctiveness with which God created you and what gifts the Holy Spirit has distributed to you.

You can learn to identify your distinctiveness by paying attention to how your mind works and what draws your interest. God has instilled within you certain *passions*: things you feel strongly about, things you're fervently interested in, things that give you a special sense of joy when you talk about them or pursue them. Those passions direct you to who, where, and what God wants you to love in life...as only you can.

Just as Mac and PC computers have different operating systems, God has also given you distinctive built-in ways of processing information and making decisions. Do you tend to be emotional or rational? Reflective or outspoken? Creative or systematic? Artistic or mechanical? These tendencies, along with your passions and interests, make up your *distinct personality*. God's love is to be clearly expressed through your distinct personality, as only you can express it.

If your parents understood that you were a one-of-a-kind individual and sought to train you up in "the way you should go," you have, no doubt, come a long way in identifying your personality type, talents, special gifts, and passions. But if you are like most people, you have only a partial understanding of who you are. You could probably use some help in figuring it out. We suggest the book *Why You Do What You Do* by Bobb Biehl.

One other thought about our personal identities. Understanding that we are God's children with a special place in his body doesn't mean unbelievers don't have talents or natural gifts. It doesn't mean they can't come to understand themselves and their uniqueness to varying degrees. What it does mean, however, is that unless and until people come to know God as their Father through Christ, they will never understand their true place in this world. A non-Christian may exercise a talent or skill, but it will never be fully expressed as it was meant to be, or it will never bring maximum meaning to that life. God made us in his image, and when we live out his way, his truth, and his life, we find both our true identity and experience pure joy because we are being what we are created to be. We are reflecting his image. Knowing who we are and living as God designed us provides a sense of meaning and purpose to life.

LIVING OUT YOUR RELATIONAL IMAGE OF GOD

Knowing you are a relational being, created in God's image, is important. But how do you live out that image in relationship to others? As we stated earlier, reflecting the image of a relational God includes certain social responsibilities, moral and ethical choices, creativity, and so on. These responsibilities spring directly from the core characteristic that defines God best—love. "God is love," John says, "and all who live in love live in God, and God lives in them. And as we live in God, our love grows more perfect" (1 John 4:16-17). It is as if God wired into us a yearning to live out our relational nature, a yearning to love someone and have someone love us deeply enough to explore the depths of who we really are as people created in God's image.

THE RELATIONAL LOVE PROCESS

The relationships that are lasting and most meaningful are those in which we come to know another person intimately and allow him or her to know us equally. That is where the relational love process of knowing and being known comes in.

Know Others

One of the words Scripture uses for lasting intimacy is the Hebrew word *yada,* meaning "to know." It denotes a deep and intimate acquaintance. A 16-year-old girl sent me (Josh) one of the best definitions of intimacy I've seen. She wrote, "It is the capacity to be real with another person…no façade, no barriers." We all want to be real and be known. It's as if those around you had a sign hung around their necks reading, *Please know me!* In Jeremiah 1:5, God uses this word to say to the prophet, "I knew you before I formed you in your mother's womb." God knew us intimately before we were born, and he wants to teach us to know others intimately.

Being made in God's image means we are complex and intricately designed. Therefore, it takes time to explore the relational depths of those you love—to discover their likes and dislikes, probe their interests and desires, and begin to uncover the wonders of who they are. As a person feels someone desires to truly know them and love them for who they are, they begin to experience relationship as God designed. And as you do, you will be replicating the DNA of God's image of love.

Be Known

King Solomon said that the Lord "offers his friendship to the godly" (Proverbs 3:32). Friendship in this verse is the Hebrew word *sod*, meaning vulnerable or transparent disclosure. In other words, God offers his friendship—a transparent disclosure of himself—to the godly. God wants us to know him intimately. The Lord said, "I want you to be merciful; I don't want your sacrifices. I want you to know God; that's more important than burnt offerings" (Hosea 6:6).

God is pleased to reveal himself to us, and he created us in his likeness to reveal ourselves to others. That is another dimension to experiencing deepened love relationships. It's not easy to open ourselves up and be vulnerable. It can be risky, and at times we may even get hurt. But it is a risk worth taking.

As you enter close relationships with others, it's important to let them get to know you for who you really are. Let them know your dreams and aspirations, your fears and hesitations, your hopes and expectations. As you learn to "self-disclose" you will be reflecting a likeness of God, and you will experience a deeper relationship with others.

Be Involved

King David wrote, "O LORD, you have examined my heart and know everything about me...Every moment you know where I am" (Psalm 139:1, 3). The Hebrew word *sakan*, translated "know" here, means a caring involvement. God had much more than simply an informational knowing of David; he was caringly involved in David's life.

For us to do the same is to be involved in the lives of those we love. This means entering their world and becoming interested in what they're interested in. When you take a sincere interest in another and demonstrate you care, you are living out the image of God, and your relationship with the other person deepens.

When I (Sean) was around ten years old I was really into sports cars. I would cut out magazine pictures of cars like the Maserati, the Lamborghini, and the Ferrari Testarossa. I pinned them up on my bedroom wall and thought they were so cool.

My dad noticed my newfound interest, and one day he really surprised me. He had looked through the Yellow Pages and picked out some of the top sports car dealerships in Beverly Hills. Then he sent each car dealer a letter that said:

> I'm a desperate dad. I'll do anything to spend time with my son, and right now he's into sports cars. Would it be possible if I pulled him out of school and brought him up to your showroom so that we could take some test drives? I want to tell you up front, I'm not interested in buying a car.

Amazingly, he got positive replies from every dealer. He called and made appointments for us, and we drove up to Beverly Hills (a distance of some 150 miles) for a day in the sports car showrooms. And what a day it was! Dad waited in the showrooms while I went out on "test drives" with salesmen and "tried out" just about every big-name car you can think of. As I came by the showroom in each car, I would wave to Dad—I was so proud.

Along with the test drives, I got posters, some of which were autographed by famous race car drivers. It was an incredible day. On the way home we discussed which cars we liked the best and went over all the flyers, books, and posters I had collected. Then Dad gently switched the subject and started talking to me about looking at all this in the light of our Christian worldview.

"You know, Sean," he said, "all these cars are fun, but they cost huge amounts of money. What we should be thinking about is what God has called us to value as a family." He then explained, "Let's look at what we did today in light of God's love for us…what Christ did on the cross…what he created us for." And with that beginning he was able to communicate to me as a ten-year-old one of the best lessons on materialism he could have possibly taught. He didn't make it preachy, but he did make the point about how we may like certain things and enjoy them, but their cost downgrades them to a very low category compared to the importance of where we are as followers of Jesus.

I never forgot that lesson on materialism. But I'm convinced the lesson would never have stuck if my dad hadn't entered my world and demonstrated he loved me by focusing on my interests. The real lesson that day that has molded and shaped me as a father and husband is that I am to enter the life of my wife and family in order to love and be loved.

TALKING ABOUT THE
RELATIONAL CONTEXT OF LIFE

Everything around us and in us reflects that we were made for relationships. You can talk about moral values or the creation around us—whatever it is, it is based in God's relationship with us.

Place God's Commands Within a Relational Context

Whenever you talk with someone about God's commands and rules, always put them within the context of his loving motivation to provide for us and protect us. This is important because so many people see his commands as restrictive and harsh. But the truth is, God's commands come from who he is and his desire to bless us. Discover the loving provision and protection behind his commands, and you will find the love that reflects his character. This is what we must teach.

God's commands are designed to bless us. For example, we are told not to steal from others nor lie or be a cheat (see Exodus 20:15-16). In other words, we are to live honest lives because God is true. "He is the Rock," Moses declared, "his works are perfect...A faithful God who does no wrong, upright and just is he" (Deuteronomy 32:4 NIV). His nature is true—he doesn't vary or deviate from his very essence of being holy and righteous. The reason the writer of Hebrews said, "It is impossible for God to lie" (6:18) is that God cannot deny his own nature. And when we live honest lives we reflect God's true nature. By doing this we're protected from guilt and enjoy a clear conscience. We're protected from shame and enjoy a reputation of integrity. We're protected from ruined relationships and enjoy relationships based on trust.

When we place God's commands within a relational context...
we can see that to be like him is for his glory and our benefit.

When my (Josh's) daughter Kelly was in fourth grade, several students in her class swiped an object off the teacher's desk while the teacher was out of the room. The children only wanted to play with the object, but it soon broke. Then they returned it to its previous place on the teacher's desk.

When the teacher discovered the damage, she asked one of Kelly's classmates what had happened. The girl yielded to the pressure of the group and lied. Then the teacher asked Kelly. Kelly explained matter-of-factly what had happened.

The next day I took Kelly out for breakfast at a local restaurant. I told her she'd done the right thing in spite of any pressure or harassment she might get from her classmates.

"Honey," I then asked, "why is lying wrong?"

"Because the Bible says it's wrong," she answered.

"Why does the Bible say it's wrong?"

"Because God commanded it."

"Why did God command it?"

"I don't know," she admitted.

I took her hands in mine and locked eyes with her. "Because God is true. By his very nature he can't be dishonest. So what you did when you told the truth was to act like God. You reflected his nature." We went on and talked about the many benefits of being an honest person.

When we place God's commands within a relational context—that is, when we see ourselves as his creatures, related to him in love and designed to experience joy when we reflect his nature—we can see that to be like him is for his glory and our benefit. This enables us to avoid seeing his rules as restrictive or legalistic.

Place Your Own Instructions Within a Relational Context

As a parent you obviously don't need to give your children a reason or benefit for everything you instruct them to do. However, they need to understand that all your instructions and rules come out of your loving heart for them and a loving desire for their best interests.

Growing up I (Sean) remember how my dad or mom wouldn't always let me go everywhere I wanted to go or buy everything I wanted to buy. Of course I'd be disappointed and even at times complain or argue with them. As I think back, what stands out to me about those times is not the arguments or disappointment I felt, but my parents' constant reminders of this one thing: They would say, "Sean, I hope you know it needs to be this way because I love you." That was the theme.

As a young person I certainly couldn't understand the depths of my parents' love. I understand it better now that I am a parent myself. But knowing they loved me and genuinely wanted my best kept me from making some costly mistakes. That doesn't mean I always listened. Like any kid, I made my share of poor choices. But knowing that my parents truly loved me was a powerful motivating force to take their wisdom to heart. None of us can be perfect parents, but we can be deeply loving parents. We can let our children know that what we do to correct them is because we love them.

Use the Fascinations of Nature to Praise God's Existence

Take advantage of our natural world to point to the existence and creativity of God. Watching a nature documentary or taking a trip to the zoo can serve as a great opportunity to wonder at the amazing design of God's world. You can pose questions like, "What does a rose tell us about God and what he likes?" or "Why did God make giraffes with such long necks?" We don't necessarily have to know all the answers in order to marvel at God's miraculous creation and praise him for it.

Some time ago the BBC produced a television series called *Planet Earth*. A lot of my (Sean's) friends were talking about it, so I decided to purchase the DVDs to see why all the commotion. I was completely blown away! The nature footage they captured was absolutely amazing. After I had shown a couple of episodes to our family, our young son, Scottie, started asking, "Can we watch *Planet Earth* tonight?"

In my favorite scene, a gigantic great white shark chases a seal. Sharks are swift and powerful; the seal is more agile. But despite its agility, the seal cannot escape earth's most feared predator. The chase ends when the shark explodes from the water and catches the seal in its jaws in midair. The slow-motion footage was worth the price. Incredible!

My wife and I took the opportunity presented by the series to celebrate the powerful forces of God's creation with our son, using nature as a springboard to share a biblical worldview: "When I consider your heavens, the work of your fingers, the moon and the stars, which you have set in place, what is man that you are mindful of him, the son of man that you care for him?" (Psalm 8:3-4 NIV).

If you have an interest in astronomy, flowers, or gardening, or if you are fascinated with honeybees, ants, whales, or the hibernation of bears, you can use those interests to wonder aloud about the miracle of creation and what it might suggest about the nature of our Creator God. Physics and the study of gravity, light, atomic energy, or electricity are other fields rich in mystery that inspire wonder of the God of creation. You don't have to be a scientist or a botanist to see the natural world as a means to glorify God to those around you. Going on a hike and marveling at God's creation can be just as effective.

Use the Miracle of Birth to Praise God's Existence

Use the birth of a baby or remembering the day a person was born to marvel at the miracle of birth. King David said, "You made all the delicate, inner parts of my body and knit me together in my mother's womb. Thank you for making me so wonderfully complex! Your workmanship is marvelous—and how well I know it" (Psalm 139:13-14).

The fascinating aspects of our complex bodies can be used to praise God for this handiwork. You might remember from high school biology that the "double helix" shape of DNA resembles a twisted ladder. Each rung is a piece of your genetic code, and amazingly, every cell in your body contains a complete DNA blueprint for everything about you. The sequence of those rungs provides the pattern for the production of every building block of life. Not only that, but within each human being's reproductive cells lies the information that, when combined with genetic information from a mate, adds up to the genetic pattern handed down to a child.

DNA, in other words, is what determines not only *who we are* but *what our children look like*. Use fascinating information like this to stand in awe of our Creator God. Wonder aloud about "What would it be like to know everything there is to know?" "What does God look like?" "What if he has a favorite color?" "Why does he love us so much?" This exercise isn't meant to humanize God, but rather to help those around you understand that while God is infinite and beyond our comprehension on one hand, on the other he is an approachable, relational God who takes notice even of how many hairs grow on our heads.

Teach Your Kids the Basics of a Biblical Worldview

As a professor, I (Sean) am constantly thinking of simple ways to teach my students a biblical worldview. I explain to them that every worldview answers three basic questions:

1. *Origin*—how did we get here?

2. *Predicament*—what went wrong?

3. *Resolution*—how do we fix it?

Since God created the world, everything was originally good (*origin*). But humans twist these good things and make them evil (*predicament*). God sent his son, Jesus, to die on the cross for our sins, so we could be restored in our relationship to him (*resolution*).

To apply this truth, I often ask my students a question such as "What gives human beings value?" The answer, of course, is they are made in the image of God (*origin*). Then I ask, "How has this truth been twisted?" Answers include the false ideas that our value comes from our possessions, appearance, success, and so on (*predicament*). Then I ask, "How do we get back to seeing ourselves as God sees us?" The answer is to replace the false ideas we accept from our culture with biblical truth (*resolution*). You can do this little exercise using anything God created, including art, sports, work, music, relationships, and more. By posing these questions on various issues, you can help young people form a biblical worldview.

SUMMARY

Because we believe the truth that a personal God exists and created us in his image, we can enjoy the benefits of his creation, especially loving relationships. Our ethics, morals, social and civic responsibilities, and the capacity to love and be loved come from the fact that we were made in God's relational image. We find our true identity in our Creator. And as we live out who we are within the context of God's image and likeness of love, it brings pleasure to him and purpose, meaning, and joy to us.

GOD'S WORD CAN BE TRUSTED

When Sean was 12 years old and his sister Kelly was 14, I (Josh) wrote a book of 15 letters to them. The book cover was inscribed: "My precious son and daughter, here are the letters I promised. They're from my heart… Love, Dad." The first letter read in part:

Dear Kelly…Dear Sean,

If letters had arms to wrap around, they would be squeezing you right now with the world's biggest hug.

For the past couple of years you both know I've crisscrossed America speaking, appearing on radio and TV and talking to young people about their sexuality. You've been with me on many of these trips.

It really hurts when I listen to personal stories guys and girls have told me. My heart has been broken as they have talked about how their lives have been messed up because they didn't understand God's plan or know how to manage their sexuality.

If there was ever a gift your mom and I want you, Kelly, and you, Sean, to have, it's the gift of sexual wholeness. And that gift can be yours if you make it through our world's minefield of teen sexual pressure without getting emotionally blown up. To help you win,

I'm giving you this book. It's sort of a road map, drawn from the best insights, experiences, tips, and secrets I've been able to learn through 20 years of marriage to your mother...

Well, dear Kelly and dear Sean, here are my letters to you. WOW, do I ever love you both!

—Dad

Even though I (Sean) was only 12 at the time, this book of letters had a profound impact on my life. It was profound because it became the motivating factor in abstaining from sexual immorality. On the surface you might think I followed the guidelines for sexual purity because they were so explicitly laid out for me. But that is not what impacted me so deeply. It was the fact that from a father's heart of love came guidelines to protect me from heartache and provide me maximum joy in my future relationships. Dad simply wanted me to experience what he had in life and marriage.

LETTERS FROM A LOVING HEART

Your earthly father may not have written you a book, but your heavenly Father did. His book, the Bible, is like letters from his heart to you. They have been written "so that your joy may be complete" (John 15:11 NIV). They are God's "road map" for you. They are his "secrets" on how you can make it through the world's "minefields" that threaten to cause you heartache and misery. The written Word of God comes from a Father's heart.

Every command and instruction from God comes out of his loving heart to provide for us and protect us.

"All Scripture is inspired by God and is useful to teach us what is true and to make us realize what is wrong in our lives. It straightens us out and teaches us to do what is right. It is God's way of preparing us in every way, fully equipped for every good thing God wants us to do" (2 Timothy 3:16-17). All the teachings of Scripture then—whether in the form of instruction, parable, admonition, precept, ordinance, or command—are intended to reveal who God really is and provide a detailed account of his ways. So when God says "avoid that attitude," "follow this way," "abstain from these actions," or "embrace these thoughts," he is not trying to restrict us from being happy. He is attempting to lead us to right living in relationship with him. That is what brings pleasure to him and happiness and joy to us.

Every command and instruction from God comes out of his loving heart to provide for us and protect us. As Moses told the nation of Israel,

> Obey the LORD's commands and laws that I am giving you today *for your own good*...I am giving you the choice between a blessing and a curse! You will be blessed if you obey the commands of the LORD your God...You will receive a curse if you reject the commands of the LORD your God and turn from his way (Deuteronomy 10:13; 11:26-28).

By commanding us to love him, God is saying in effect, "Devote yourself to knowing me intimately and open yourself to me fully so my ways will become your ways." God's design is such that an intimate relationship with him is the only way humans can succeed in living meaningful lives of joy. Moses understood this, and he begged God, "If you are pleased with me, teach me your ways so I may know you" (Exodus 33:13 NIV). Following God's ways leads to knowing him; knowing him leads to being and living like him; being and living like him leads to joy.

God's commands and instructions to act in certain ways flow out of who he is and how he himself acts. When we seek to know him intimately—love him—we can take on his ways and reap the benefits. The psalmist David said in Psalm 19 that the ways of the Lord revive the soul, make us wise, bring us joy, and give us insight for living. That is his loving provision. Life apart from him results in guilt, emotional distress, shame, loneliness, and disrupted relationships. That is what he wants to protect us from.

Thus, we can say the Bible is a perfectly right set of laws and guidelines that flow out of a perfectly right God to instruct us to live as God designed us to live. Therefore:

> **We believe the truth that the Bible is God's revelation of himself to us, which declares his ways for us to follow.**

It reveals a relational God, the God who "would speak to Moses face to face, as a man speaks to his friend" (Exodus 33:11). It is the revelation of "a God who is passionate about his relationship with you" (Exodus 34:14). And it is a revelation that, from the first words Moses penned in the book of Genesis to the last word John wrote in Revelation, reflects the loving heart of a God who wants us to be in right relationship with him so we can enjoy all the benefits that relationship offers.

To sum it up: Scripture is the means by which God has chosen to introduce and reveal himself to you so he can enjoy a relationship with you. God's Word—the record of all his ways—is given to you for a relational purpose: so you may know him and enjoy all the blessings of a relationship with your loving Creator.

DOES IT MATTER IF IT'S RELIABLE OR NOT?

Imagine a college-age group of Christians gathering for a Bible study. Listen to how the conversation turns as they begin to discuss the purpose of the Bible.

"I'd like to start a new series," begins Chad, the small group leader. "What would you say to doing this study on 'How to Get the Most out of Your Bible'?" he asks as he holds up a study booklet. The group nods in approval.

"Okay, let me start by asking this question: What's the purpose of the Bible?" He looks around the room at the expectant faces. "How would you describe what it does for us?"

Moments pass. Finally Allen speaks up. "It's God's truth. It's the inspired Word of God."

Chad nods. "Okay, good. What else?"

"It's…the book of Christian teachings," Sara offers.

"It's the teachings of the Jewish religion too," Megan adds. "The Old Testament is, anyway."

Several others in the group speak up.

"All right," Chad says, "those are all good responses. But let me give you a little different description of the Bible and see what you think." He glances down at his booklet as he reads, "The Bible is God's instruction manual for living. It is our road map to heaven. It is God's love letter to us. It's the means we use to get to know him." He allows the words to sink in for a moment, then holds up his Bible in one hand and continues. "So if people don't study this book, they can't very well know him."

"What if we don't have all of the Bible?" Allen interrupts. "What if there's, like, missing books or chapters? Does that mean we can't know God?"

"Yeah," Sara interjects. "What if God really gave 15 commandments, but we have only 10 of them?"

"Now, slow down," Chad says, holding his hand in the air as if trying to stop traffic. "Let's not get carried away."

"But Sara and Allen are right," Megan protests. "What if the people writing the Bible didn't put down everything God said…or maybe they got it all wrong or something. Does that mean we're all out of luck? Is that what you're saying?"

The questions these college students are asking might overwhelm even the most seasoned Bible teacher. But they're good questions—ones that must be answered if we expect to develop a deep, solid, and lasting understanding of the Bible. And they are questions that will inevitably confront each of us and our children in a postmodern society that considers religious truth something that can be determined subjectively.

If the Bible is just a helpful collection of nice thoughts, then it doesn't matter too much if parts have disappeared or been mistranslated over the years. If the Bible is merely another version of truth, then it makes little difference whether it is accurate. But if the Bible is what Chad claims—God's instruction manual for living, and the primary means by which we can know God—then it becomes extremely important to know whether it's reliable, whether it was recorded exactly as God gave it, and whether it's been accurately passed down to us. As Megan the college student asked, "What if the people writing the Bible didn't put down everything God said…or maybe they got it all wrong or something. Does that mean we're all out of luck?"

As it happens, Megan's question has already been answered in the Bible itself, in an incident that's recorded in the Old Testament.

When the Book of the Law Was Lost

The incident took place in Judah, during a period when a young man named Josiah reigned as king. At that time, the people of Judah had been worshipping idols for many years, and many of the old ways had been neglected or lost. But Josiah "began to seek the God of his ancestor David" (2 Chronicles 34:3). He decreed the destruction of the pagan idols and altars that dotted the land and began an effort to repair, restore, and reconsecrate the temple in Jerusalem.

One day, as Hilkiah the high priest was working amid the flurry of the temple restoration efforts, a long and ancient scroll was discovered. The priest's hands must have trembled as he rolled through the scroll, reading words that had been lost many years earlier. Recognizing its importance, Hilkiah conveyed the scroll to a man named Shaphan, the king's private secretary.

As Shaphan read from the scroll to Josiah, the king no doubt recognized the words. Even though he had never heard them before, much of what Shaphan read had been circulated for years by word of mouth, from parent to child and sage to student. Josiah, like Shaphan and Hilkiah, recognized this as "the Book of the Law of the LORD as it had been given through Moses" (verse 14).

But soon Josiah's fascination turned to worry and then quickly to horror as Shaphan read:

> If you fully obey the LORD your God by keeping all the commands I am giving you today, the LORD your God will exalt you above all the nations of the world. You will experience all these blessings if you obey the LORD your God…
>
> *But* if you refuse to listen to the LORD your God and *do not obey* all the commands and laws I am giving you today…you will be cursed wherever you go…[with] curses, confusion, and disillusionment

in everything you do, until at last you are completely destroyed (Deuteronomy 28:1-20).

When the king heard those words, he tore his clothes with his bare hands. "We have not been doing what this scroll says we must do" (2 Chronicles 34:21). He understood that God had not been revealed to his people because they had been without the written revelation of God. Fearful for himself and his people, Josiah gathered the people together. He read to them from the lost scroll, and together they pledged to obey the Lord and his Word.

A Distorted Revelation Produces Distorted Results

The story of King Josiah emphasizes how dangerous it would be if God's Word were lost...or distorted, altered, or misrepresented to us through inaccurate copying over hundreds or thousands of years. Before the written word, God spoke directly to Moses, Abraham, and the prophets. God also revealed himself in the flesh and spoke to us through his Son, Jesus (see Hebrews 1:1-2). These revelations of God have been recorded in written form and preserved in the pages of Scripture. But if the facts and events of the Bible weren't carefully and truthfully recorded, then the Bible we have today is a distorted reflection of God's nature and character.

So knowing God and living in relationship with him are dependent on our receiving and possessing an accurate revelation of him. Unless the Bible is reliable, we have no assurance its teachings are true at all. Imagine, for example, God really did give Moses 15 commandments, and some scribe along the way decided to eliminate five of them. We would—at best—possess an incomplete picture of what God is like and what he requires of us. And at worst, as Josiah realized, we would be courting disaster, inviting "curses, confusion, and disillusionment in everything [we] do" (Deuteronomy 28:20).[1]

If we hope to enjoy the benefits of knowing God, we must be sure we have a Bible that accurately represents what God inspired people to write on his behalf. Because if the Word of God was not accurately recorded and relayed to us, then we and our children, like Josiah and the nation of Judah, will be cheated in our efforts to know God and may be exposed to "curses, confusion, and disillusionment."

EVIDENCE GOD'S WORD IS RELIABLE

How can you be sure the Bible you read is what God actually said? It was written thousands of years ago. How can you be sure it was copied correctly? Who's to say large passages haven't been left out or distorted by people adding their own ideas? Is there evidence that the Bible we have today is a reliable reproduction of what God inspired his writers to write? Let's explore these questions.

GOD'S WORDS HAVE BEEN RELAYED ACCURATELY

This God-inspired book called the Bible was written during a 1,500-year span through more than 40 generations by more than 40 different authors from every walk of life—shepherds, soldiers, prophets, poets, monarchs, scholars, statesmen, masters, servants, tax collectors, fishermen, and tentmakers. Its God-breathed words were written in a variety of places: in the wilderness, in a palace, in a dungeon, on a hillside, in a prison, and in exile. It was penned on the continents of Asia, Africa, and Europe and was written in three languages: Hebrew, Aramaic, and Greek. It tells hundreds of stories, records hundreds of songs, and addresses hundreds of controversial subjects. Yet with all its variety of authors, origins, and content, it achieves a miraculous continuity of theme—God's redemption of his children and the restoration of all things to his original design.

Because of the redemptive and relational purpose of the Bible, God cannot allow it to be lost, twisted, or distorted. As Jesus said, "I assure you, until heaven and earth disappear, even the smallest detail of God's law will remain until its purpose is achieved" (Matthew 5:18). He will permit nothing to impede his purpose. "Heaven and earth will disappear," Jesus said, "but my words will remain forever" (Matthew 24:35).

God is so passionate about his relationship with us that he has personally—and miraculously—provided the inspiration of his Word and supervised its transmission. He repeatedly reinforced its reliability so that all those who have open eyes and open hearts may believe it with assurance and confidence. Nations have rejected it, tyrants have tried to stamp it out, heretics have tried to distort it, but the evidence for the Bible's reliability is sufficient to assure us and our kids that it has remained a true reflection of reality—of who God is.

It's not difficult to see the superintending work of God in the composition of the Old and New Testaments. Considering the process of writing and preserving manuscripts in ancient times, the fact we can be confident we have an accurate Bible is truly miraculous. None of the original manuscripts that God inspired authors to write—called *autographs*—are known to exist today. What we read now are printed copies based on ancient handwritten copies of yet other copies of the original. This is because the Bible was composed and transmitted in an era before printing presses. All manuscripts had to be written by hand. Over time, the ink would fade, and the material it was written on would deteriorate. So if a document was to be preserved and passed down to the next generation, new copies would have to be made or the document would be lost forever. Of course, these copies were made just like the originals—by hand, with fading ink, on deteriorating materials.

But, you may rightly wonder, doesn't the making of hand-copied reproductions open up the whole transmission process to error? How do we know that a weary copier, blurry-eyed from lack of sleep, didn't skip a few critical words or leave out whole sections or misquote some key verses? Indeed, our manuscripts of the Bible differ from each other because people make mistakes when they copy something by hand. Or what if, during the copying of Mark's Gospel some hundred years after he wrote it, some agenda-driven, meddling scribe added five chapters of his own or twisted around the things Jesus said or did? If the words God gave to Moses, David, Matthew, or Peter were later changed or carelessly copied, how could we be sure we are coming to know the one true God? How could we be confident that the commands we obey are a true reflection of God's nature and character? What if it's true, as some critics say, that the Bible is a collection of outdated writings riddled with inaccuracies and distortions? How can we be sure the manuscripts available to us today are an accurate transmission of the originals?

God has not left us to wonder. He has miraculously supervised the transmission of his Word to ensure that it was relayed accurately from one generation to another.*[2]

---

* This chapter has been adapted from *Beyond Belief to Convictions*, chapter 8; *Evidence That Demands a Verdict*, chapters 3 and 4; and "Can the New Testament Be Trusted?" article by Sean McDowell. Please see these two McDowell books and the article at www.seanmcdowell.org for more details on the reliability of Scripture.

The Case of the Meticulous Scribes

One of the ways God ensured his Word would be relayed accurately was by choosing, calling, and cultivating a nation of men and women who took the Book of the Law very seriously. God commanded and instilled in the Jewish people a great reverence for his Word. From their very first days as a nation, God told them, "Listen closely, Israel, to everything I say...Commit yourselves wholeheartedly to these commands I am giving you today. Repeat them again and again to your children. Talk about them when you are at home and when you are away on a journey, when you are lying down and when you are getting up again. Tie them to your hands as a reminder, and wear them on your forehead. Write them on the doorposts of your house and on your gates" (Deuteronomy 6:3, 6-9).

That attitude toward the commands of God became such a part of the Jewish identity that a class of Jewish scholars called the *Sopherim,* from a Hebrew word meaning "scribes," arose between the fifth and third centuries BC, even though some of the Old Testament books were written even earlier. These custodians of the Hebrew Scriptures dedicated themselves to carefully preserving the ancient manuscripts and producing new copies when necessary. The Sopherim were eclipsed by the Talmudic scribes, who guarded, interpreted, and commented on the sacred texts from AD 100–500. In turn, the Talmudic scribes were followed by the better-known Masoretic scribes (AD 500–900).

The zeal of the Masoretes surpassed that of even their most dedicated predecessors. They established detailed and stringent disciplines for copying a manuscript. Their rules were so rigorous that when a new copy was complete, they would give the reproduction equal authority to that of its parent because they were thoroughly convinced they had an exact duplicate.

This was the class of people who, in the providence of God, were chosen to preserve the Old Testament text for centuries. A scribe would begin his day of transcribing by ceremonially washing his entire body. He would then garb himself in full Jewish dress before sitting at his desk. As he wrote, if he came to the Hebrew name of God, he could not begin writing the name with a quill newly dipped in ink for fear it would smear the page. Once he began writing the name of God, he could not stop or allow himself to be distracted; even if a king was to enter the room, the scribe was obligated to continue without interruption until he finished penning the holy name of the one true God.

The Masoretic guidelines for copying manuscripts also required the following:

- The scroll must be written on the skin of a clean animal.

- Each skin must contain a specified number of columns, equal throughout the entire book.

- The length of each column must extend no less than 48 lines or more than 60 lines.

- The column breadth must consist of exactly 30 letters.

- The space of a thread must appear between every consonant.

- The breadth of nine consonants had to be inserted between each section.

- A space of three lines had to appear between each book.

- The fifth book of Moses (Deuteronomy) had to conclude exactly with a full line.

- Nothing—not even the shortest word—could be copied from memory; it had to be copied letter by letter.

- The scribe must count the number of times each letter of the alphabet occurred in each book and compare it to the original.

- If a manuscript was found to contain even one mistake, it was discarded.[3]

God instilled in the Masoretes such a painstaking reverence for the Hebrew Scriptures to ensure the amazingly accurate transmission of the Book of the Law so you and I—and our children—would have an accurate revelation of God. Until recently, however, we had no way of knowing just how amazing the preservation of the Old Testament has been.

Before 1947, the oldest complete Hebrew manuscript dated to AD 900. But with the discovery of 223 manuscripts in caves on the west side of the

Dead Sea, we now have Old Testament manuscripts that have been dated by paleographers at around 125 BC. These Dead Sea Scrolls, as they are called, are a thousand years older than any previously known manuscripts.[4] But here's the exciting part: Once the Dead Sea Scrolls were translated and compared with modern versions, the Hebrew Bible proved to be identical, word for word, in more than 95 percent of the text. (The variation of 5 percent consisted mainly of spelling variations. For example, of the 166 words in Isaiah 53, only 17 letters were in question. Of those, 10 letters were a matter of spelling, and 4 were stylistic changes; the remaining 3 letters comprised the word *light,* which was added in verse 11).[5]

In other words, the greatest manuscript discovery of all time revealed that a thousand years of copying the Old Testament had produced only excruciatingly minor variations, none of which altered the clear meaning of the text or brought the manuscript's fundamental integrity into question. It is true that the Masoretic scribes developed their strict rules roughly one thousand years after many of the Old Testament books were written. Nonetheless, this discovery shows the text has remained largely intact for a millennium, which suggests deep care and reverence for passing on the Scriptures long before the Masoretes came on the scene.

A strong case can be made that God has preserved his Word and accurately relayed it through the centuries so when you pick up an Old Testament today, you can be confident you are holding a well-preserved, fully reliable document.

The Case of the New Testament Text

The Hebrew scribes did not copy the manuscripts of the New Testament. There were several reasons. The official Jewish leadership did not endorse Christianity; the letters and histories circulated by the New Testament writers were not then thought of as official Scripture; and these documents were not written in the Hebrew language, but rather in Greek. Thus, the same formal disciplines were not followed in the transmission of these writings from one generation to another. In the case of the New Testament, God did a new thing to ensure that the blessing of his Word would be preserved for us and our children.

One way of evaluating the textual reliability of ancient literature is to consider two factors: 1) the time interval between the original and the earliest copy and 2) how many manuscript copies are available.

For example, virtually everything we know today about Julius Caesar's exploits in the Gallic Wars is derived from 251 copies, the earliest of which dates to almost 1,000 years after the time *The Gallic Wars* was written. Our modern text of Livy's *History of Rome* relies on about 470 manuscripts that are dated from 400 to 1,000 years after the original writing (see chart below).[6] By comparison, the text of Homer's *Iliad* is much more reliable. It is supported by more than 1,900 manuscript copies in existence today, with a 400-year time gap between the date of composition and the earliest of these copies.

TEXTUAL RELIABILITY STANDARDS APPLIED TO CLASSICAL LITERATURE					
Author	Book	Date written	Earliest copies	Time gap	Number of copies
Homer	*Iliad*	800 BC	c. 415 BC	c. 400 yrs.	1,900+
Herodotus	*History*	480–425 BC	c. 150–50 BC	c. 350 yrs.	About 106
Thucydides	*History*	460–400 BC	c. 300–200 BC	c. 100 yrs.	188
Plato	*Tetralogies*	400 BC	c. 300–200 BC	c. 100 yrs.	238
Demosthenes	*Speeches*	300 BC	c. 100 BC	c. 200 yrs.	444
Caesar	*Gallic Wars*	100–44 BC	c. AD 900	c. 1000 yrs.	251
Livy	*History of Rome*	59 BC–AD 17	c. AD 300–400	c. 400 yrs. c. 1000 yrs.	About 470
Tacitus	*Annals*	AD 100	c. AD 850	c. 750 yrs.	36
Pliny Secundus	*Natural History*	AD 61–113	c. AD 400–500	c. 350 yrs.	200+

The textual reliability for Livy, Homer, and these other ancient sources is considered more than adequate for historians to work with, but this evidence pales in comparison to what God performed in the case of the New Testament text. We have more than 5,800 manuscripts of the Greek New Testament, plus another eighteen thousand manuscripts of the New Testament translated into other languages. The earliest of these is a fragment of John's Gospel currently in the John Rylands Library of Manchester, England. It has been dated to within *50 years* of the date when the apostle John penned the original.[7]

Keep in mind that earlier manuscripts are generally more reliable because the number of copies between the original and the early manuscripts tend to be fewer, giving less chance for mistakes to have crept in. Early manuscripts, however, also tend to be small fragments rather than complete books. This may leave us wondering if we have enough useful data across all of our earliest manuscripts to reconstruct the entire New Testament.

We do. According to New Testament manuscript specialist Dan Wallace, "Today we have as many as 12 MSS [manuscripts] from the second century, 64 from the third, and 48 from the fourth—a total of 124 MSS within 300 years of the composition of the New Testament. Most of these are fragmentary, but the whole NT [New Testament] text is found in this collection multiple times."[8]

Given all of the manuscript evidence available for the New Testament, scholars are able to apply a number of common-sensical methods to cross-check the manuscripts against each other and use contextual clues to reconstruct the original wording with a high degree of confidence. Their work is not done in secret, either. Anyone with knowledge of biblical Greek can pick up a Greek Bible with a so-called critical apparatus. The apparatus details the most significant differences across the manuscripts and the important manuscripts that contain each different reading. You will find a handful of challenging spots to be sure, but most ambiguous spots of the text make little difference in the meaning, and no important theological issue is jeopardized by the manuscripts.[9]

Since the time the original manuscripts were written—more than nineteen hundred years ago—skeptics have tried to refute the Bible, infidels have tried to stamp it out, and dictators have tried to burn it. However, God's Word has not only prevailed but proliferated. Voltaire, the noted eighteenth-century French skeptic, predicted that within a hundred years of his time, Christianity would be but a footnote in history. Ironically, in 1828, 50 years after Voltaire's death, the Geneva Bible Society moved into his house and used his printing press to produce thousands of Bibles to distribute worldwide. "People are like grass that dies away," Peter wrote, quoting Isaiah the prophet, "but the word of the Lord will last forever" (1 Peter 1:24-25).

GOD'S WORD HAS BEEN RECORDED ACCURATELY

We can be confident the manuscripts of both the Old and New Testaments have been handed down over the centuries with care. In other words, we can have confidence that what was written down initially is remarkably close to what we have today. But a more basic question arises. When these inspired writers were recording historical events, were they chronologically close to those events so we can have confidence in the accuracy of what they wrote?

Such careful inspiration and supervision of the Bible underlines God's purpose, that not a single piece of this revelation about himself or the human condition be left to chance or recorded incorrectly.

You see, many ancient writings adhered only loosely to the facts of the events they reported. Some highly regarded authors of the ancient world, for example, reported events that took place many years before they were born and in countries they had never visited. While their writing may be largely factual, historians admit that greater credibility must be granted to writers who were both geographically and chronologically close to the events they report.

With that in mind, look at the loving care God took when he inspired the writing of the New Testament. There is good reason to believe that the accounts of Jesus' life, the history of the early church, and the letters that form the bulk of the New Testament were all written by men who were either eyewitnesses to the events they recorded or contemporaries of eyewitnesses. God selected Matthew, Mark, and John to write three of the four Gospels. These were men who could say such things as, "This report is from an eyewitness giving an accurate account" (John 19:35). God spoke through Luke the physician to record the third Gospel and the book of Acts. Although not an eyewitness, Luke was a careful writer who used as "source material the reports circulating among us from the early disciples and other eyewitnesses of what God [did] in fulfillment of his promises" (Luke 1:2).

God could have spoken through anyone, from anywhere, to write his words about Christ. But to give us additional confidence in the truth, he worked through eyewitnesses such as John, who said, "We are telling you about what we ourselves have actually seen and heard" (1 John 1:3). He worked through Peter, who declared, "We did not follow cunningly devised fables when we made known to you the power and coming of our Lord Jesus Christ, but were eyewitnesses of His majesty" (2 Peter 1:16 NKJV). And whom did he choose as his most prolific writer? The apostle Paul, whose dramatic conversion from persecutor of Christians to planter of churches made him perhaps the most credible witness of all!

But God didn't stop there. Those through whom he transmitted his inspired Word were also apostles. These men could rely on their own eyewitness experiences, and they could appeal to the firsthand knowledge of their contemporaries, even their most severe opponents (see Acts 2:32; 3:15; 13:31; 1 Corinthians 15:3-8). They not only said, "Look, we saw this," or "We heard that," but they were also so confident in what they wrote as to say, in effect, "Check it out," "Ask around," and "You know it as well as I do!" Such challenges demonstrate a supreme confidence that the "God-breathed" Word was recorded exactly as God spoke it (2 Timothy 3:16 NIV).

Such careful inspiration and supervision of the Bible underlines God's purpose: to ensure the reliability of his revelation to humankind. Ample evidence exists to suggest God was very selective in the people he chose to record his words— people who for the most part had firsthand knowledge of key events and who were credible channels to carefully record those truths he wanted us to know.*

GOD'S WORD HAS BEEN REINFORCED EXTERNALLY

God did not stop working after he had brought about the development of the massive textual evidence for the reliability of his Word. He has since

---

* A comprehensive treatment of the internal evidence test is covered in chapters 3, 4, and 23 of *Evidence That Demands a Verdict.*

worked to reinforce the evidence through external means. A routine criterion in examining the reliability of a historical document is whether *other* historical material confirms or denies the internal testimony of the document itself. Historians ask, "What sources, apart from the literature under examination, substantiate its accuracy and reliability?"

In all of history, the Bible is by far the most widely referenced and quoted book. For example, the New Testament alone is so extensively quoted in the ancient manuscripts of nonbiblical authors that all 27 books, from Matthew through Revelation, could be reconstructed virtually word for word from those sources.

The writings of early Christians like Eusebius (AD 339) in his *Ecclesiastical History* III.39 and Irenaeus (AD 180) in his *Against Heresies* III reinforce the text of the apostle John's writings. Clement of Rome (AD 95), Ignatius (AD 70–110), Polycarp (AD 70–156), and Titian (AD 170) offer external confirmation of other New Testament accounts. Non-Christian historians such as the first-century Roman historian Tacitus (AD 55–117) and the Jewish historian Josephus (AD 37–100) confirm the substance of many scriptural accounts. These and other outside sources substantiate the accuracy of the biblical record like that of no other book in history.*[10]

These extrabiblical references, however, are not the only external evidences. Although some questions remain, and much archaeological work needs to be done, the historical record consistently supports the biblical account. Archaeologist Titus Kennedy published a book called *Unearthing the Bible: 101 Archaeological Discoveries That Bring the Bible to Life*. We have summarized and adapted Dr. Kennedy's words in seven of the findings he discusses from the Old Testament. Keep in mind, these are only a small sample of what archaeologists have uncovered in support of the Bible.

1. **Stele of Hammurabi**. A stele is a monument of stone or wooden slab erected for commemorative purposes. This stele is roughly 7.5 feet and is inscribed in laws from the 18th-century BC Code of Hammurabi. It contains information about customs, contracts, social

---

* For more information on the confirmation of the Bible's reliability in extrabiblical sources, see chapters 3 and 4 of *Evidence That Demands a Verdict*.

practices, economics, and punishments. Since it dates approximately to the time of Jacob and Joseph, and the laws and customs overlap with the book of Genesis, we can compare the two accounts. One case is particularly illuminating: the Code of Hammurabi records the price of a slave as 20 shekels, which coincides with the biblical account (Genesis 37:28).[11]

2. **Papyrus Brooklyn**. This is an Egyptian papyrus that contains a list of domestic servants from about the 17th century, which corresponds to the time the Hebrews lived in Egypt as settlers and then as slaves. Roughly thirty of the servants have Semitic names and nine of them appear to have Hebrew names. Dr. Kennedy concludes, "Therefore, this list is a clear attestation of Hebrews living in Egypt prior to the Exodus under Moses, in their earlier period of residence in the country prior to their total enslavement, and perhaps shows that a group may have migrated south or was taken south for work."[12]

3. **The Merneptah Stele**. This stele is an Egyptian stone standing nearly 10.4 feet. The text mentions that Canaan was plundered and "Israel is laid waste and its seed (grain) is not." This is perhaps the earliest inscription mentioning the people of Israel. Dr. Kennedy concludes, "If the Israelites began to settle Canaan after 1400 BC as the books of Joshua and Judges describe, then by the time of Merneptah they would have been the main occupants of the land rather than the Canaanites, just as the stele indicates."[13]

4. **The Goliath Ostracon**. This inscribed piece of pottery comes from the 10th or 9th century and was discovered at the ancient Philistine city of Gath. Although there is some debate about the translation of the text, the name appears to be a form of the name "Goliath," and it dates to the time shortly after the wars between David and the giants of Gath.[14]

5. **Tel Dan Stele**. Many scholars rejected the existence of David because there was no convincing evidence for his existence and reign outside

biblical references. In 1993, in ancient Dan (northern Israel), an inscription was discovered that refers to the "house of David." Dating to the 9th century BC, this is the earliest known reference to King David. Given that the inscription is found on a victory stele from the Arameans, a known enemy of Israel, David was undeniably a historical figure.[15]

6. **Bulla of Isaiah.** Isaiah is the most quoted Old Testament book for the authors of the New Testament. He was a prophet who ministered from roughly 740–686 BC and may have been executed in the reign of Manasseh. A bulla (a lump of clay molded around a cord and stamped with a seal) was discovered in Jerusalem and may refer to Isaiah the prophet. It was discovered alongside 32 other bullas, including one of King Hezekiah. It contains the name Isaiah and appears to have the word "prophet" in archaic Hebrew script.[16]

7. **Cylinder of Nabonidus.** Until 1854, there was no source outside of Daniel referring to Belshazzar, king of Babylon. In the 6th century BC, the Babylonian king Nabonidus placed four identical cylinders as foundation deposits in Ur. The cylinders refer to Belshazzar as the eldest son of king Nabonidus, which confirms his existence in the time and place the Bible describes.[17]

Repeatedly throughout history, the astounding accuracy of God's Word has been confirmed externally. This is very different from the Book of Mormon, for example, for which there is no external support. The external evidence for the Bible sets it apart from other religious writings of the world. It is also a clear and praiseworthy indication of how God lovingly supervised its transmission so that he might preserve for us—and our children—all the blessings that come from knowing him and obeying his Word.

THE PROTECTION AND PROVISION OF GOD'S WORD

As we discussed earlier in the book, the majority of people today have been conditioned to believe moral and spiritual claims are true only *when they choose to believe them.* When people hold this view of truth, the meaning and power of God's Word in their lives is diminished to the point of having little effect.

THE TWO MODELS FOR VIEWING TRUTH

In our culture there are two distinct models for knowing that something is true. Each model affects how we see and apply God's Word.

- *Model #1:* Truth is when a belief matches up with reality; it is objective and universal. The truth is known through discovering God and his Word.

- *Model #2:* What is true is defined by the individual; it is subjective and situational. Truth is determined through simply choosing to believe something.

The second model—a subjective (relativistic) model—is the model many people use today when it comes to issues of morality and religion. It is the lens through which they understand themselves and the basis on which they make life's decisions.

It is certainly true that some choices in life are subjective. Should I go bowling tonight or watch a movie? Do I prefer chocolate peanut butter ice cream or cookies and cream? Should I wear my green shirt or my black one? These are personal choices relative to the individual. The phrase *Chocolate peanut butter ice cream is the best* may be true for me, since it's my favorite, but it may not be true for you. Subjective claims depend on the feelings or preferences of the individual. In fact, saying chocolate peanut butter ice cream is the best is really a claim about *my* experience of the ice cream (the subject) rather than the ice cream itself (the object).

On the other hand, *objective* claims depend not on feelings or beliefs but on the external world. They are true or false independently of how we think or feel. For example, the statements "1 + 2 = 3," "George Washington was the first president of the United States," and "Water = H_2O" are all objective truths.

Where would you place the moral claim "Abortion is wrong"? Your gut reaction might be to consider it a subjective claim, like ice cream. After all, don't people disagree about the answer? But think about it for a moment. If all moral claims were like ice cream, could we ever condemn any action as wrong? No! We couldn't condemn racism, sexism, war crimes, or any other action as actually being immoral. If morality were subjective, then there would be no real difference between a father who has nurtured and cared for his children and a father who has molested his children. Each father made a personal choice, and that choice was "true" for him.

In the case of abortion, either the unborn is human or it is not. And either humans have the right to life or they don't. These are questions of fact, not opinion. Upon reflection, we all know there is moral truth, just as there is mathematical truth. And the same is true with religious claims. Either the world was created or it wasn't. Either God exists or he doesn't. Either Jesus rose from the grave or he didn't. We may choose to believe these claims, or not, but they all deal with objective claims about reality that are either true or false.

We may not always know the truth immediately. But as believers in God, we don't make up a truth that's comfortable to us at the moment. We know objective truth exists—it's out there waiting to be discovered. And when it seems unclear to us, we seek to discover it. When making decisions, we consider facts and weigh evidence. We do our best to arrive at truth, and then we live accordingly even if it is uncomfortable and costly. But to a relativist, there is no objective truth outside of the self. The relativist will argue that since everyone has a different viewpoint, truth is unknowable.

Without reference to an objective standard, people struggle with the impossible challenge of trying to define truth or falsehood, right or wrong, good or evil. When we stray from the objective standard—the Word of God—and attempt to devise our own moral standards, the picture not only becomes indistinct and muddy but the relevance of Scripture and its positive benefits of protection and provision are lost.

GOD AND HIS WORD AS OUR STANDARD

The town of Sèvres, a suburb of Paris, hosts the headquarters of the International Bureau of Weights and Measures. This bureau establishes and ensures reliable standards for all physical measurements—mass, length, volume, and weight—throughout most of the industrialized world.

If you wanted to be absolutely certain the millimeter divisions on your ruler were accurate, you would compare them against the bureau's linear standards. If you wanted to know whether the bottle of Coke in your refrigerator contained exactly two liters of liquid, you could check it against the bureau's volume measurements.

The relevance of God's Word as our standard for living provides both the means to know God for who he is, and the way or guidelines to live in a godly manner.

In a similar manner, we know a standard for right and wrong that exists outside, above, and beyond ourselves. That standard is the nature of God himself as revealed in the Scriptures. The relevance of God's Word as our standard for living provides both the means to know God for who he is, and the way or guidelines to live in a godly manner. This results in God being honored and us living a life of joy. That is why choosing God's definition of what is right and wrong and living accordingly grants us the benefits of his protection and provision.[18]

LIVING UNDER THE PROTECTION AND PROVISION OF GOD

Some people react to God's laws negatively. They see his commands as constricting and biblical morality as confining. They don't see the benefits to a moral lifestyle. They fail to realize God's commands, like those of a loving parent—"Don't touch the stove," "Look both ways before you cross the street," "Eat your vegetables"—are not meant to spoil our fun and make us miserable. God gave commands—"Flee sexual immorality"; "Husbands, love your wives"; "You shall not commit adultery" and all the others—because he wanted to protect us and provide for us. He didn't concoct those rules to be a killjoy or to throw his weight around; he gave them because he knew some things we didn't. He knew, for example, that sexual immorality is a path, not to pleasure and fulfillment, but to emptiness and frustration.

Moses acknowledged this truth when he challenged the nation of Israel:

> Now, Israel, what does the LORD your God require from you, but to fear the LORD your God, to walk in all his ways and love him, and to serve the LORD your God with all your heart and with all your soul, and to keep the LORD's commandments and His statutes *which I am commanding you today for your good*? (Deuteronomy 10:12-13 NASB).

The relevance of God's Word to each of us is simply this—*it is for our good!* Looking down from an eternal, omniscient perspective, God can see things we cannot. He's like a general directing soldiers from a helicopter. He can see the entire battlefield. He knows where the enemy is hiding and has set traps. From his superior viewpoint he can direct his troops to avoid the enemy and his traps. Every truth, every rule, and every guideline coming from God's Word flows from the loving heart and character of God for our own good.

"I know the plans I have for you," God told the nation of Israel, "they are plans for good and not for disaster, to give you a future and a hope" (Jeremiah 29:11). He went on to express his desire for his children to have "one heart and mind to worship me forever, for their own good and for the good of all their descendants" (32:39). Choosing God's way instead of choosing wrong does not sap all the fun and excitement out of life; on the contrary, it accomplishes our good, because we were created to reflect his likeness and image. When we live godly lives—lives that reflect the character of God—we inevitably experience true joy. Paradoxically, joy doesn't come from seeking joy. As the title of C.S. Lewis' spiritual autobiography, *Surprised by Joy*, indicates, true joy comes from the last place critics of God's laws would think to look. It comes from seeking God and following his ways.

Words of Warning

In discussing the joy of God's protection and provision that results from knowing and following God's ways, we must take care not to give the impression that bad things do not happen to moral people, or that people who engage in immorality are never happy. Indeed, the prophet Jeremiah asked, "Why are the wicked so prosperous? Why are evil people so happy?" (Jeremiah 12:1), and King David confessed he had seen "proud and evil people thriving like mighty trees" (Psalm 37:35).

Living out God's ways does not mean that in the short term morality is always immediately rewarded and immorality is always immediately punished. Sin does promise immediate satisfaction, and it does often deliver pleasure for a period of time. Some of the rewards of morality and the consequences of sin may not be measured out until after this life is over.

We must also be careful not to communicate the impression that God's commands are true simply because they are beneficial. To illustrate this point, think back to when you were in the third or fourth grade. You were taught the multiplication tables. That knowledge has paid off many times over for you. It helps you complete your tax return and compare prices in the grocery store. You might say that you get something good from your relationship with the multiplication tables. But $5 \times 6 = 30$ is not true *because* you get something good out of it. It is true because it is true, because it reflects certain laws—it reflects reality.

The multiplication tables are true whether you benefit from them or not. But as you make use of the truth of the multiplication tables, you indeed gain benefit. Similarly, those things that are true and right in God's Word are not so *because* of any benefit you may derive from them; they are true because they are true.

Seeing God's Protection

There was a young man we'll call Greg. He lived down the block from a family who had an in-ground swimming pool in their backyard. Greg had never gone swimming in their pool; he barely knew the people, and a high wooden fence enclosed the pool.

One dark evening when Greg knew his neighbors were away, he and his girlfriend snuck behind the house, scaled the fence, and entered the pool area to go for a swim. Greg threw off his shoes, climbed the ladder and, while his girlfriend was still taking off her shoes and socks, leaped off the end of the diving board.

He heard his girlfriend scream just before he lost consciousness. The pool held only a few feet of water; Greg's dive ended with a shallow splat of water and a sickening crunch of bones. His late-night dive paralyzed him from the neck down for the rest of his life.

Greg ignored the fence his neighbors had erected around the pool. He probably assumed it was there only to keep people like him and his girlfriend from having fun. In reality, it was meant for protection, and his disregard of that boundary cost him dearly. Similarly, when we disregard the moral boundaries God has erected to protect us from harm, the cost can be devastating.

More than 50 years ago Dr. S.I. McMillen wrote a brilliant book called *None of These Diseases.* He demonstrated how over two dozen divine commands or standards served to prevent such disorders as heart disease, cervical cancer, and arthritis long before the advent of modern medicine! McMillen wrote in the preface: "When God led the Israelites out of afflicted Egypt, he promised them that if they would obey his statutes, he would put 'none of these diseases' upon them. God guaranteed a freedom from disease that modern medicine cannot duplicate."[19]

That doesn't mean if we always obey God we'll never get sick. But God's commandments do act as an umbrella. When you put up an umbrella, it shields you from the rain. But if you choose to move out from under that umbrella during a storm, you're bound to get wet. As long as you and I stay under the umbrella of God's commands, we'll be shielded from many consequences. However, if we step out from under that protective cover, we should not be surprised if we suffer the negative effects of sinful behavior.

Seeing God's Provision

So far, most of what we've written about the benefits of God's Word has emphasized how it protects us from evil. But protection is only one side of the coin. The other side is provision. Adhering to God's instructions not only protects us from the consequences of evil, it also provides positive benefits. To illustrate, I (Josh) went hiking years ago in the Great Smoky Mountains National Park with my son and daughter. We set out in the morning to hike to the top of Clingmans Dome, the highest point in the park, a towering 6643 feet.

It was a long hike from our campsite, much longer than I had expected. We really got tired, but we plodded on. Sean started to complain, so did his sister. And their groans and complaints seemed to increase in volume and intensity with the altitude. I began to wonder if I was being cruel by pushing my kids too hard.

But eventually we reached the "dome," the bald spot at what seemed to be the top of the earth. We all gazed in wonder at the breathtaking vista. The magnificent view made us forget about our aching legs and throbbing lungs. Sean actually wrapped his arms around me and whispered, "Thanks, Dad. This is great." His sister joined us in an embrace.

That view—and the sense of accomplishment at having completed a taxing hike—turned complaints into appreciation. My insistence on completing the hike had provided us with an experience no painting of the Smoky Mountains could match.

That sort of thing may be what the psalmist had in mind when he wrote, "He [God] makes me as surefooted as a deer, leading me safely along the mountain" (Psalm 18:33). Obedience to God's commands not only protects us from harm; it also allows God to provide for us, sometimes in breathtaking ways.

When Jesus said, "You will know the truth, and the truth will set you free" (John 8:32), he spoke not only of freedom *from* things like disease, disillusionment, and disappointment, but of freedom *to*. Being obedient to God's Word means being free to enjoy *maximum* leisure, *maximum* satisfaction, and *maximum* liberty—in the way God intended. God's prohibitions and directives to us come out of a heart of love that in effect says, "Follow in my ways and your joy will be made complete." God always has our best interest at heart.

LIVING UNDER GOD'S PROTECTION
AND ENJOYING HIS PROVISIONS

Missouri is called the "Show-me State." And there is a little bit of that attitude in all of us. Most of us are interested in seeing how things work and knowing why they function as they do. Well, when God gives us instructions to act in a certain way, there is a clear picture of how our obedience results in protection from harm and a provision of blessing. We could give countless examples here, but chapter length will limit us to two.[20]

GOD'S WORD ON SEXUAL IMMORALITY

In biblical terms, sexual immorality is all sex that occurs outside of a marriage between one man and one woman (extramarital and premarital sex). Scripture states:

- "Abstain from...sexual immorality" (Acts 15:29).

- "Run away from sexual sin" (1 Corinthians 6:18).

- "Among you there must not be even a hint of sexual immorality... because these are improper for God's holy people" (Ephesians 5:3 NIV).

- "God wants you to be holy, so you should keep clear of all sexual sin" (1 Thessalonians 4:3).

Sexual Immorality Violates God's Nature

God's very nature is pure. "Everyone who has this hope [of glory] in him purifies himself, just as he [God] is pure" (1 John 3:3 NIV). Because we are to reflect his image and follow in his ways, we are commanded to "have nothing to do with sexual sin, impurity, lust, and shameful desires" (Colossians 3:5).

God's very nature is faithful. "Understand...that the LORD your God is indeed God," Moses told the Israelites. "He is the faithful God who keeps his covenant for a thousand generations" (Deuteronomy 7:9). Because we are to reflect God's image of faithfulness and follow in his ways, we are commanded to "give honor to marriage, and remain faithful to one another in marriage" (Hebrews 13:4). Faithfulness can, of course, be broken even *before* one is married. To engage in premarital sex is to connect with another in a way intended only for a covenant relationship, thus having no ground for a solid commitment to being faithful.

The Protection and Provision of Living Sexually Pure and Faithful

Living sexually pure lives and remaining faithful to a present or future marriage relationship results in the following benefits:

PROTECTS FROM:	PROVIDES FOR:
guilt	spiritual rewards
unplanned pregnancy	optimum atmosphere for child raising
sexually transmitted diseases	peace of mind
sexual insecurity	trust
emotional distress	true intimacy

Both of us (Josh and Sean) decided early on to wait until the loving commitment of marriage before expressing ourselves sexually. As a result, we have been protected from feelings of guilt and have enjoyed an uninterrupted relationship with God.

We have never had to go through the heartache of an unplanned pregnancy. And consequently, our children, conceived out of a loving married relationship, have had the opportunity to be raised by their biological mother and father.

We have been protected from the fear that any sexually transmitted disease might come into our marriage bed.

We have been protected from the sexual insecurity that can occur from being compared to past sexual lovers one's spouses may have had. And consequently, we have experienced the provision of trust in our relationship.

We have been protected from the emotional distress premarital sex can bring and the feelings of betrayal an extramarital affair can cause. As a result we have enjoyed relational intimacy with our wives unobstructed by breaches of trust or ghosts from the past. Reflecting God's character in terms of purity and faithfulness in our human relationships brings glory to God and blessings to us.

Not everyone has remained faithful prior to marriage or during marriage. It is important for people who have made these mistakes to know that God is a faithful and forgiving God who can restore broken hearts, broken emotions, and broken marriages. For six years of his life, Joshua Broome was one of the most successful adult film stars in the world. He was the male performer of the year in 2012 and participated in more than a thousand pornographic films. On his journey to becoming a Christian, he battled depression and suicidal thoughts. Josh is now married, has three sons, and has committed his life to communicating biblical truth. He is truly a changed man and wants the world to know about the saving power of Jesus Christ. Our faithful God is the God of new beginnings. If you want to hear Josh's story, check out my (Sean's) interview with him on YouTube.[21]

Examples of Mentoring Others in Purity and Faithfulness in Marriage

Celebrate anniversaries. Wedding anniversaries are ideal times to let children and friends know how faithfulness and purity have protected and provided for you in the areas discussed above. (This can include people who have suffered divorce, experienced God's grace and healing, and are now pursuing a faithful oneness in their marriage.) Make your own anniversary a family celebration. Let others know how much marital fidelity means to you. Explain what the marriage commitment has done for your relationship. The more that people, especially members of your own family, see how faithfulness and purity have benefited your lives and theirs, the more impact it will have on them.

Don't underestimate the ability of younger children (six, five, or four years old, for example) to understand the principles of sexual purity and marital fidelity. You have an excellent opportunity to build a foundation for their sexual chastity by helping them understand the principles of faithfulness and purity. You can explain your faithfulness to your spouse by putting it in the form of promise-keeping: "I promised I would love your mother always, and that's what I am going to do because I love your mother more than anyone, and God would be disappointed in me if I broke my promise to her." You can explain marital fidelity by saying, "I live only with your father and with no one else because I love him so much and because God created a wife to love only one man in that way." Teach them early of your commitment to each other and how you are exclusively devoted to each other. Your modeling and teaching will pay off in a decade or so when their hormones start raging.

Pastors and youth workers, you can take advantage of your anniversary or that of a mature couple in your church. Have your spouse come into the youth group or adult small group for a faithfulness and purity celebration. Explain how those principles have brought provision and protection into the marriage.

Take full advantage of weddings. Whether you are a youth worker, pastor, or parent, you can use a wedding to celebrate God's principle of faithfulness and purity. Take time prior to and following the ceremony to emphasize the commitment the couple is making and their promise to be faithful for a lifetime. Get a copy of the marriage vows and read them together with your friends or younger children. Weddings are an ideal time to reinforce God's way of love and sex within the marriage commitment—and how that reflects the relational character of God. Also consider showing your kids your wedding video.

Use opportunities presented by TV, news, and current affairs. When you and your kids, for example, see something on television or in the movies that contradicts God's standard for sex, discuss the benefits of obeying God's command and the consequences of violating them. You may be surprised how insightful young people are in detecting the benefits and consequences of people's actions once they begin to see life through the lens of God and his commands. One of our friends calls this game Spot the Lie. If you do this, just be sure not to be overly critical. Look for positive aspects too.

GOD'S WORD ON THE FAMILY

For century upon century, faithful Jews have begun their daily prayers by reciting the *shema,* the phrase Moses spoke to the Israelites after delivering the Ten Commandments to them: "Hear, O Israel: The LORD our God, *the* LORD *is one*" (Deuteronomy 6:4 NIV).

The *shema* reveals the singularity of God. "See now," God says in his Word, "there is no god besides me" (Deuteronomy 32:39 NIV). "Understand that I alone am God," he declares, "There is no other God; there never has been and never will be" (Isaiah 43:10). The *shema* also testifies to his unity. Long before Jesus Christ was revealed to humans as the Son of God, long before the Holy Spirit was given to the church at Pentecost, God revealed himself as a mysterious unity. The Genesis account of creation reports that God said, "Let *us* make people in *our* image" (Genesis 1:26), yet "the LORD is *one.*" The Bible reports that God responded to the Tower of Babel by saying, "Come, let *us* go down and confuse their language so they will not understand each other" (Genesis 11:7 NIV), yet "the LORD is *one.*" The divine name *Elohim,* applied to God throughout the Pentateuch, is a plural in the Hebrew, yet "the LORD is *one.*"

Even in Old Testament times, the concept of a plural Godhead—what Christians now call the Trinity—existed. The oneness of God represents a perfect relationship of unity. The *shema* makes it clear that God is not a partnership. He is not a conglomeration. He is not a committee. He is a *unity*: "Hear, O Israel: The LORD our God, *the LORD is one.*"

God cannot be separated. He cannot be divided. His perfect oneness in loving relationship is not something he strives for; it is not even something he manufactures. It is something he *is.* "The Father and I are one," Jesus said (John 10:30).

Divided Families Violate God's Character of Unity

Unity is part of God's nature and character. He is relationally one. And it is that unity he wishes us to reflect in our marriages and family relationships. When the Bible says "a man will leave his father and mother and be united to his wife, and they will become one flesh" (Genesis 2:24 NIV), it is saying marriage should reflect God's nature of oneness and unity. God went on to amplify this unity theme regarding marriage. Jesus, speaking specifically of the marriage commitment, added, "Since they are no longer two but one, let no one separate them" (Mark 10:8-9).

The Protection and Provision of Moms and Dads

When marriages and families are bound by unity and love, the relationship results in the following benefits:

PROTECTS FROM:	PROVIDES FOR:
parental inattention	parental involvement
emotional insecurity	emotional security
relational problems	healthy role models

It doesn't take vast university and government research studies to tell us kids benefit from having a father and mother married to each other in their lives. Why? For one, the sociological data reveals men and women tend to approach parenting differently. Moms and dads treat sons and daughters differently, and kids ideally need both for their well-being. According to sociologist Rob Palkovitz, "Even in families with egalitarian ideals, parents still have different styles, voices, histories, and connections to their children as well as gendered relationships toward their sons and daughters."[22]

Specifically, how do involved fathers benefit children? According to Palkovitz, father involvement with young children is associated with overall life satisfaction, happiness, and psychological well-being. Further, father involvement in married parent families "is associated with lower psychological distress and fewer depressive episodes in teens."[23] Fathers who play with their kids tend to encourage them to be positive about the world and take risks. Additionally, positive father involvement is the single greatest factor discouraging teen pregnancy for girls. The conclusion is obvious: Involved fathers make a huge difference. And mothers have powerful impacts too.[24]

Jesus had good reason to say, "Since they [a married man and woman] are no longer two but one, let no one separate them, for God has joined them together" (Matthew 19:6). A united marriage and family fosters feelings of consistency, permanence, and stability. It helps a child know who they belong to, who belongs to them, who they can trust, and what their lives will be like tomorrow.

I (Josh) grew up in an alcoholic home. I knew what a divided and dysfunctional home was like. And even today I suffer some of the emotional fallout of growing up in a home that was not unified. The greatest security you can give your children is the experiential knowledge that you love your spouse. If you want to provide real security for your child, demonstrate how much you love your spouse.

When Sean was six years old, I noticed he wasn't quite himself one day when he came home from school. I asked what was wrong.

"Aw, nothing, Dad," he said.

Sean and I had pretty good communication, so I said, "Come on. Share with me what you're feeling."

He hesitated and then asked, "Daddy, are you going to leave Mommy?"

"What makes you ask that?"

Three of his friends' dads had just divorced their mothers, Sean told me, and he was afraid I might do the same.

I sat down with Sean, looked him in the eye, and said, "I want you to know one thing. I love your mother very much. I'm committed to her, and I'll never leave her. Period."

That little six-year-old breathed a sigh of relief, smiled at me, and said, "Thanks, Dad." At that moment he didn't need reinforcement of my love for him as much as he needed the security that comes from knowing his mother and I love each other and are committed to a permanent relationship. The loving oneness of a marriage reflects the nature of God's unity, and it is that unbreakable bond of love that communicates security to younger generations.

Examples for Parents of Mentoring Unity in the Family

Openly communicate your love to your spouse today. Take advantage of every opportunity to let your children know how much you love your mate. Be affectionate with each other around them. Kisses, roses, special dates, favorite meals—there are a hundred and one ways to openly demonstrate before your children how you love each other. Your kids will also love it when you involve them in helping plan a special meal or a surprise that demonstrates your love and appreciation for your spouse. Your kids' participation in helping you plan these things also increases their awareness of—and confidence in—your loving commitment to each other.

Pull out your wedding album. You may be surprised at how fascinated your children are—even your teenagers—by the story and pictures of your wedding. Pull out the wedding photos and use them as a way to share your deep convictions about marriage, the vows you made to your spouse, and how that commitment stands today. Sharing stories of your courtship and marriage—and how honoring marriage has resulted in God's protection and provision in your life—will reinforce your child's beliefs in God's way for marriage and family.

Examples for Parents and Others of Mentoring Unity

Make birthdays special. Whether you are 5, 15, or 50, hearing about the details of the day you were born is always fascinating. Use that fascination to provide your child with a greater sense of belonging. Emphasize to your children the fact that they came from the union of your love for your mate. Explain how they have inherited distinct characteristics and features from each of you. Explain to a friend how his or her being in the world has brought you meaning. The more that people gain a sense of their heritage or significance, the more unity they will feel with their family and friends.

Use opportunities presented by TV, news, and current affairs. Use movies or news events of divorces or pending marriages as topics of discussion. Rather than condemning a person who has suffered a divorce, talk about the protection and provision they will be missing. If you know the person, discuss how you and your children or friends can be supportive and helpful. Using current events can be an ideal way to discuss the negative consequences of violating God's standard of unity in marriage and family and a good way to point out the positive rewards of living by his way.

SUMMARY

God has given us his reliable Word that accurately reflects who he is (pure, faithful, a unity, and so on). Because he created us in his image, he provides instructions in his Word that show us how to conduct our lives in a way that reflects his nature. By following these instructions, we can live godly lives and enjoy the protection and provision he planned for us. This truth of God and his Word is another component in the building of a Christian worldview. The more we understand God's character and nature and how they are reflected in the commands and instructions found in his Word, the more we gain a perspective on life as God intended it.

ALL HAVE SINNED

S cottie, our firstborn son, was a precious bundle of love Stephanie and I (Sean) cherished from day one. We did nothing but shower him with love and devotion and did everything we could to model a giving, trusting relationship. Yet despite our loving efforts, and with no influence from the outside culture, one day Scottie grabbed a toy from me and declared authoritatively, "Mine." I wasn't surprised or appalled by his actions—in fact I chuckled inside. Knowing human nature, I had been expecting that at some point my son would exhibit self-centeredness.

If you have been around children very long, you too can testify that a child without any training has an independent streak that is "me-centered." From infancy there appears to be a struggle for control to get what we want when we want it. In one form or another this independent drive to be in charge lies behind every struggle for power, every prejudice, every conflict, and every abuse of relationship since the dawn of time. Why is this? Humans were created in the image of a triune God whose Persons are in harmonious relationship with one another. Yet how can the human race, fashioned in the likeness of this perfect God, be so self-centered from birth? The answer is found in the beginning when sin originally entered the world.

THE PERFECT CIRCLE OF RELATIONSHIPS

Imagine spending a day with the first man and the first woman in perfect relationship with God. At sunrise Adam and Eve awaken refreshed and cheerful, without a trace of morning grumpiness. They hug and kiss each other, then march off to work in the garden. Though they apply themselves diligently to every task, they never tire. In fact they seem to find immense joy in tending and shaping their property and nourishing and guiding the creatures that fawn on them. When they grow hungry, they pause and eat from the abundant food growing all about them. They quench their thirst from crystal streams. As evening approaches they leave their work, plunge into a clear lake and swim for half an hour, then dry off by chasing through the cool woods unblighted by stickers or poison ivy. Reaching the blossom-covered bower that is their home, they sit drinking fresh juice from a coconut shell as they eagerly await the highlight of their day.

"Is he coming yet?" Eve asks, looking down the path through the forest.

"Listen," replies Adam. "I think I hear something."

In moments the familiar, soft sound of movement through the grass is unmistakable.

"Oh, he's coming!" Eve cannot contain her excitement. She bounds joyfully up the path as Adam closes the distance behind her. They run to God like children to a father returning home at the end of a workday. And until sundown, the happy pair walks the paths of the garden and chats with their Creator as their souls burn with ecstatic joy.

While the details of this scene are fictional, it is a true picture of how Adam and Eve must have loved God and responded to him. They looked forward to his presence with all the anticipation of a lover. God loved them and delighted in them. Man and woman loved God and each other. The two had joined the Godhead's circle of relationship, and together they experienced its indescribable goodness. They felt the joy of freely giving of themselves to one another. They experienced the security of being accepted without conditions. They felt valued by the all-sufficient God who wanted to spend time with them. The praise and appreciation God must have given them for their excellent tending of the garden made them feel significant. And the affection and gratitude they all offered one another was expressive of a devoted relationship of love.

This perfect circle of loving relationship was God's ultimate intention for all humanity from creation forward. He intended Adam and Eve and all their descendants to be ecstatically happy with him and each other forever. And in Eden, it all worked perfectly.[1]

WHAT'S IN A CHOICE?

Obviously, somewhere along the way something went wrong. This world we live in is hardly the Garden of Eden. Far from delighting in God, many people today feel quite the opposite toward him. Some see God as something like a strict judge watching their every move with a stern, disapproving eye. Some find the idea of God so far-fetched they don't even believe he exists. And if he does exist, they think he is remote and uncaring—somewhere off in his distant heaven, leaving us to struggle alone with problems in a world filled with every kind of evil.

Many people actually want God to remain distant. In fact, this is one common motivation for atheism. Aldous Huxley, author of *Brave New World*, explained that he and his atheist friends desired a world without the meaning God could give it because such a world gave them "liberation from a certain system of morality. We objected to the morality because it interfered with our sexual freedom."[2]

Such views of God are almost infinitely removed from the way Adam and Eve saw him in Genesis. How did we humans move from intimacy with God in a perfect world to alienation from him in today's messed-up world?

Freedom to Trust

There is no hint in Scripture that continuing a perfect relationship between humans and God would be automatic. The relationship was based on an authentic love that was to be expressed freely and voluntarily. Therefore the close relationship involved a choice and was to bear the fruit of trust.

Of course, God was all-powerful and could have created humans with no choice capacity at all. He could have manipulated their every move and made them conform to his every wish. But had he done this, humans would not have been created in his own image. God is free to choose, and he gave humans that same capacity.

So, in the pristine perfection of the Garden, God offered Adam and Eve a tangible way of expressing their unselfish love and trust in him. He gave them a command not to eat a certain fruit. And so there it was; they had a voluntary choice to believe God was acting unselfishly and had their best interest at heart, or that he was selfishly keeping something good from them.

God is passionate about us loving him and jealous if we turn away from him because he knows loving him is the only way for us to truly find joy and completeness.

There was a risk within God's masterly plan to create humans in his relational image and likeness. The risk was that they could choose to reject such a relationship. Authentic love cannot be forced. God knew this, as well as the consequences if they rejected him. That is why the very hint of his created humans trying to satisfy their needs outside of him would produce jealousy. His first commandment says, "Do not worship any other god, for the LORD, whose name is Jealous, is a jealous God" (Exodus 34:14 NIV). The New Living Translation renders "a jealous God" as "a God who is passionate about his relationship with you."

God's jealousy is far from being selfish. He wanted Adam and Eve and all their descendants to worship him and him exclusively—but not because his pride was hurt if they didn't or because he couldn't stand rejection. Rather, he is passionate about us loving him and jealous if we turn away from him because he knows loving him is the only way for us to truly find joy and completeness.

God is love, joy, peace, goodness, and everything needed to bring pure happiness and joy. "Whatever is good and perfect," James declares, "comes to us from God" (James 1:17). So when God told Adam and Eve to avoid that fruit, he was actually attempting to lead them to unselfish, other-focused living in relationship with him. That kind of relationship would bring great pleasure to him and deep happiness to them.

Separation from God

But as we all know, Adam and Eve chose another course. Satan, the enemy of God, entered the Garden of Eden and convinced the humans to make a choice that ruined God's intended relationship with humans and inflicted on the world untold agony and devastation. "Toward evening they heard the LORD God walking about in the garden, so they hid themselves among the trees. The LORD God called to Adam, 'Where are you?' He replied, 'I heard you, so I hid. I was afraid because I was naked'" (Genesis 3:8-10).

Just a day before, Adam and Eve couldn't contain their excitement over the arrival of their Creator. On this particular evening, however, their reaction was altogether different. Fear had driven a wedge between humans and God, which is why they hid from him in shame. This fear and hiding was the result of their self-centered act, which is what we call sin. But Adam and Eve's disobedience involved more than simply eating from a "do not take" tree. It involved rejecting God as the source of what is right and true. That rebellion against God brought death to the relationship. Both the man and the woman were sent out of the Garden of Eden (see Genesis 3:23-24).

Their act resulted in more tragedy than just Adam and Eve's expulsion from the Garden. The consequences were dreadful and devastating, affecting the planet itself. Every plant and animal and every human born since that day became subject to pain, disease, decay, sorrow, and death (see Romans 8:20-22).

The entrance of sin drove life from the world. By sinning, Adam and Eve disrupted their relational connection to a perfect and holy God—who is life itself and from whom all life comes (see John 1:4; 5:26). Gone were their shared moments of intimacy and joy with their Father God. Gone were the thrills of laughter they enjoyed together.

Their sin brought into the world not only the living death of separation from God, but hunger, disease, hatred, and heartache that would end in their physical death and eternal separation from God. Sin and death reigned over the whole human race from that moment forward. Scripture states, "When Adam sinned, sin entered the entire human race. Adam's sin brought death, so death spread to everyone, for everyone sinned" (Romans 5:12).

Think of the worst that can happen. What is the greatest tragedy of life? What saps all the joy out of living? The answer is death. Death is humanity's greatest curse, for it is the absence of the God of all life and goodness.

"The wages of sin," Scripture states, "is death" (Romans 6:23). And there is nothing we humans can do in and of ourselves to reverse the payoff of sin. The apostle Paul said we are "utterly helpless" (Romans 5:6).

WHEN GOODNESS IS NO GOOD

According to a recent study on theology in America, 71 percent of adults believe everyone is born innocent in the eyes of God.[3] As a result, many also believe they will go to heaven. According to this view, if you and I commit more good deeds than bad deeds in our lifetimes, God will likely grant us entrance into heaven. After all, we can all think of people who are worse than us.

What this belief fails to take into account is the biblical teaching about death. Death is more than what happens when you stop breathing and they bury you. Even as we humans breathe and walk about on the face of the planet, we are already dead spiritually. Dead people have no ability to save themselves, good works or no good works. They have no ability to do anything—they are dead! Doing good works no more means we're spiritually alive than the rigor mortis spasms of a corpse means it's physically alive. Scripture tells us plainly, "Salvation is not a reward for the good things we have done" (Ephesians 2:9). Strict adherence to God's law won't even help. "The law of Moses could not save us," Paul said, "because of our sinful nature" (Romans 8:3). There is absolutely nothing we can do on our own to solve our sin problem because we are all dead spiritually and will soon be dead physically.

The boundary of trust God drew was crossed with the first humans. The self-centered choice of Adam and Eve brought death and a helpless dilemma for the entire human race.

To summarize what we've said up to now:

> *We believe the truth that God created humans in his image to relate to him lovingly, but that relationship was destroyed because of original sin. Sin was passed to the entire human race, and consequently all are born spiritually dead and utterly helpless to gain favor with God.*

As a result of sin and death, the universe is in a state of entropy—moving from order to disorder. Everything is dying, and no amount of human ingenuity or technology or medical advances can permanently reverse the inevitable doom of us all. That is, nothing apart from a miraculous intervention by God.

There are, however, those who would say humans are born naturally good. And in time the evolutionary process will work out and the best and strongest of human nature will survive. To some, the problems of humans have a natural explanation with natural solutions. Yet Scripture paints another story, a story that records the fact that human sin has consequences. This is the subject of the next section.

EVIDENCE THAT SIN HAS CONSEQUENCES

Stop right now and try a simple experiment. Check the news. What kinds of stories do you see? Almost undoubtedly most will be about murder, deception, natural disasters, and other such calamities. What does this tell us? Sure, as the saying goes, "If it bleeds, it reads." Dramatic stories do draw attention. But we think they reveal something far deeper: *The world is deeply broken.* And we all know it.

Every newspaper and every online news source around the globe today is full of headlines and stories telling of the earth's population caught up in greed, robberies, conflict, killings, war, destruction, and death. Could this really be the result of self-centered humans choosing to disregard God and his ways?

Marxists blame capitalism and the unequal distribution of wealth for much of the evil of the world. Secular humanists blame religion. And certain forms of Buddhism say all evil in the world is simply an illusion. But Jesus said it's not outside circumstances that cause evil in the world. "From the heart come evil thoughts, murder, adultery, all other sexual immorality, theft, lying, and slander" (Matthew 15:19). The core problem of sin isn't sociological, economic, or intellectual; it is a spiritual or heart problem. As another saying goes, "The heart of the problem is the problem of the heart." All of us have hearts that are naturally in rebellion against God and his purposes for the world.

You may need no further evidence other than your life's observations and the daily news to confirm that sin results in negative consequences. But if that isn't enough, thousands of years of recorded history of a particular family of people serves as a living testimony. This historic record is documented in the Hebrew Bible, the Old Testament. God has given us the accurate stories of his people, the children of Israel, that demonstrate how living in relationship with him brings blessing and choosing a self-centered path (sin) brings negative consequences. The following is but a small sampling of headlines drawn from the pages of Scripture.

RESENTMENT AND JEALOUSY PRODUCE MURDER
From Genesis 4

Cain was the first child of Adam and Eve. He became a farmer. Abel was the couple's second son. He became a sheepherder. As the boys grew to manhood, both brought offerings before God. Cain brought produce and Abel brought choice lambs. God accepted the offerings of Abel, but not of Cain. And Cain was furious.

"'Why are you so angry?' the LORD asked him. 'Why do you look so dejected? You will be accepted if you respond in the right way. But if you refuse to respond correctly, then watch out! Sin is waiting to attack and destroy you, and you must subdue it'" (Genesis 4:6-7).

If Adam and Eve learned anything from their own sin, they would have surely shared it with their boys. You would think they must have stressed to their sons that a Godlike relationship is based on an unselfish focus for another and a trust that God is good—his ways are always best. But Cain obviously didn't get it. Because when God said, in effect, "Believe that my ways are right and follow them, and they will work for you because I have your best interest at heart," Cain responded in anger.

Cain rejected God's warning that sin was waiting to attack and destroy him. When he refused to lovingly relate to God, his resentment and jealousy drove him to murder his brother.

LUST, RAPE, AND MASS KILLINGS
From Genesis 34

Jacob was the son of Isaac, the grandson of Abraham. He, along with his large family, settled outside of the town of Shechem in Canaan. The town was named after its prince, Shechem.

One day Dinah, Jacob's daughter, was visiting some friends in the area. Prince Shechem saw Dinah and just had to have her. To Dinah's horror, the prince forced himself on her and raped her.

Prince Shechem decided he wanted Dinah for his wife and started negotiations with Jacob through his own father. In fact, the proposal was that the men of Shechem take all of Jacob's daughters for marriage and Jacob's sons take all the daughters of Shechem for marriage.

Jacob's sons counteroffered. They proposed that if the men of Shechem got circumcised, the exchange deal would be acceptable. Shechem agreed and the entire male population of the town got circumcised. But this was nothing but a ploy by the sons of Jacob. They had revenge in mind.

Three days after the circumcisions, when the men were still sore and less-than-agile, Jacob's sons slaughtered every man in town. Then they "seized all the flocks and herds and donkeys—everything they could lay their hands on, both inside the town and outside in the fields. They also took all the women and children and wealth of every kind" (Genesis 34:28-29). But after the mass killings, Jacob was so fearful of retaliation from the neighboring cities that he moved his entire family out of the area.

A woman was sexually abused because a man wanted what he wanted. Shechem's lust was a self-centered, brutal act of aggression that resulted in a tragic domino effect. It bred retaliatory sins in its wake and left a trail of tragedy—lies and deception, death and destruction, women becoming widows, children becoming orphans, families being ripped apart and displaced.

A LUST FOR POWER LEADS TO SLAVERY
From Exodus 1

Soon after the debacle in Shechem, God changed Jacob's name to *Israel*. And eventually Israel moved his family to Egypt. In a few generations the children of Israel populated much of the land. This explosive growth concerned the new king of Egypt. "He told his people, 'These Israelites are becoming a threat to us because there are so many of them. We must find a way to put an end to this. If we don't and if war breaks out, they will join our enemies and fight against us'" (Exodus 1:9-10).

The lust for power drove the Egyptian king to a brutal solution: slavery. This lustful thirst for power forced free men and women into chains and bondage. But even during their captivity the children of Israel continued to multiply. Afraid of an uprising by the masses, the king had an idea to keep the Israelites to a manageable minimum. He called for the murder of all the newborn male population of the Israelites. But it didn't work. God's people continued to multiply.

Eventually, a baby would miraculously be saved from the male killings and grow to become the deliverer of Israel. Moses would lead his people out of slavery in Egypt and march them toward God's Promised Land.

A lust for power caused an entire nation of people to suffer the brutality of enslavement. This sinful appetite for dominance resulted in physical pain, emotional suffering, and the loss of human dignity.

THE PRICE OF SIN

As we've seen in the illustrations above, there are negative consequences to sin. In fact, God warned the children of Israel repeatedly.

> If you refuse to listen to the LORD your God and do not obey all the commands and laws I am giving you today...[you will experience] curses, confusion, and disillusionment in everything you do, until at last you are completely destroyed for doing evil and forsaking me (Deuteronomy 28:15-20).

The price of sin is high. The result is always the same: pain and suffering, heartache and ruin, destruction and death. Death ultimately is the wages of sin, just as God proclaimed to Adam and Eve.

We need go no further than the mirror to see the effects of original sin. The apostle Paul made the case "that all people, whether Jews or Gentiles, are under the power of sin" (Romans 3:9). That includes you. And that includes us. Paul then went on to quote from the Old Testament, saying, "No one is good—not even one. No one has real understanding; no one is seeking God. All have turned away from God; all have gone wrong. No one does good, not even one" (Romans 3:10-12).

The McDowell family, your family, and each of us personally suffer the fallout of our own sins. The Old Testament stories may give us clear examples, but each of us has personal examples of the negative consequences of sin in our lives. The sins of a sharp tongue, an explosive temper, lust, racism, jealousy, greed, family neglect, are the sins that bring us and those around us heartache and pain. Big or small, committed in secret or in the open, we all must admit we struggle with the issue of sin.

EVIL ACTS ARE NOT INHUMANE

When I (Sean) was in high school, I referred to an evil act on TV as inhumane. My dad graciously and firmly corrected me. He said, "Son, that act is not inhumane. Inhumane means not human. But that act was done by a human being just like you and me." We don't like to hear that. We like to think evil acts occur only when people act against their human nature. But if Scripture is right, then evil acts—the evil and suffering imposed on the millions of Jews in Nazi Germany; the atrocities committed against the "counterrevolutionaries" across decades in communist China; the ill treatment and killings of tens of thousands under the name of apartheid in South Africa; the ethnic cleansings in Croatia, Bosnia, and Herzegovina; the slavery practiced in the United States—are not the doings of a small number of deranged individuals, desperate for power. But a serious study of Scripture shows that to take God's Word seriously, we have to recognize man's inhumanity to others isn't inhuman but sadly and horribly *human*. Humans have done these things against one another since the beginning of time, right down to our current day.

Although humans are made in God's image, and thus have both inherent value and a moral conscience, our natures have been deeply tainted by sin. Scripture declares corruption is primarily a matter of the heart. For example, the apostle John wrote, "Whoever hates his brother is a murderer" (1 John 3:15 NKJV). In other words, you can be a murderer even if you don't actually kill. In John 7:7, Jesus said the world hated him "because I testify that its works are evil" (NIV). The message that humankind is desperately sinful—which, again, includes you and me—is as unpopular a message as there has ever been.

As author and apologist Clay Jones puts it,

Humans don't want to hear about the depths of human depravity, but, as it is for both drunks and cancer victims, the road to recovery begins by understanding the seriousness of the problem. That's why Jesus said the well didn't need a doctor but the sick, and that he didn't "come to call the righteous, but sinners" [Matthew 9:12-13]. Jesus wasn't suggesting there were righteous, healthy people who didn't need Him, but that only those who regard themselves as sick or sinner will come to Him. The others are no less sick or sinful; they just refuse to see it.[4]

Theologian Langdon Gilkey is someone who believed humans were basically good until he was interned by the Japanese with two thousand others—men, women, and children—during World War II. Like so many people are, he had been confident that "when the chips are down, and we are revealed for what we 'really are,' we will all be good to each other." But his conclusion was this: "Nothing could be so totally in error."[5] Our niceness, he says, is "the thin polish of easy morality."[6]

The truth of our depravity is well illustrated by the Lord's warning to Israel in Deuteronomy 28: If they disobeyed, they would come under siege, and then "the most gentle and sensitive woman among you…will begrudge the husband she loves and her own son or daughter the afterbirth from her womb…For…she intends to eat them secretly because of the suffering your enemy will inflict on you during the siege in your cities" (verses 56-57 NIV). We shouldn't be surprised by this, because the Bible tells us that "there is *no one* who does good, not even one" (Romans 3:12 NIV). "Their throats are open graves…," wrote Paul. "Their mouths are full of cursing…Their feet are swift to shed blood" (Romans 3:13-15 NIV; see also Psalm 53:1-3).

Stemming from a question that Aleksandr Solzhenitsyn himself posed as a result of suffering eight years in a Soviet gulag, Clay Jones writes, "I think we must [all] ask: If my life had turned out differently, might I have been a guard in Auschwitz?" Or for a more contemporary example, might you have been one of Saddam Hussein's soldiers releasing nerve gas on the Kurds or torturing the Kuwaitis to death? To "conclude that we were somehow born innately better than the millions who [have] murdered or condoned murder is without logical or scientific foundation," declares Jones. "A belief in one's innate superiority is the father of genocide. On the other hand, if we admit that we could have murdered, except for the grace of God, then we understand the depravity of humankind."[7]

In spite of our inherent sinfulness and capacity for evil, however, we do have a choice. Just as Adam and Eve were free to choose God's way or their own way, we, too, can make moral choices that affect our everyday lives. God has not left us without instructions. He has provided us with a formula for turning our back on sin, choosing him, and making right choices in life. The question is how we make those right choices.

CHOOSING RIGHT FROM WRONG

Satan's disguise was perfect. Serpents were wise and subtle, and the innocent Eve would not suspect a thing if such a creature started a conversation with her. He slipped into the Garden of Eden and approached the woman.

"What is it with this relationship between you and God?" he asked Eve. "Look at you—it's all about what he wants. But what about what you want? He's robbing you of your true identity." The creature rolled his eyes upward. "That God of yours has fooled you into thinking that listening to him is in your best interest. But how can you think it's in your best interest to never be free enough to make your own decisions? He's not even allowing you to decide what is good for you to eat."

"Oh, it's not like that at all," answered Eve. "He gives us the run of this garden, we have plenty of delicious food to eat, and he doesn't tell us to do anything except what makes us happy." She paused to wrap an ivy tendril around an oak limb. "Why should we want anything different?"

"But he did forbid you to eat one fruit, did he not?" replied the serpent. "Why can't you eat that sweet-smelling, juicy morsel hanging on that tree right there?" He pointed to the leafy tree in the center of the garden, its branches heavy with glistening orbs of fruit.

"Well, you're right. God did tell us not to eat that fruit," said the woman. "He said if we ate it we would die."

"Ah, but I happen to know better," replied Satan. "That fruit won't kill you. Do you want to know the real reason God forbids it?" He leaned close to her ear and lowered his voice to little more than a whisper. "It will make you equal to him, and he doesn't want rivals. He wants to keep you ignorant so he can control you. If you really want to be like God, you must be independent enough to call your own shots and eat what you want to eat. Let him know you won't be kept down any longer."

The more Eve listened to the smooth-talking serpent, the more God's warning faded. His words became hazy; they didn't seem to make sense anymore. Maybe that snake was right. Maybe God didn't have her best interest at heart. Maybe she needed to break free to become her own person. With her heart racing, Eve reached out and gingerly touched the fruit. Nothing happened. She touched it again, tentatively closing her fingers around it. Nothing happened. Then she gripped it firmly, pulled it from the tree, and took a quick bite before she could change her mind. Immediately she ran to Adam and managed to cajole him into eating it with her.[8]

Obviously the infamous encounter between Satan and Eve recounted in Genesis 3 has been greatly amplified here. But we believe this expansion of the story provides telling insights that help us understand the nature of Satan's temptation and Eve's fatal decision. That decision has had a catastrophic effect on the human race and the entire universe from that time forward. In fact, your own concept of right and wrong and how you make moral decisions has been distorted by the aftermath of Eve's decision. No matter how close your relationship with God may be right now, knowledge of what is good no longer comes naturally. It now requires a deliberate process of spiritual discipline to keep God in the center of each decision.

What was the real sin Adam and Eve committed that day? Was it that they didn't love God enough to do what he asked them to do? Was it that they failed to be "other-focused" in their relationship with God? Was it that they didn't trust him enough to believe that the prohibition of the fruit was for their own good? All those things are part of the picture. What is central to all of them is that of independence—self-sovereignty. Eve felt she had the right to choose for herself whether or not she should eat the fruit.

When the serpent told Eve that in making her choice she would become a god of her own, he hit the nail on the head. What he didn't tell her is that

God alone is the arbiter of right and wrong. He is the absolute standard of rightness. When Adam, Eve, or anyone else decides that they alone know what is right for them, they are in effect worshipping the god of self. Right, godly choices that bring fulfillment and joy to our lives are those that relationally align with the person and character of a holy, righteous God. He and he alone establishes the boundaries of right and wrong—which, by the way, are always in our best interest.

THE FOUR "CS" OF RIGHT CHOICES

There is a relational process of making right moral choices that, if followed, will bring God's protection and provision in life every time. We have distilled this process into an easy-to-remember formula we call the "4-Cs." Each time you and I are confronted with a moral choice we can follow this process.

1. Consider the Choice

When it comes to considering moral choices, we need to pause and realize we are at a crossroads. The choices we make—to be less than honest, to advance a flirtation to the next level, to enhance our score by "borrowing" someone else's answers, or to show mercy to someone—are often made without considering the gravity of what we are really doing. To make right moral choices, we must first pause long enough to remind ourselves we are facing an opportunity for a right or wrong decision.

2. Compare the Choice to God

Eve seemed to pause long enough to realize she was about to make a right or wrong choice. But she failed to compare her attitude and action to him, which would have meant looking at the choice in relation to the commands that emanate from his nature. This, of course, would have required that she believe God was her absolute standard for right—not herself. When we choose to obey God, we are in effect telling him, "I love you enough to place your interests first in my life. You are the sovereign God whose character and nature defines what is right for me."

When we justify our actions or attitudes based on what *we* think is right, we are, as we say, rationalizing. To rationalize is to convince ourselves with "rational lies" that an action is right when it's actually in opposition to God's character. We are actually usurping God's role as the sovereign arbiter of what is right or wrong.

God's commands come out of his nature, and his nature is absolute truth. His actions do not deviate from his character of integrity. God always does what he says he will do. When we make our moral decision in light of the character of God, our choice becomes crystal clear.

3. Commit to God's Way

Committing to God's way is easier said than done. It means we have to admit we are not the ruler over our lives—God is. The present-day concept of deciding what is "right for you" appeals to so many people because it puts us in charge. Giving ourselves the capacity to decide our own morality feels independent and empowering. And it has the added advantage of making us feel we're being moral because we're not being judgmental. We allow everyone to make his or her own moral decisions without judging their choices. What could be fairer than that?

To think this way is simply to fool ourselves with more "rational lies." But even when we see through our rationalizations and recognize that what we want to do may be self-serving, we still find it hard to commit to God's way. What we want to do fights with what we ought to do because we are plagued with a sin nature that wants what it wants when it wants it. That is why Paul said to "put to death the sinful, earthly things lurking within you" (Colossians 3:5). We must turn our backs on the appetites and desires that don't measure up to our holy God. When we deny our self-serving ways and commit to following him, we are loving him. And in response he gives us the power to walk in his ways. And then finally we can...

4. Count on God's Protection and Provision

When we humbly admit God's sovereignty and lovingly seek to please him, not only can we begin to clearly see the distinctions between right and wrong, but we can also begin to count on God's protection and provision.

This doesn't mean everything will be rosy. In fact, God says bluntly that we may sometimes suffer for righteousness' sake. But even such suffering has rewards. Living according to God's way brings many spiritual blessings, like freedom from guilt, a clear conscience, and the joy of God's smile upon our lives. We can also enjoy many physical, emotional, psychological, and relational benefits when we commit to God's ways. Of course, God's protection and provision should not be the primary motivation for obeying God; we should obey him simply because we love him, trust him, and want to be like him. But the practical and spiritual benefits of obeying certainly provide powerful encouragement for choosing right and rejecting wrong.

Adam and Eve failed to go through the 4-Cs process. Today we all suffer the consequences of their poor choice.

God has made a way to redeem us from eternal consequences. But as followers of Christ we still need to learn how to resist our natural tendency to decide for ourselves what is right or wrong and choose God's way (*consider, compare, commit,* and *count*). Then we can experience the joy that results with being in a loving relationship with God and following his ways.

A PRACTICAL EXAMPLE OF
HOW TO MAKE RIGHT CHOICES

To help understand this process better we have created a "case study" that gives a practical example. Discuss these with your family and friends and make the 4-Cs process a pattern of life.

CASE STUDY: MERCY
"What Goes Around Comes Around"

Geena, a bank loan officer, was grocery shopping on her day off. As she was loading her trunk with groceries in the parking lot, a woman put a bad scrape in Geena's car with a cart.

"Excuse me, ma'am," Geena said, "you just scratched my car with that cart."

"You shouldn't have parked so close to the cart return," the woman replied. "It's your problem, not mine."

"Now wait a minute," Geena responded. "I want this taken care of. Please give me your insurance information."

"I'm out of here," came the reply. "My insurance won't cover that." And she walked quickly to her car and drove off. In her frustration, Geena failed to write down the woman's license plate number.

A week later Geena was on the job at her bank, processing a car loan application that was on the borderline of being approved. The bank manager told Geena it was her call. The applicant came in to determine whether she was approved for the car loan. When she sat down in front of Geena's desk, Geena was surprised to see it was the same woman who had put the scratch in her car. The woman, however, didn't recognize Geena.

Consider the choice. It would be very tempting to deny the loan. The woman had been discourteous and irresponsible in not repairing the damage she had caused to Geena's car. Geena had a choice to consider—show mercy, forgive the woman, and approve the loan or give her a taste of her own medicine. What should Geena do? What would you do?

Compare it to God. "This is what the LORD Almighty says: Judge fairly and honestly, and show mercy and kindness to one another" (Zechariah 7:9). Mercy is right and a virtue because it comes from the very nature of God. As Micah declared, he is one who "delight[s] to show mercy" (Micah 7:18 NIV). King David said God's "mercy endures forever" (Psalm 107:1 NKJV). Paul noted that "God is so rich in mercy" (Ephesians 2:4).

If Geena is to reflect God's nature of mercy, she must show mercy.

Commit to God's ways. Geena has a problem. Showing mercy to this woman would, in effect, be rewarding an irresponsible person who showed no mercy on her. The interesting thing is that the car scratcher doesn't even recognize Geena. So Geena could deny the loan and no one would be the wiser.

Geena chose to approve the loan. What did she gain by showing mercy?

Count on God's protection and provision. Jesus promised, "If you give, you will receive...Whatever measure you use in giving—large or small—it will be used to measure what is given back to you" (Luke 6:38).

- By showing mercy Geena can count on God to protect her from want. "If you forgive those who sin against you, your heavenly Father will forgive you" (Matthew 6:14).

- Showing mercy protects us from God's judgment and provides for forgiveness. It's relatively easy to show mercy on the merciful. But it requires a commitment to God's ways to show mercy on the undeserving. Jesus said, "Blessed are the merciful, for they will be shown mercy" (Matthew 5:7 NIV).

We are born in sin, and even though God forgives us of our wrongdoing we are still faced with the desires of the sin nature. The 4-Cs process is a means of training ourselves to resist the natural impulse to follow our nature and commit instead to God's ways. Paul said, "I discipline my body like an athlete, training it to do what it should" (1 Corinthians 9:27). And as we do, we can count on God's protection and provision.

SUMMARY

The Christian faith puts forth the truth that a relational Creator God exists, he reveals himself through his reliable Word, and sin has destroyed the God/human relationship. If that were where the human story ended, it would be tragic beyond words. But the story doesn't end there. Next, we lay out what we believe about the solution to the great human dilemma of sin and death: *the truth of the incarnation.*

GOD BECAME HUMAN

N ow you build a house out of these blocks, Joslin," the second-grade teacher demanded, tapping her foot ominously and holding a ruler threateningly in her right hand. Mrs. Lenard had me (Josh) sit down at the small table of blocks to teach me a lesson—to use my right hand.

I was born left-handed, but my teacher was trying with all her might to make me switch to being a right-hander. When I reached out with my left hand, she smacked it with the ruler and said, "Stop—think it through. Do it with your right hand." I was terrified and confused. I was only doing what came naturally, but I was severely punished for it. This experience significantly affected how I saw myself. I began to think I was defective, a factory reject.

The trauma of this experience also caused me to develop a speech impediment. Whenever I became frightened, anxious, or tired—usually at school— I stuttered. My stuttering was a great embarrassment to me. In the fifth grade I was told to memorize and recite the Gettysburg Address. I was so nervous when I stood up that I began to stutter. In front of the entire class, my teacher demanded, "Say it! Say it! Stop stuttering, and say it!" Mortified in front of my friends, I ran out of the classroom crying.

Because my parents' education had stopped at the second grade, they had never learned good grammar. As a result, I usually mangled the language. If my English teachers emphasized correct grammar, it never got through to me. Somehow I got by. But when I entered college, my down-home grammar caught up with me, and I again became the object of ridicule. I was embarrassed to speak up in class. One day in freshman English, the professor asked me, "Where's Bob?" I said, "He doesn't feel good." In front of everyone, the professor corrected me: "Mr. McDowell, you mean 'Bob doesn't feel *well*.'" I looked at her perplexed, wondering what the big deal was. To me it seemed just as well to say "good"! Experiences like these further solidified my perception that I was an inferior human being and a totally unacceptable person.

ACCEPTING THE UNACCEPTABLE

Adam and Eve must have felt that way after they sinned. At first they had experienced a wonderful love relationship with God in the perfect Garden of Eden. But after they sinned, they were banished from the garden.

They were no longer innocent—instead they were guilty. They no longer delighted in God—instead they felt fear and shame. Rather than basking in God's favor and enjoying his provisions, they worked the cursed ground and sweated to make ends meet. Their sin had left them feeling alone and unacceptable.

But how did God feel? Was he angry and vindictive? Did he never again want anything to do with the human creation that had rebelled against him? Instead of anger, God felt grief and sadness. One generation after another, his cherished humans lived a life of sin and rebellion and "it broke his heart" (Genesis 6:6).

We rejected God, yet he still accepted us.

Imagine God as he watches in grief and sadness while your own generation sins and suffers the consequences of those sins. He was there when you were born into the very world where he and the first human couple once walked in perfect relationship. And instead of rejecting you, he longs to relate to you as intimately as he once did to them. He wants to take pleasure in us. He wants to see in our eyes the delight that only his life and love can bring. But that's not possible, because from the moment we were conceived, our sin has separated us from the life that is found in him. While his heart accepts us without condition, his holiness cannot embrace our life of self-ishness. For each of us have followed in Adam and Eve's footsteps, becoming God's *enemy* by repeatedly and selfishly choosing our own sinful ways instead of his holy ways.

So what did God do? He took the initiative. We are the ones who desperately needed him, but we didn't seek him out. We are the ones who should have been crying out for help. Yet the all-sufficient Lord, who "has no needs... [but] gives life and breath to everything, and...satisfies every need there is" *wants you and wants me* (Acts 17:25). We rejected him, yet he still accepted us. He wants to relate to us—to enjoy and delight and take pleasure in a personal relationship with us. He wants to complete our joy.

So God entered our world to cancel the curse of sin and death that has power over us. He "became human and lived here on earth among us" (John 1:14). "Because God's children are human beings—made of flesh and blood—Jesus also became flesh and blood by being born in human form. For only as a human being could he die, and only by dying could he break the power of the Devil, who had the power of death" (Hebrews 2:14). Only the Son of the living God could wrench the power of death out of the hand of our archenemy, Satan, so that God could be reconnected to his children in a personal, one-on-one relationship.

The incarnation is the miracle of God's Son taking on human form. Therefore:

> *We believe the truth of the incarnation (God becoming human), in which God accepted us without condition and sent Jesus Christ, born of the Virgin Mary, to redeem us and restore us to a relationship with him.*

The incarnation says, "You may have turned away from me, but I'm not turning away from you. You are so important to me that I will go to extraordinary lengths to have a personal relationship with you. I'll enter your world and become human like you to save you from death and eternal aloneness without me." Faced with the issue of restoring a relationship with humans, God did not merely send a prophet or even an angel; he sent the ultimate gift—himself!

EVIDENCE THAT GOD BECAME HUMAN TO REDEEM US

December 25 is a date celebrated by billions of people all over the world each year. We celebrate the birth of Jesus Christ. We proclaim the miraculous incarnation of God taking on human form. We preach about a God full of love and acceptance, who entered our world to save us from eternal death. And though the Scripture says God "became human and lived here on earth among us" (John 1:14), how can we really know if God actually showed up to demonstrate his acceptance and love for us?

That question may sound cynical, but the reality is, God himself wants to assure us that he actually came to earth to redeem us. That is why he had an angel declare to shepherds, "I bring you good news of great joy for everyone! The Savior—yes, the Messiah, the Lord—has been born tonight in Bethlehem...!" (Luke 2:10-11). God wanted to assure those living at the time that Mary's baby was actually the Son of God—the Supreme Being that came to redeem them. God wants us to believe with confidence that his Son is our redeemer as well.

Jesus of Nazareth, born in Bethlehem of Judea some 2000 years ago, is the person of history who claimed to be God's Son. His claim was exclusive. No other but the Incarnate One could redeem the human race. In fact, he made that truth central to all he said and did. He made believing in him as the Incarnate One the pivotal point. Jesus told his skeptics, "You are of this world; I am not...Unless you believe that I am who I say I am, you will die in your sins" (John 8:23-24). "I am the way, the truth, and the life," Jesus said. "No one can come to the Father except through me" (John 14:6).

LORD, LIAR, OR LUNATIC?

Some say Jesus Christ's claim to deity is not really the important thing here. They suggest it is the *teachings* of Jesus that are really important—love your neighbor, feed the hungry, make this planet a better place, and so on. So they point to Jesus as a great moral teacher and discount his claim to deity. But C.S. Lewis, professor at Oxford University and once an atheist, understood this issue clearly. He wrote:

> A man who was merely a man and said the sort of things Jesus said would not be a great moral teacher. He would either be a lunatic—on a level with the man who says he is a poached egg—or else he would be the Devil of Hell. You must make your choice. Either this man was, and is, the Son of God: or else a madman or something worse.

Then Lewis added:

> You can shut Him up for a fool, you can spit at Him and kill Him as a demon, or you can fall at His feet and call Him Lord and God. But let us not come up with any patronizing nonsense about his being a great human teacher. He has not left that open to us. He did not intend to.[1]

Jesus' claim to be God (Deity) leaves us with two alternatives: Either his claim is true or it is false. If his claim is false, we are left with two added options: He either knew it was false, or he didn't know it was false (see the diagram on page 118).

JESUS' CLAIMS TO BE GOD[2]

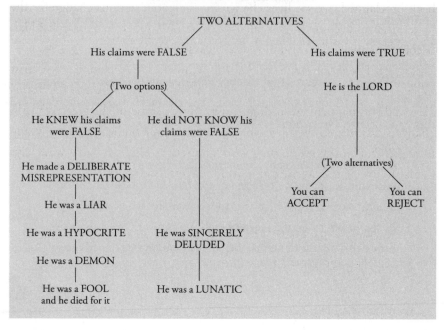

Was Jesus a Liar?

If, when Jesus made his claims, he knew that he was not God, then he was lying and deliberately deceiving his followers. If he was a liar, then he was also a hypocrite because he taught others to be honest whatever the cost. Worse than that, if he was lying, he was evil because he told others to trust him for their eternal destiny. If he couldn't back up his claims and knew it, then he was unspeakably wicked for deceiving his followers with such a false hope. Last, he would also be a fool because his claims to being God led to his crucifixion—claims he could have backed away from to save himself even at the last minute.

How could Jesus ever be considered a great moral teacher if he was wrong about his claims to deity? This means he would be knowingly misleading people about the most important issue of his teachings—believing in him as the Son of God.

To conclude that Jesus was a deliberate liar doesn't coincide with what we know either of him or of the results of his life and teachings. While it might be logically possible, it seems eminently unreasonable. Wherever Jesus has been proclaimed, we see lives change for the good, nations change for the better, thieves become honest, alcoholics become sober, hateful individuals become channels of love, and unjust persons embrace justice.

Dr. Jeff Myers, president of Summit Ministries, talks about how Christ-followers have transformed the world in his book *Truth Changes Everything*. How did this happen? According to Dr. Myers, some of the greatest world-changers committed their lives to Jesus, embraced a biblical worldview, and lived out that worldview in their work and relationships. In what ways have Christ-followers transformed the world? Myers lists a few:

- Fighting for human rights
- Loving our neighbors
- Learning and growing in education
- Fostering the scientific revolution
- Cultivating the arts
- Pursuing justice
- Seeing work as valuable

While this is only a sample of the ways that Christ-followers have changed the world, the point is powerful: The truth of Jesus transforms lives and cultures.[3]

Was Jesus a Lunatic?

If we find it inconceivable Jesus was a liar, then couldn't he have mistakenly thought himself to be God? After all, it's possible to be both sincere and wrong. But we must remember for someone to mistakenly think himself God, especially in the context of a fiercely monotheistic culture as Judaism was, and then to tell others their eternal destiny depends on believing in him is no small matter. In fact, these claims led Jesus to his death at the hands of the religious leaders. Is it possible Jesus really believed he was God but wasn't?

Today we would treat someone who believes himself to be God the same way we would treat someone who believes he is Napoleon. Unless it was an obvious power grab, of which Jesus portrayed the *opposite*, we would see him as deluded and self-deceived. Yet in Jesus we don't observe the abnormalities and imbalance that go along with such derangement. If he was insane, his poise and composure were nothing short of amazing.

In light of the life, example, and teachings of Jesus, it's hard to imagine he was mentally disturbed. Here is a man who spoke the most profound words ever recorded. His instructions have liberated many people from mental bondage. Although we have to be careful diagnosing someone from such a historical distance, psychologist Gary R. Collins concludes that Jesus

> was loving but didn't let his compassion immobilize him; he didn't have a bloated ego, even though he was often surrounded by adoring crowds; he maintained balance despite an often demanding lifestyle; he always knew what he was doing and where he was going; he cared deeply about people, including women and children, who weren't seen as important back then; he was able to accept people while not merely winking at their sin; he responded to individuals based on where they were at and what they uniquely needed. All in all, I just don't see signs that Jesus was suffering from any known mental illness... He was much healthier than anyone else I know—including me![4]

Was Jesus Lord?

As we can see, it would be very difficult for anyone to conclude Jesus was a liar or a lunatic. If Jesus has truly claimed to be God, and we have his words recorded accurately, then the only remaining alternative is that he was—and is—the Christ, the Son of God, as he claimed. Yet in spite of the logic and evidence, many people cannot seem to bring themselves to accept this conclusion.

The issue with these three alternatives concerning Jesus is not which is possible. Obviously all three are possible. Rather, the question is, "Which is most probable?" We cannot, as so many people want to do, put Jesus on the shelf merely as a great moral teacher or a prophet. That is not a valid option. He is a liar, a lunatic, or Lord and God. We must make a choice. Our decision about Jesus must be more than an idle intellectual exercise. As the apostle John wrote, "These are written so that you may believe that Jesus is the Messiah, the Son of God, and"—more important—"that by believing in him you will have life" (John 20:31).[5]

JESUS DID CLAIM TO BE GOD

There are some today who would say Jesus never really claimed to be the Son of God—he only said he was the Son of man, implying he wasn't making a claim to deity. But this is mistaken.

According to the Gospels, Jesus repeatedly made it clear he was the unique Son of God, an assertion that did not go unnoticed by the religious leaders of his day. In fact, that claim was the very reason they tried to discredit him and, eventually, the reason they put him to death: "The Jewish leaders tried all the more to kill him. In addition to disobeying the Sabbath rules, he had spoken of God as his Father, thereby making himself equal with God" (John 5:18).

On more than one occasion, Jesus' clear assertion of his own deity caused his fellow Jews to want to stone him. One of those times, when Jesus asked why they wanted to kill him, they retorted, "for blasphemy, because you, a mere man, *have made yourself God*" (John 10:33).

Yet another time, Jesus told a paralyzed man, "My son, your sins are forgiven" and again the religious leaders reacted with outrage. "What?" they said. "This is blasphemy! *Who but God* can forgive sins!" (Mark 2:5-7).

In the final days prior to Jesus' death, he made it clear—even to the Sanhedrin (the Jewish high council)—just who he was: "The high priest asked him, 'Are you the Messiah, the Son of the blessed God?' Jesus said, 'I am…'" In response to the proclamation, they "condemned him to death" (Mark 14:61-64). Jesus' actions and words point to his identity as Deity and the Messiah, and all of it points to the purpose for which he came to earth.

Given the three options considered above, it is fully reasonable to conclude Jesus is Lord. But we have much more evidence of his deity than this. Let's consider the virgin birth.

JESUS WAS BORN OF A VIRGIN

Long before there was the written Word, before anyone had heard of the Messiah, God erected in the Garden of Eden a signpost that pointed directly to the means by which his Son would be born. When God cursed the serpent who tempted Eve, he said to it, "I will put enmity between you and the woman, and between your seed and her seed; he shall bruise you on the head, and you shall bruise him on the heel" (Genesis 3:15 NASB). This verse is prophetic, for the offspring of the woman is, of course, Christ.

It is highly significant that Genesis 3:15 refers specifically to the offspring of the woman and not of the man. The natural process of conceiving and giving birth involves the ovum of a woman and the sperm of a man. These are the "seeds" from the two sexes that are necessary for human birth. When God promised the serpent that he would be crushed by the seed of the woman, he referred to a *supernatural* process: Satan would be defeated by a person conceived from the seed of a woman only, without the usual requirement of the seed of a man.

Scripture foretold that same supernatural process again, 700 years before God was born as a child, when the prophet Isaiah said, "The LORD himself will choose the sign. Look! The virgin will conceive a child! She will give birth to a son and will call him Immanuel—'God is with us'" (Isaiah 7:14).

What striking words: "The *virgin* will *conceive.*" In the course of nature, virgins don't conceive. But God promised something human history had never seen before (nor has it since): A child would be born outside the natural process of conception. Instead, the Holy Spirit of God himself would form, in the dark ocean of a virgin's womb, a child of divine origin. This person would bear a unique identity because the infinite God would be his father and a finite human virgin would be his mother—thus the God-man would be born.

If that really happened—if the historical Jesus truly was born to a virgin—it would provide compelling evidence for his deity. But is there evidence that what had been promised in the Genesis record and Isaiah's prophecy actually came to pass? Is there any reliable way to investigate the circumstances of Jesus' birth?

The Accounts of the Event

Let's begin with the historical record. Seven centuries after Isaiah's prophecy, Matthew reported the extraordinary circumstances of the birth of a child called Jesus of Nazareth:

> This is how Jesus the Messiah was born. His mother, Mary, was engaged to be married to Joseph. But while she was still a virgin,

she became pregnant by the Holy Spirit...All of this happened to fulfill the Lord's message through his prophet. "Look! The virgin will conceive a child! She will give birth to a son, and he will be called Immanuel (meaning, God is with us)" (Matthew 1:18, 22-23).

The Gospel of Luke, the careful historian whose writings have been repeatedly supported by archaeology, records the appearance of the angel Gabriel to Mary and his announcement that she would give birth to the Messiah. Mary answered with a question: "But how can I have a baby? I am a virgin." Gabriel replied, "The Holy Spirit will come upon you, and the power of the Most High will overshadow you. So the baby born to you will be holy, and he will be called the Son of God" (Luke 1:34-35).

These two historical accounts give us a record of the event of the virgin birth, but they give us no evidence to assure us the event actually occurred. As we continue to look at the record, however, evidences begin to appear, and these evidences give us confidence the overall account is true.

Reactions of Jesus' Contemporaries

Among the most significant of these evidences are those contained in the accounts of how the people of Jesus' hometown, Nazareth, reacted to him after he began his public ministry.

On one occasion, after he had taught in the synagogue, the people he had grown up with said, "'He's just the carpenter, the son of Mary'...They were deeply offended and refused to believe in him" (Mark 6:3). The label "son of Mary" was an unambiguous insult in a society that called children by the name of their fathers—except, of course, in the case of children whose paternity was doubted.

At another time, Jesus' opponents threw a sharply pointed barb at him when they said, "*We* were not born out of wedlock!" (John 8:41).

These insults imply it was common knowledge in Jesus' hometown that he had been conceived before Mary's wedding to—and without the help of—Joseph. In other words, it seems very likely the circumstances of Jesus' miraculous birth caused him to be labeled as an illegitimate child in the society of his day.

These insults hurled at Jesus give us evidence that his hometown people knew he was not Joseph's son. This gives us a leg up in believing in the virgin birth, but it is not a clincher. How do we judge whether the birth was indeed miraculous or whether Mary was lying and Joseph was deceived? For answers let's look first at Mary's story and then at Matthew's account of Jesus' birth.

The Responses of Mary and Joseph

When Mary turned up pregnant, why would she have insisted that she was a virgin? She knew such a story would certainly be too wild to believe; why didn't she come up with a more believable story? She could have claimed she was raped, or she could have claimed Joseph pressured her into yielding to his desire. Joseph would have known better, but no one else would have. But instead of a rational explanation that would fit the known laws of nature, she tells people she is pregnant by God's Holy Spirit. Why would she say such a thing when it is so certain to be the least believable of explanations? Only one reason makes sense. It was true.

Now let's look at her pregnancy from her fiancé Joseph's point of view. Here is what Matthew tells us about Joseph's reaction:

> This is how Jesus the Messiah was born. His mother, Mary, was engaged to be married to Joseph. But before the marriage took place, while she was still a virgin, she became pregnant through the power of the Holy Spirit. Joseph, her fiancé, was a good man and did not want to disgrace her publicly, so he decided to break the engagement quietly.
>
> As he considered this, an angel of the Lord appeared to him in a dream. "Joseph, son of David," the angel said, "do not be afraid to take Mary as your wife. For the child within her was conceived by the Holy Spirit"…When Joseph woke up, he did as the angel of the Lord commanded and took Mary as his wife (Matthew 1:18-20, 24).

As you can see, Joseph knew all about the birds and the bees. He knew how babies were made, and he had not had sex with his fiancée. So when

Mary turned up pregnant, he was naturally convinced she had committed fornication. So he resolved to do what any man would—call off the engagement. Matthew's account, however, tells us that an angel told Joseph the truth about Mary's pregnancy. And based on that communication, he believed and went on with the wedding.

Think about what this tells us. Joseph would have been the hardest man on the planet to convince of Mary's story that she was a virgin. He was directly affected! He was the man who would, for the rest of his life, be ridiculed for marrying an unfaithful, pregnant woman who was bearing another man's child. He would have to endure the contempt of the men in the town, who would forever look on him as too stupid not to believe Mary's wild story.

Yet it's clear Joseph was not stupid and made his decision fully aware of the implications of violating social expectations about purity and the sanctity of marriage. A good and prudent man, as Matthew calls him, would be well aware of how marrying Mary would mar his reputation for the rest of his life. So why would he go on and marry the girl? Only one reason makes any sense at all. He actually received a message from an angel, and that message was the absolute truth: Mary was a virgin who was bearing in her womb the Son of God. The fact that Joseph believed this truth, knew the lifelong consequences, and yet took under his protective wing the Son of God and his earthly mother is what makes this man one of the great heroes of the Bible.

The evidence for the virgin birth not only points to the conclusion that Jesus of Nazareth is who he claimed to be; it also shows how much he identified with us. Though he was God, he humbled himself and willingly endured the sneers and scorn of those who didn't believe in him. The evidence of Christ's deity through the miracle of the virgin birth is just one of the truths God has given us to reinforce that he accepted us in spite of our sin and sent the one and only person who could redeem us.[6]

WHAT GOD'S UNCONDITIONAL ACCEPTANCE PRODUCES

It was time for the big season to start. I (Sean) was 12 and ready to play Little League baseball. Prior to the first game my dad, Josh, got an idea about how to teach me—and my teammates—an important lesson. He bought 12 coupons good for ice cream sundaes at a local restaurant and took them to my coach.

"Coach, these are for the kids," he said.

"This is great," the coach said with a big smile. "I wish more dads took an interest like this. I'll take them for sundaes after our first win."

"No," Josh said quickly. "I want you to take them for sundaes after their first *loss*."

My coach looked at my dad strangely. What Dad was saying wasn't computing. So Dad proceeded to explain his thinking.

"Coach, I don't know about you, but as I raise my kids I don't want to acknowledge their success as much as their effort. And I don't want to acknowledge their effort as much as their being created in the image of God. I believe my son is created in the image of God and that he has infinite value, dignity, and worth. None of these things have anything to do with playing baseball. If he never played baseball an inning in his life, I would love and accept him just as much."

My coach looked at Josh for a long moment. Finally, all he could muster was, "That's weird!" But he agreed to use the coupons as Dad instructed.

The season started, and our team won our first few games. But we lost the third or fourth game, and the coach was true to his word. He gave each player an ice cream sundae coupon, and we all went out to "celebrate" our loss.

Of course, my teammates and I certainly appreciated the sundaes. But there was an even greater benefit to my dad's generosity. Over the next two weeks three of the kids on my team came up and thanked him for the special treat. One of my teammates, a boy named Jesse, came up to Dad and said, "Thanks a lot for the ice cream sundaes, Mr. McDowell. Wow! It doesn't matter to you if we win or not—you love us anyway." The lesson I learned so powerfully that day was that my dad accepted me no matter what.

GOD'S ACCEPTANCE IS EVEN "WEIRDER"

A father rewarding his son and the baseball team when they lose a game may be weird. But God's acceptance of us is even weirder. The apostle Paul said, "You were [God's] enemies, separated from him by your evil thoughts and actions" (Colossians 1:21). We as humans didn't just lose a sports game. We rejected God's ways and his love and brought evil into his perfect world of absolute good. Yet Jesus came to die for us "while we were still his enemies" (Romans 5:10). It's not just that we were undeserving—we were rebels against God. And because we were dead spiritually, we couldn't do anything to change our enemy status.

If we were so undeserving and enemies of God, what kind of acceptance is it that motivated him to come to earth to die for us? It was a unique kind of acceptance that finds its roots only in God. It was a love that accepted you and me without any conditions whatsoever. God was motivated by a love that embraced us for exactly who we were—undeserving rebellious sinners.

There is perhaps nothing that brings greater joy to the human heart than for another person to know all your faults and failures and, despite them, love you for being you.

God coming to earth isn't based on anything you have done or could do in the future. It is purely the result of his grace. Every other religion in the world teaches that human effort is required to attain some type of "salvation." But what some religions call salvation is essentially escape from evil with no prospect of joy. Buddhists explain that a person must go through countless cycles of reincarnation to reach what is called nirvana, which is essentially a state of personal oblivion. Islam teaches Muslims they must work very hard to qualify for rewards that Allah may choose to give them. Mormons declare grace is obtained only after a person does all he or she can do to receive salvation. But Christianity teaches that humans are helpless and can do nothing to merit salvation. It is God who takes the initiative to reach out to his enemies. "God saved you by his special favor when you believed. And you can't take credit for this; it is a gift from God. Salvation is not a reward for the good things we have done, so none of us can boast about it" (Ephesians 2:8-9).

We state it again for emphasis: His grace was extended to us while we were gripped by death—sinners by birth and enemies of God. "When we were utterly helpless, Christ came at just the right time…God showed his great love for us by sending Christ to die for us while we were still sinners" (Romans 5:6, 8). "Can we boast, then, that we have done anything to be accepted by God? No, because our acquittal is not based on our good deeds" (Romans 3:27). Regardless of all you've done—or haven't done—he offers grace. *God accepts you* completely without any conditions, and in spite of your sin he provides a way back to him.

The relational meaning of the incarnation is that you and I are unconditionally loved and accepted. There is perhaps nothing that brings greater joy to the human heart than for another person to know all your faults and failures and, despite them, love you for being you.

When Josh gave me (Sean) and my team ice cream sundaes after we lost our first baseball game, his gift said, "I know you messed up and didn't really play that well, but despite your failure I love you." How much more does God know us for all that we are, including our faults, failures, and sin—yet he accepts us without conditions.

Accepted in Spite of Our Weaknesses

After I (Josh) became a Christian, I transferred to Wheaton College, a Christian school. The more I grew in my faith, the more I struggled over the challenge to give myself entirely to God. I resisted because I thought he might want me to go into Christian ministry, which meant only one thing to me—public speaking. At that time my poor grammar and stuttering problem were still very evident. As a result, it seemed to me that giving "everything" to God was giving him very little he could use.

Finally I said, "God, I don't think I have any speaking talents or other gifts you can use in ministry. I stutter when I'm scared, and I speak horrible English. I have all these limitations, so you surely don't want me in ministry. But if you can take these limitations and glorify yourself, then I will serve you the rest of my life with every breath I breathe."

God accepted all of me, regardless of my limitations. And because he accepted me without any conditions, I could give him myself without reservation. And amazingly he did something with my limitations. I truly believe I am living a supernatural life because I am living beyond my human limitations.

I have now been privileged to speak about Christ to millions of people in over half the countries of the world. I am humbled when I realize how many have been reached through the writings in my books. After all these years, I still struggle a little with my grammar when I speak and write. Every time I address a crowd or begin work on a book, I am aware of both my weakness and the grace of God. He accepts me for who I am, weakness and all, and I couldn't be happier. God's unconditional acceptance of us evokes a deep joy that is hard to explain. While it takes the pressure off to perform, it creates a motivation to do our best. And when we do mess up, we are not condemned. The freedom of being accepted without conditions produces a relationship that is secure.

ACCEPTANCE WITHOUT CONDITIONS CREATES A SECURE RELATIONSHIP

When someone accepts you for who you are, it gives you a sense of security. Since that kind of relationship is not based upon performance, it creates a natural vulnerability where you open up and trust another. It engenders a security that gives you confidence that, no matter what, you'll be loved.

The incarnation is a reflection of the Godlike acceptance that produces a secure relationship. We see this in Jesus dying for us while we were sinners and enemies of God. But we also see it in how he interacted with others. Take, for example, the Samaritan woman in John 4. She had three strikes against her socially: 1) She was a woman, therefore considered inferior to men in that culture; 2) she was a Samaritan, a race of people despised by the Jews; and 3) she was immoral, living with a man who was not her husband. While Jesus exposed her sin, he engaged her in conversation without judgment or condemnation. As a result, the woman welcomed the truth when Jesus shared it, and her life was changed.

The Pharisees of his day criticized Jesus for fraternizing with "tax collectors and many other notorious 'sinners.'" Jesus replied, "Healthy people don't need a doctor—sick people do" (Matthew 9:11-12). How does a doctor respond to a person who comes to him or her with an illness or injury? Can you imagine a doctor condemning the poor patient for being sick? "How stupid can you be? If you had been paying better attention, you wouldn't have hit your thumb with the hammer." No, the physician accepts the patient right where he or she is and focuses on providing the comfort and healing needed.

This is how the Incarnate One connects with us when we are in pain, trouble, or crisis. He doesn't condemn us or criticize us, even though we may be in the wrong. God does not condone or overlook our sin either; it must be dealt with on his terms. But he loves us for who we are and accepts us at the point of our failure. Embracing such love and acceptance from God gives us the joy of a secure relationship. We can say like Paul, "I am convinced that nothing can ever separate us from his love" (Romans 8:38).

ACCEPTANCE THAT IDENTIFIES WITH US CREATES AN INTIMATE RELATIONSHIP

Jesus not only accepts us for who we are, he identifies with all that we feel. He knows what we are going through, and he understands it like no other. And that creates a bond and intimacy like nothing else can.

Remember, he experienced life as a human baby, child, teenager, and man. He suffered embarrassment, humiliation, and rejection. As God, Christ understood his creation perfectly. But by becoming a human being, he let us know how intimately and completely he identifies with us—and with all we experience.

Christ wanted me (Josh) to know he identified with my humiliation as the son of the town drunk and with my sense of aloneness. He wants you to know he identifies with your feelings of rejection when your child is not chosen for the basketball team or when you're overlooked for a job promotion. He identified with you as you were teased cruelly by classmates or shunned by "friends." He can identify with what you feel when you are betrayed by a girlfriend or boyfriend, a coworker, or a spouse.

Think of it: He is the all-sufficient Lord, yet when he was born to Mary he became as dependent as you were when you were a baby. He was the one who fashioned the human body, yet like you he had to learn to walk. He was the preexistent Word, yet he had to learn to speak, just as you did. He created clouds and rivers and lakes, yet he got thirsty. He endured the taunts of those who knew only part of his family's story. He must have felt the almost unbearable weight of grief when his earthly father, Joseph, died. He suffered not only the physical torture of the cross as he died for you but also the anguish of being rejected, humiliated, denied, abandoned, and even betrayed by his closest friends. Why did he willingly go through all of that?

Because he wants you to know that he understands. The writer of Hebrews tells us that Christ "has gone through suffering and temptation...[and] is able to help us when we are being tempted...[He] understands our weaknesses, for he faced all of the same temptations we do, yet he did not sin. So let us come boldly...and we will find grace to help us when we need it" (2:18; 4:15-16). There is nothing you have experienced that God in Christ does not understand firsthand! He, like you, has experienced

- rejection—by his own people
- abandonment—by his own disciples
- misunderstanding—by his own followers
- ridicule—at his own trial
- betrayal—by a close friend
- criticism—by the religious leaders of his day[7]

He has also experienced human achievement and victories. He knows what it's like to feel loved and accepted. He knows the joy of completing a job well done. He has heard the voice of his Father say, "This is My beloved Son, in whom I am well pleased" (Matthew 17:5 NKJV). He has known the victory of conquering what no one has ever conquered: death.

He has experienced all the ups—and downs—of human existence. He's "been there, done that"—wherever you have been. The incarnation is Jesus' way of saying, "No matter what emotion you may be feeling, no matter what experience you may be enduring, I can identify with what you're going through and I'm here for you."

HOW TO ACCEPT OTHERS AS GOD ACCEPTS US

God's coming to earth says to each of us, "Regardless of your sin I will give my life to redeem you." That kind of unconditional acceptance is the basis for a relationship with God that is both intimate and secure. But that God-like acceptance isn't just for God to express to us—he wants us to express that same kind of acceptance toward others.

If we are to live out Godlike acceptance in our lives, we must learn to accept others for who they are, no matter what.

Paul the apostle exhorts us to "accept each other just as Christ has accepted you; then God will be glorified" (Romans 15:7). God did not wait until we were believing right or living right before he invited us into a relationship with him; he gave himself for us "while we were still sinners" (Romans 5:8). That is a key message Jesus was conveying in the story of the prodigal son in Luke 15. It was the response of the Father—a response of unconditional acceptance. Yes, the son came back home...but only to ask to live as a servant, not as a son. The father, however, was "filled with love and compassion, he ran to his son, embraced him, and kissed him" (verse 20). The father broke the custom of the day, took the initiative toward the wayward boy, and unconditionally received him with all the rights of sonship. That is true, Godlike acceptance.

If we are to live out Godlike acceptance in our own lives, we must learn to accept others for who they are, no matter what. Then God will be glorified, and others will experience a relational connection that reflects Christ's connection to us. And that kind of connection will foster the joy of secure relationships and will help us to pass on our faith to others.

ACCEPTANCE INVOLVES MAKING YOURSELF AVAILABLE TO OTHERS

Accepting others as Christ accepts us means we must take the time to be *with* people.

The pressure was on. The book deadline was fast approaching, and I (Josh) needed to focus. Although the memory of this experience takes me back many years, I recall it vividly. I was right in the middle of editing a chapter when two-year-old Sean wandered in.

"Want to play, Daddy?" he chirped expectantly.

As an experienced parent (having already been through the two-year-old stage with Kelly), I should have realized Sean really wanted only a hug and a minute or two to show me his new ball. But I was working on an "important" chapter and felt I just didn't have even two minutes to spare.

"Son, how about playing a little later?" I replied. "I'm right in the middle of a chapter."

Sean didn't know what a chapter was, but he got the message. Daddy was too busy, and he'd have to leave now. He trotted off without complaining, and I returned to my manuscript. But my relief was short-lived. Dottie soon came in and sat down for a "little chat."

She began, "Honey, Sean just told me you were too busy to play with him. I know this book is important, but I'd like to point something out."

"What is that?" I asked rather impatiently, because now my wife was keeping me from my all-important project.

"I think you have to realize you are always going to have writing to do, and you are always going to have deadlines. Your whole life will be researching and doing similar projects. But you're not always going to have a two-year-old son who wants to sit on your lap and show you his new ball."

"I hear what you're saying," I said, "and you make a lot of sense as usual. But right now I've got to finish this chapter."

"All right, Josh," she said. "But please think about it. You know, if we spend time with our kids now, they will spend time with us later."

I did think about it, and the more I thought, the more Dottie's gentle words were like a knife slicing me to the core. She was right. I would always have deadlines to meet, contracts to fulfill, phone calls to answer, and people to see. But my children would only be children for a short time. Soon the years would sweep by. Would I have any more time for them next year than I did this year?

I knew what the answer would be if I didn't change my ways. Quietly, without any big speeches or fanfare, I made a decision. I took Sean out in the yard and tossed the ball with him for a while. Ever since, I have tried to place my children ahead of my contracts, deadlines, and the clamor of a world that wants me to get back to them ASAP. And it has paid off.

I (Sean) have often been the beneficiary of Josh's decision. I don't remember that day when my dad didn't take time with me. But I do remember my dad doing his best to plan his speaking schedule around my basketball games and working hard to be involved in my life, as well as the lives of my sisters. The older I get, the more I appreciate the sacrifice my father made to build a relationship with me—especially now that I have my own family. He refused to sacrifice his family on the altar of success, fame, or popularity. This doesn't mean it wasn't hard, at times, having a father who was so busy and who traveled so much. I missed him often—badly. What got me through was knowing how passionately he loved us kids.

To demonstrate that you accept a child, a spouse, or a loved one for who they are involves taking the time to be there for them when they need you.

ACCEPTANCE INVOLVES
ENTERING ANOTHER'S WORLD

I (Josh) remember talking to one father who told me that he had taken time to spend with his son, but he now regretted it. The son and father did not maintain a good relationship, and he saw the time with his son as a big failure.

"What did you do together?" I asked.

"Well, I love to golf," he said, "so I took him golfing, and it was a disaster."

"Does your son like to golf?" I inquired.

"No, but I do," he responded.

The Incarnate One stepped into our world; he did not demand that we enter his. He came to us and accepted us in order to deal with *our* problem. We too must enter the world of others and focus on *their* interests and issues if they are going to sense we love and accept them. You can't do this without truly getting to know the other person. If people you care about could verbalize this deep longing to be loved for who they are, it might sound like this: "I long for you to take thought of me and show an interest in what I do and what I like, caring about my dreams and aspirations. But it doesn't help me if you enter my world just because I want you to; it has meaning only if you do it because *you* want to, because you truly love and accept me for who I am."

Dottie, who is my (Sean's) mother, tells a story of what her own mother did to enter her world and accept her imaginative spirit. She tells it in her own words:

As a little girl, my hero was Peter Pan. Just hearing the story took my breath away. I spent much of my playtime living and reliving each scene, and I couldn't get enough of it. Each time I dreamed about the boy who could fly, I felt inspired and energized.

I remember clearly the day I wandered down into our basement when I was about five years old. I spotted a box of Ivory Snow, a popular laundry detergent in those days, next to my mother's washing machine. In my well-developed imagination, each handful of soap flakes looked like the pixie dust that Tinker Bell sprinkled on Wendy, Michael, and John to enable them to fly. Thrilled at the prospect, I decided to relive the Tinker Bell scene. I'll never forget the exhilaration I felt as I took handfuls of "pixie dust" and sprinkled them generously throughout the entire basement. It was a magical moment in my young life.

When I was done, everything in the basement was covered with soap. When my mom discovered what I had done, she listened to my explanation, lovingly understood my childish fantasy, and recognized how much the experience meant to me. Instead of reacting in anger or frustration at the mess I had created, she laughed with me and encouraged me to repeat the whole story of Peter Pan to her. Later, still in a lighthearted mood, we cleaned up the enormous mess together.

What did this experience communicate to me? It assured me that my mom accepted me and my wild imagination. She unselfishly chose to encourage my childish dreams and that made me feel accepted. I shall never forget it!

Even as an adult my mother would dream my dreams with me, wanting to know every detail and delighting in every interest that I pursued. Mom is with the Lord now. But her interest in knowing the details of my pursuits communicates that she accepted me for who I am. And it has taught me how to demonstrate acceptance of my husband, children, and those around me.

ACCEPTANCE INVOLVES ACCEPTING THE FAULTS OF OTHERS

We all have the need for others to accept us for who we are, "warts and all." Genuine acceptance is able to separate the person from his or her behavior, just as Christ loves and accepts us in spite of our sin.

When someone you love does something different from how you would do it or makes a costly mistake, acceptance will focus on the person you love, not the difference or the failure. Godlike acceptance says: "Even if nothing about you changed, I would love you anyway"; "I want to know how you're feeling, because how you feel is important to me"; "I'm so proud of how you handled that situation"; "What happened to the car in the fender-bender isn't important—I'm just glad you're all right, because you are the one who matters to me."

After a disagreement or a clash of wills, it's likely your acceptance needs to be expressed again. This might take the form of fixing a person a favorite meal, sending a bouquet of flowers, or any outward expression that communicates, "We may not always see eye to eye, but I always love you."[8]

The more we take the time to understand another person, the more accepted he or she feels. The Incarnate One who entered our world and accepted us without condition is our perfect role model.

CELEBRATING THE INCARNATION AT CHRISTMAS

The Christmas season provides rich opportunities to focus on the awesome truth of the incarnation—"God wants to have a relationship with you!" Here are some practical ways to accomplish that goal.

While trimming the tree. Some people say that the Christmas tree tradition began when Martin Luther, struck by the beauty of a forest of starlit fir trees, brought one indoors and decorated it with candles to remind his children of God's creation. When you and your family are trimming your Christmas tree, you can have this conversation:

Ask, "What can the lights on the tree tell us about the meaning of Christmas?" After fielding questions, turn off the Christmas lights on the tree and say, "This is what all of us are like without Jesus—empty bulbs without light or life." Turn on the lights and say, "This is what all of us are like when we connect to God. He gives life and light to all who believe in Christ as their Savior. When you see the Christmas tree lit up, think of the true meaning of Christmas—that God sent his Son to earth because he wants so very much to have a relationship with you."

Ask, "What can the evergreen tree tell us about the meaning of Christmas?" After the answers and discussion, say, "You know the leaves of other trees turn brown and die in the fall. But the evergreen tree never turns brown. Its leaves remain green year-round. Before Christ was in our lives, we were like other trees. We could never live forever. But because of Christ we have the promise of eternal life. When you see the evergreen tree, remember Christ came so you can remain alive forever if you have a relationship with him."

On singing or listening to Christmas music. Christmas music is an excellent tool to reinforce the meaning of the incarnation. When the word *Immanuel* is used in a song, ask what the word means. Explain that Christ was called Immanuel, meaning "God is with us," because Jesus is God who came to live with us. And why did Jesus come to earth? He came to offer himself as a sacrifice so we could have a relationship with God.

When hearing "Silent Night," ask, "What does it mean that Jesus was a 'holy infant so tender and mild'?" This phrase gives you the opportunity to point out that Jesus was the "holy infant" because his birth father was not Joseph but rather the Holy God of the universe. Thus, Jesus was born of a virgin with God as his birth father.

When hearing "Angels We Have Heard on High," ask, "Why did the angels sing 'Gloria in excelsis deo'?" Explain that the phrase means "Glory to God in the highest." The angels sang it because it was a most glorious day when God became a human being as part of his wonderful plan to restore us to a relationship with him.

When "decking the halls." Young people generally love Christmas and all the decoration that accompanies the season. They may not, however, give much thought to the deeper reasons for decorating. Use the time of decorating your home or church to emphasize the purpose: "We decorate to express how very thankful we are that God did what he did in sending Christ to earth so we can enjoy a relationship with God."

Write a Christmas card to Jesus. Christmas cards are used primarily to express holiday wishes and sentiments to one another. But you can also use cards to teach young people the relational meaning of Christmas. Ask them to write a card to Jesus, expressing their thankfulness for his becoming human and for what he says to them through the incarnation.

Suggest: "First, tell Jesus that you know he sees and knows everything you do and think (good or bad), yet he accepts you just the way you are. And then tell Jesus how that makes you feel. Thank him for accepting you without any conditions."[9]

JESUS WAS GOD'S PERFECT SACRIFICE

I (Sean) grew up in the small mountain town of Julian, California. Most of my shopping was done at the general store in town. That is where I got candy, school supplies, crafts, and so on. My parents had dropped me, two of my school friends, and Katie, my five-year-old sister, off to do some shopping while they sat in the car. When we came out of the store, Katie had a handful of lapel pins and colorful craft pencils. As we walked to the car she handed them to my two friends and said, "Here, I bought these things for you."

We got in the car, and Dad and Mom looked at each other in a strange way. Mom then got out and asked Katie to join her. My parents had sensed something was up because they hadn't given Katie any money to buy things. Within minutes I found out my sister was a shoplifter!

My dad and mom conferred with each other for a moment. Then Mom collected the stolen goods, took her little thief by the hand, and walked her right back into the store.

There are laws against shoplifting in California. Stealing is punishable by fines and jail time. Of course, I wasn't too worried. I figured with Katie returning the stolen stash and giving an apology, she'd be forgiven and go free. But what if the store owner was really ticked at Katie? What if he refused to forgive and pressed charges?

Of course, that didn't happen. Forgiveness was offered, and Katie was set free of the consequences of stealing.

But what about the higher court of heaven? Can God just say, "Sure, you sinned, but that's okay, forget it—I'll forgive you and we'll be friends"? The reality is that God by nature is holy. He can't just overlook sin. The Bible says of God, "Your eyes are too pure to look on evil; you cannot tolerate wrong" (Habakkuk 1:13 NIV). God is so holy that he "cannot allow sin in any form" (Habakkuk 1:13). So by his very nature he is unable to have a relationship with those infected with sin.

Therefore, even though he is "rich in mercy" (Ephesians 2:4), sin separates us from him. And that separation is a big deal because sin has caused a dreadful consequence: death. The apostle Paul said we "were dead, doomed forever because of [our] many sins" (Ephesians 2:1). Dead people can't accept forgiveness even when it's offered, because they're dead. So that presents quite a dilemma. In order for God to forgive us he had to address our sin. And to do that he put in place an amazing and miraculous plan. One that carried with it a very high price.

A SACRIFICE IS NEEDED

They had traveled for three days. The young boy couldn't remember ever being on such a long journey with his father. It was exciting.

When his father saw their destination in the distance, he told his two servants, "'The boy and I will travel a little farther. We will worship there, and then we will come right back.' Abraham placed the wood for the burnt offering on Isaac's shoulders, while he himself carried the knife and the fire" (Genesis 22:5-6).

Isaac knew about burnt offerings, and he knew something was missing from his father's preparations. "'We have the wood and the fire,' said the boy, 'but where is the lamb for the sacrifice?'" (verse 7). Isaac had been taught there was a price to be paid to obtain forgiveness. A living, breathing creature had to die as a blood sacrifice.

You know the story. Abraham placed his son on the altar to sacrifice him as God had told him. But just as he lifted his knife to sacrifice his son to God, "the angel of the LORD shouted to him from heaven, 'Abraham! Abraham!... Lay down the knife...Do not hurt the boy in any way, for now I know that you truly fear God. You have not withheld even your beloved son from me.' Then Abraham looked up and saw a ram caught by its horns in a bush. So he took the ram and *sacrificed it* as a burnt offering on the altar *in place of his son*" (verses 11-13).

Accepting a Substitute

Abraham, like all of us, had sinned and was dead spiritually and separated from God. But in this dramatic example, God was showing him that he had a miraculous plan in place by which Abraham and the rest of us could be brought back to spiritual life in exchange for another life. A blood sacrifice would be made in our place and, in a real sense, purchase our resurrection to a new life in relationship with God.

But this "life-for-a-life" exchange was very specific. Scripture tells us that "the LORD called to Moses from the Tabernacle and said to him, 'Give the following instruction to the people of Israel. When you present an animal as an offering to the LORD...it must be a male with no defects...Lay your hand on the animal's head, and the LORD *will accept its death in your place* to purify you, making you right with him'" (Leviticus 1:1-4 NLT). The priests were then instructed to offer the sacrifice before God, as a substitute, to atone for the person's sin. People were guilty of the sins, but the animal without defects became a holy sacrifice that God accepted. The death of the holy animal substituted for the death of the sinner.

However, the annual sacrifices were not God's permanent solution to our dilemma of sin and death. They were only a symbol of what was to come. In order for the consequences of sin (death) to be reversed so we could be made alive to God, a more powerful and perfect sacrifice had to be made.

The Perfect Redeeming Sacrifice of Christ

Since we were born dead spiritually, sin has all of us enslaved. The apostle Paul said, "I am sold into slavery, with sin as my master" (Romans 7:14). Paul said he was a prisoner to sin and declared, "What a wretched man I am! Who will rescue me from this body of death?" (verse 24 NIV). He then answers his own question: "Thanks be to God—through Jesus Christ our Lord" (verse 25 NIV).

Our freedom from the enslavement of sin and death was through the "redemption that came by Christ Jesus. God presented him as a sacrifice of atonement" (Romans 3:24-25 NIV). Redemption in this verse is a commercial term. It is a reference to the high price paid to purchase a slave in that day—a price so high it not only purchased the slave but also purchased the legal paperwork to buy the slave completely out of slavery. This redemptive price brought total freedom so the person would never again be sold back into slavery.

There it is! God's miraculous and merciful redemptive plan to set us free of our sins and bring us back to life in relationship with him. "God is so rich in mercy, and he loved us so very much, that even while we were dead because of our sins, he gave us life when he raised Christ from the dead" (Ephesians 2:4-5). The blood sacrifices of bulls and goats were not sufficient or powerful enough for a just God to cancel our death sentence. You see, a sacrificial death was just part of the redemptive plan. The sacrifice also had to rise to life again so that we too could be brought back to life.

It is an amazing miracle. Even though the "wages of sin is death" (Romans 6:23), "God paid a ransom [your wages]...And the ransom he paid was not mere gold or silver. He paid for you with the precious lifeblood of Christ, the sinless, spotless Lamb of God" (1 Peter 1:18-19). It is Jesus' death on the cross that atones for your sins. He became your sacrifice for sin. His death substitutes for your death, and then his resurrection to life is your resurrection to new life in him. So because of his atoning sacrifice you can be set free, forgiven of your sins, and escape eternal banishment from the presence of God. "For Christ died for sin, once for all, the righteous for the unrighteous, to bring you to God" (1 Peter 3:18 NIV).

Just as the priests of old took the sin offering into the holy tabernacle and made a sacrifice to God to redeem the people, "so Christ has now become the High Priest over all good things that have come. He has entered that great, perfect sanctuary in heaven...Once for all time he took blood into that Most Holy Place, but not the blood of goats and calves. He took his own blood, and with it he secured our salvation forever" (Hebrews 9:11-12).

Therefore:

> *We believe the truth that Jesus, as the sinless Son of God, atoned for our sin through his death on the cross. And the offering of his blood as a sacrifice for sin redeems us so we are forgiven—set free—and raises us to new life in him.*

Some would say Jesus' death as the "spotless Lamb of God" satisfies the demands of both God's holiness and his justice. His holiness is satisfied because Jesus was sinless—a perfect sacrifice. His justice is satisfied in that Christ's death paid our "wages of sin," which is death.

While there is some disagreement over the distinction as to whether Christ "suffered for us" or whether he was "punished instead of us" (biblically speaking, both views are true), there is common agreement that through Jesus' death we are redeemed—forgiven of our sin, raised to new life, and reconciled to God. "God made Christ, who never sinned, to be the offering for our sin, so that we could be made right with God through Christ" (2 Corinthians 5:21).

EVIDENCE THAT JESUS WAS
GOD'S PERFECT SACRIFICE

When you are put on the justice scales of God, there is only one thing that can outweigh your sin. It isn't your good deeds, a life of penance, or even the sacrifice of your own life. The only thing that will cancel out your sin and satisfy the justice scales of a holy God is a pure and holy sacrifice.

God wants us to feel confident in our faith that
Jesus of Nazareth is the holy Lamb of God. That
is why he has given us such clear signs.

The book of Hebrews tells us that not only did Jesus die for us, but he "is the kind of high priest we need because he is holy and blameless, unstained by sin…He does not need to offer sacrifices every day like the other high priests…Jesus did this once for all when he sacrificed himself on the cross… [God's] Son has been made perfect forever" (7:26-28).

If the Jesus of history born in Bethlehem some 2000 years ago was truly God's Son, then it is clear he was the perfect sacrifice needed to secure our salvation. And God wants us to feel confident that Jesus of Nazareth is the holy Lamb of God. That is why he has given us such clear signs.

First, God gave John the Baptist a sign to identify Jesus as God's Son. John saw Jesus coming toward him the day after he baptized him and said,

> "Look! There is the Lamb of God who takes away the sin of the world!"…Then John said, "I saw the Holy Spirit descending like a dove from heaven and resting upon him. I didn't know he was the one, but when God sent me to baptize with water, he told me, 'When you see the Holy Spirit descending and resting upon someone…he is the one who baptizes with the Holy Spirit.' I saw this happen to Jesus, so I testify that he is the Son of God [the Chosen One of God]" (John 1:29-34).

God has also given us convincing means to identify his Son through what are called *messianic prophecies*.

MESSIANIC PROPHECIES POINT TO JESUS

Imagine God, several millennia ago, devising the plan to send his only Son to earth. If we could have spoken down the corridors of time, we might have asked, "How will we know him? How will we recognize him as the Messiah, the holy Lamb of God—your acceptable sacrifice for sin?"

God might have responded, "I will give you prophecies about him in the Old Testament so you can recognize him when he comes. Some of these prophecies may make sense only after he has come and you look back with new eyes, but many will make sense in advance."

"What are some of those predictive prophecies?" you would likely ask. "Well, for starters," God might say, "let me give you 12."

The issue of the fulfilment of prophecy is somewhat complex. It involves understanding the language and culture of the Old Testament and also biblical ideas such as the concept of a "type." But for sake of simplicity, we list 12 predictive prophecies of the Old Testament and their fulfilment in the New Testament (all Scripture quotations here are from the NLT):

1. **The messiah would be pre-existent and divine.** Isaiah 9:6 says, "For a child is born to us, a son is given to us. The government will rest on his shoulders. And he will be called: Wonderful Counselor, Mighty God, Everlasting Father, Prince of Peace." Colossians 1:17 indicates this was true with Jesus: "He existed before anything else, and he holds all creation together."

2. **The messiah would be a prophet.** Deuteronomy 18:18 says, "I will raise up a prophet like you from among their fellow Israelites. I will put my words in his mouth, and he will tell the people everything I command him." The Gospels report Jesus being called a prophet from Nazareth in Galilee (Matthew 21:11).

3. **The messiah would be from the line of Jesse and the house of David.** Isaiah 11:1 says, "Out of the stump of David's family will grow a shoot—yes, a new Branch bearing fruit from the old root." Paul describes that Jesus was "born into King David's family line" (Romans 1:3).

4. **The messiah would be a judge.** The prophet Ezekiel describes the future messiah as a shepherd, judge, and ruler. Paul reports that Jesus will "judge the living and the dead when he comes to set up his Kingdom" (2 Timothy 4:1).

5. **The messiah would be a king.** Psalm 2:6 says, "For the Lord declares, 'I have placed my chosen king on the throne in Jerusalem, on my holy mountain.'" When Jesus was crucified, they placed a

sign announcing the charge against him: "This is Jesus, the King of the Jews" (Matthew 27:37).

6. **The messiah would have a special presence of the Holy Spirit.** Isaiah 11:2 says, "And the Spirit of the LORD will rest on him—the Spirit of wisdom and understanding." According to Mark 1:10, "As Jesus came up out of the water, he saw the heavens splitting apart and the Holy Spirit descending on him like a dove."

7. **The messiah would be preceded by a messenger.** Isaiah 40:3 says, "Listen! It's the voice of someone shouting, 'Clear the way through the wilderness for the LORD! Make a straight highway through the wasteland for our God!'" Mark 1:1-3 confirms that this announcement was about Jesus, and the messenger was John the Baptist.

8. **The messiah would have a ministry that began in Galilee.** Isaiah 9:1 says, "Nevertheless, that time of darkness and despair will not go on forever. The land of Zebulun and Naphtali will be humbled, but there will be a time in the future when Galilee of the Gentiles, which lies along the road that runs between the Jordan and the sea, will be filled with glory." Matthew 4:12-17 makes it clear Jesus began his ministry in Galilee, just as predicted by Isaiah.

9. **The messiah would perform miracles.** Isaiah 35:5-6 says, "And when he comes, he will open the eyes of the blind and unplug the ears of the deaf. The lame will leap like a deer, and those who cannot speak will sing for joy!" All four Gospels make it clear Jesus performed a range of different miracles (see Matthew 9:35).

10. **The messiah would enter the temple.** Malachi 3:1 says, "'Look! I am sending my messenger, and he will prepare the way before me. Then the Lord you are seeking will suddenly come to his Temple. The messenger of the covenant, whom you look for so eagerly, is surely coming,' says the LORD of Heaven's Armies." In Matthew 21:12, Jesus enters the Temple to knock over tables of moneychangers and drive out people buying and selling sacrifices.

11. **The messiah would ride into Jerusalem on a donkey**. Zechariah 9:9 says, "Rejoice, O people of Zion! Shout in triumph, O people of Jerusalem! Look, your king is coming to you. He is righteous and victorious, yet he is humble, riding on a donkey—riding on a donkey's colt." The disciples of Jesus brought him a colt so he could come into Jerusalem with a triumphal entry (Luke 19:35-37).

12. **The messiah would be a light to the gentiles**. Isaiah 42:6 says, "I, the LORD, have called you to demonstrate my righteousness. I will take you by the hand and guard you, and I will give you to my people, Israel, as a symbol of my covenant with them. And you will be a light to guide the nations." Acts 13:47-48 makes it clear the apostles, in fulfilment of this prophecy, began preaching the gospel beyond Israel to all the nations.

This is only a sample of the many prophecies fulfilled by Jesus.* So much more could be said, but this should be sufficient to help explain why so many people came to believe that Jesus was (and is) the unique messenger of God.

Before we wrap up this section, let's consider a common objection: The Gospel authors deliberately crafted their biographies of Jesus to make it appear as if he fulfilled the Old Testament Scriptures. Is this reasonable?

One response to this objection is to point out the historicity of specific messianic prophecies. For instance, it is incontrovertible that Jesus uniquely brought representatives of all nations to a recognition of the God of Israel, fulfilling Isaiah 49:6. There is also good evidence Jesus was born in Bethlehem, fulfilling Micah 5:2. And there is compelling evidence of the destruction of the temple within a generation of the life and ministry of Jesus, fulfilling Daniel 9:26. These are just a few of the examples that cumulatively challenge the idea that the Gospel writers made it appear as if Jesus fulfilled the Old Testament Scriptures. In many cases, we can historically establish that the prophets' predictions came true.

Further, at the time the Gospels were written, the Christian church was undergoing considerable persecution. Many Christians were martyred in

---

* An extensive list of Old Testament prophecies fulfilled in Christ can be found in *Evidence That Demands a Verdict*, chapter 9.

excruciating ways, such as by being crucified, by being burned alive, or by being fed to wild animals. Since the Gospel writers had nothing obvious to gain from inventing a new religion and everything to lose, this suggests they recorded what actually happened and what Jesus really said.

What is the purpose of these prophecies? So we can be confident in the truth that Jesus truly is God's perfect atonement for our sins. That truth causes us to join with the angels as they sing, "Worthy is the Lamb, who was slain, to receive power and wealth and wisdom and strength and honor and glory and praise!" (Revelation 5:12 NIV).

THE TRUE MEANING OF LOVE

The cross fell into the hole with a loud thud, sending shock waves of agony through Jesus' legs and arms. Prior to being nailed to the cross he had been beaten almost beyond recognition. Now he hung there on the tree in excruciating pain. Soldiers below him gambled for his clothes. Religious leaders mocked him. He pushed himself up from his nail-pierced feet in his attempts to get deep breaths. Each time he did this, pain shot up his legs. But he finally managed to draw enough breath to speak: "Father, forgive these people, because they don't know what they are doing" (Luke 23:34).

That kind of love is so amazing it defies our understanding.

The crowd laughed and jeered. "'He saved others,' they said, 'let him save himself if he is really God's Chosen One, the Messiah'" (Luke 23:35).

Two guilty criminals were crucified on either side of Jesus. One of them scoffed, "'So you're the Messiah, are you? Prove it by saving yourself—and us, too, while you're at it!' But the other criminal protested, 'Don't you fear God even when you are dying? We deserve to die for our evil deeds, but this man hasn't done anything wrong.' Then he said, 'Jesus, remember me when you come into your Kingdom.'"

"Jesus replied, 'I assure you, today you will be with me in paradise'" (Luke 23:39-43). Though guilty and dying alone, this criminal who deserved his punishment experienced the forgiving love of the Savior.

YOU ARE LOVED AND FORGIVEN

The criminal hanging there beside Jesus was as good as dead. So are you. Like that dying criminal, you are guilty of sin as charged. Your sin stands between you and a holy God without hope of forgiveness. You are dead to him with no ability in yourself to change your death status. That is, unless Christ remembers you as he did the criminal crucified beside him.

It was a Saturday morning. I (Josh) was 11 years old. I dressed before dawn and hurriedly got my morning chores done before the workers arrived.

A team of men had been working for days to jack up a small house on my parents' farm, preparing it to be moved to a new location. My grown brother, Wilmont, was having it moved over the objections of my father. Wilmont had been engaged in a bitter feud with my dad, which had escalated into an all-out war for half of the family farm. Having successfully sued my father, Wilmont had arrived that morning with a sheriff, a deputy, and a court order authorizing him to move the house.

I hated to see my dad and brother fight, but that was between them. Today I just wanted to savor the excitement of watching an entire house being towed down the road.

Just as the tractors were being attached to the house, my father, drunk as usual, began yelling at Wilmont. The sheriff moved quickly toward the staggering man to prevent an ugly scene. But it was too late for that. My brother, expecting something like this, had arranged for numerous families from our small farming community to be on hand to provide moral support for him. Many of them began chanting obscenities at my father as the sheriff restrained the old man.

I watched in horror, my excitement turning to embarrassment. Frightened by the escalating conflict and humiliated to see our family's feud played out in full view of my friends and neighbors, I ran from the shameful scene and into our nearby barn. Slamming the barn door behind me, I scrambled into the corn bin and buried myself up to my neck in corn.

Dark, quiet, and alone, my shame slowly turned to anger. I was angry that my father's drinking brought such division to my home. I was angry that he was rarely sober. And I was angry that he had caused such pain to my mother's life. But more than anything, I felt alone.

I lay there in the corn for what must have been hours. No one came looking for me. No one seemed to even notice I was gone. I felt forgotten.

You and I were on the mind and within the heart of a
loving God the day Jesus sacrificed himself on the cross.

It's not hard to feel alone even in a world full of busyness and activity. But I really wasn't forgotten in that corn bin. And neither are you in your loneliest moments. Though a sinner by birth, deserving nothing except your sentence of death, your holy and blameless Creator spreads his arms the width of the cross and says, "I love you, and you are forgiven."

THE MEANING OF LOVE

As alone as you may feel at times in life, you are not forgotten by God. You and I were on the mind and within the heart of a loving God the day Jesus sacrificed himself on the cross.

"God showed how much he loved us by sending his only Son into the world so that we might have eternal life through him. This is real love. It is not that we loved God, but that he loved us" (1 John 4:9-10). The high price for your forgiveness was worth the sacrifice to God. Even when you were an enemy of God, separated and alone, he loved you. He saw your need, identified with your pain of death, and sacrificed himself so you might be forgiven of your sins and be raised to new life in relationship with him forever. That is the true meaning of Christ's atoning sacrifice for you.

It is hard to comprehend that Christ would love each of us that much. The great songwriter and preacher Charles Wesley couldn't understand it either and penned the words to "And Can It Be?"

> And can it be that I should gain
> An interest in the Savior's blood?
> Died He for me, who caused His pain—

For me, who Him to death pursued?
Amazing love! how can it be
That Thou, my God, shouldst die for me?

He left His Father's throne above,
So free, so infinite His grace—
Emptied Himself of all but love,
And bled for Adam's helpless race:
'Tis mercy all, immense and free,
For O my God, it found out me![1]

HOW TO LOVE OTHERS AS GOD LOVES US

"We know what real love is because Christ gave up his life for us. And so we also ought to give up our lives for our Christian brothers and sisters" (1 John 3:16). Yes, "God so loved the world that he [sacrificially] gave his only Son" (John 3:16). But how can our human love for others ever match his infinite love? Our efforts to love don't compare to God's love any more than a preschooler's coloring book compares to God's multicolored sunset or a hand-molded vase by a potter compares to God's delicate crafting of a newborn baby. Yet his love stands as a pattern to follow.

Let's look at two dimensions of Godlike love and see how God completes our joy as we love as he loves.

REAL LOVE SACRIFICES

"Observe how Christ loved us," Paul stated, "He didn't love in order to get something from us but to give everything of himself to us" (Ephesians 5:2 MSG). "Love...doesn't think about itself" (1 Corinthians 13:4-5 GWT). God wants us to love others like he loves us, and that means sacrificing something. Perhaps we don't literally sacrifice our physical life, but it does mean loving and living unselfishly. That may mean giving up our comforts for another, giving freely of our time, and giving unselfishly of our possessions. That is how we demonstrate a Godlike love to others.

Real Love Sacrifices Comfort

When Stephanie and I (Sean) had our first child, we didn't realize all it would mean to love and care for our bundle of joy. Scottie was a healthy and active baby. I knew I would enjoy feeding and rocking him and even singing to him. And I did. But I guess I just didn't realize it was such a 24/7 proposition. Stephanie and I would alternate caring for Scottie at night. So at times I found myself up at two o'clock in the morning attending to the needs of a crying baby. Sometimes at four o'clock Stephanie or I walked a crying Scottie during some of his stomachaches. It was uncomfortable losing valuable sleep and dragging off to work the next day. As a young married couple we missed going out at night with friends because we had to stay home with our baby. However, we gave up some of our past comforts willingly and, in a strange way, joyfully, because we loved our little boy. That's what sacrificial love does.

Max Lucado, in his book entitled *3:16: The Numbers of Hope,* tells of a father who loved his son sacrificially.

> I know a father who, out of love for his son, spends each night in a recliner, never sleeping more than a couple of consecutive hours. A car accident paralyzed the teenager. To maintain the boy's circulation, therapists massage his limbs every few hours. At night the father takes the place of the therapists. Though he's worked all day and will work again the next, he sets the alarm to wake himself every other hour until sunrise.[2]

A sacrificial love forgoes personal comforts to give of ourselves freely. We shouldn't love others sacrificially with personal gain in mind, but let me (Josh) tell you something surprising. Spending sleepless nights with a baby, traveling long hours to get home for a child's basketball game, enduring some of the struggles of a boy's teen years and all the ongoing, smaller yet tedious sacrifices of raising a child definitely have a payoff. The sacrifices Dottie and I made to raise Sean to adulthood have produced more joy than I can explain. A father could not be more proud of a son than I am. I won't embarrass him here by citing all his qualities as a son, a husband, a father, a speaker, and an educator. But my life has been worth living just to be married to the most wonderful woman in the world and to watch a baby boy and three baby girls grow up to become people who are sacrificially loving God, their families, and the world around them. God's gift of my family has made my joy complete. Love your family sacrificially, and that kind of joy can be yours as well.

The smaller sacrifices of life can at times be more difficult than the big sacrifices. But don't be discouraged that loving another unselfishly causes some personal and temporary discomfort. God will give back more than you can ever imagine. The apostle Peter said, "Be truly glad! There is wonderful joy ahead, even though it is necessary for you to endure many trials for a while" (1 Peter 1:6). The big payoff for enduring the discomforts of sacrificial love is joy—some on this earth and the rest in eternity.

Real Love Sacrifices Possessions

After the apostle John told us to "give up our lives for our brothers and sisters," he went on to say, "If someone has enough money to live well and sees a brother or sister in need but shows no compassion—how can God's love be in that person?" (1 John 3:17). "Pure and lasting religion in the sight of God our Father," Jesus stated, "means that we must care for orphans and widows in their troubles, and refuse to let the world corrupt us" (James 1:27). A sacrificial love means giving of our possessions to others.

We don't have to be wealthy in the world's eyes to give of our possessions. And the gift doesn't have to be of Bill Gates proportions in order to mean something. When the widow dropped two pennies in the temple collection box, Jesus said, "I assure you, this poor widow has given more than all the others have given. For they gave a tiny part of their surplus, but she, poor as she is, has given everything she has" (Mark 12:43). Giving isn't as important as giving sacrificially.

God doesn't ask for just 10 percent of your possessions; he asks that you give him your all—and when you do that, your possessions are included. Jesus said, "You must love the Lord your God with *all* your heart, *all* your soul, and *all* your mind...[and] love your neighbor as yourself" (Matthew 22:37-39). "Give your bodies to God," Paul admonishes. "Let them be a living and holy sacrifice—the kind he will accept. When you think of what he has done for you, is this too much to ask?" (Romans 12:1).

Possession is more a matter of stewardship than ownership. He has given all of us certain possessions, and he wants us to be good stewards of those possessions by using them to meet the needs of others. That is why Scripture says, "You should look not only to your own interests, but also to the interests of others" (Philippians 2:4 NIV).

In his book *The Faith,* Chuck Colson challenges us to see the world of possessions through God's eyes:

> As we see the world through God's eyes, we actually do put others' needs ahead of ours. This is why, when the great novelist Flannery O'Connor was asked by one of her correspondents how he could experience God's love, her reply was, "Give alms." She meant do something for the poor, for those in need, which in fact is one of the most telling marks of Christian holiness, as the apostle James reminds us (1:27; 2:17).
>
> When we care for God's favorites, the poor, who include the destitute, the widowed, the fatherless, the sick, prisoners, and anyone suffering injustice, we plunge immediately into the cosmic battle that's always raging between good and evil. We choose sides. Once on God's side, we come to understand God's point of view and position ourselves to experience God's love and friendship in a whole new way.[3]

Christ's kind of love—a sacrificial love—is love in action that includes giving to others of what God has given you.

Real Love Sacrifices Time

We both have done our share of traveling and speaking to young people. And if there is one thing we hear consistently from today's kids, it's this: "I have a problem with my dad—he won't spend time with me." It's not that these kids don't need their mothers, but their perception is, "My mom's there for me, but my dad is just not there. And when he is home it's like he's not really there, you know?"

What we sense kids are saying is that love is spelled T-I-M-E. In fact, we all spell love that way. When someone says they love us but don't take the time to be with us, their declaration of love rings untrue. Dads who don't spend time with their kids often make up for it by bringing home expensive gifts. But what we want from those we love is their time. We don't want more stuff; we want the person. Philosopher and poet Ralph Waldo Emerson is credited with saying that a gift is an excuse for not giving yourself. Gifts are important, but they don't replace the ultimate gift of our time.

Some people try to get around the need to spend time with their loved ones by saying it's not the quantity of time that counts but the quality. One of the biggest myths going today is the myth of "quality time." Of course we all want quality moments with our families. But you don't get them by appointment or on some kind of schedule. You get quality moments by spending larger quantities of time with your family. We must have both!

One of the biggest advantages of quantity time spent with your children is that you are able to serve as a role model for them. Whenever you run an errand, try to take one of your kids with you. When they are with us, their parents or grandparents, they can see how we respond to the world: how we act when another driver cuts us off or when a pushy salesclerk or a slow waitress irritates us. Our kids learn more about living their life when they are with us, watching us, and experiencing our reactions to others than they can learn in any classroom.

Another myth we fall victim to is the one that says, "It's the big moments that count." You might call them the "Disney World experiences"—those major excursions that take all day or all week and usually cost a lot of money. For parents, these "big moments" include trips to the amusement park, movie theater, or zoo; for youth leaders, activities such as ski trips or youth camp or big vacations. The truth is, your kids may remember the "big moments," but it's the consistent small day-in and day-out moments that will truly mold them. It's not that the big events are wrong or harmful; we plan big events with our own kids and they have created some amazing memories. But big events can never replace the consistent little moments of just *being with* them.

Dr. Jeff Myers, president of Summit Ministries, stresses the importance of knowing how to ask questions to engage a person and let them know you're there *with* them. Jeff says:

> My goal in asking questions is not for an opportunity to give instruction, but to help my students solve problems for themselves.
>
> "What do you think about that?"
>
> "Why is that happening?"
>
> "What took place?"[4]

Based on Jeff's approach, here are some suggested questions you can ask your kids when you're taking time to be with them.

- Let's share our favorite color, food, music, sport, vacation spot, and so on. Now let's think about this—why do we like some of the same things and yet have some other interests that are different?

- Describe your most embarrassing moment, happiest moment, saddest moment. Why did you feel that way? What was happening then?

- If you could ask God one question, what would it be?

Sacrificing your time to demonstrate a Christlike love requires a relational mindset. Consistently focusing your attention on the interests of another will convince him or her to believe, "I'm really loved."

REAL LOVE AFFIRMS

Because Jesus suffered torture and death for us, we know we are recipients of his sacrificial love. But when we go to him in prayer and pour out our grief over the loss of a loved one, our hurt over a betrayal by a "friend," or our feeling of being abandoned by a colleague, how does he respond? He responds with an affirming love. He is with us in these hurts, saying, "I hurt for you. I know you are hurting, and I'll be there for you." Christ's kind of love is our pattern to be there for those who are suffering or struggling with the problems of life—and also for being happy with them when their life is going great.

Every day we encounter situations that enable us to model affirming love. Consider the following common situations:

Your spouse arrives home from a trip to the store and confesses to a minor accident that bent the fender of the car. How do you respond?

Your 14-year-old daughter, a B-plus student, brings home a report card with three Cs and a D. What is the first thing you will say to her?

Your friend calls in frustration, saying he got into a fight with his supervisor and got fired today. What do you say to him?

At these moments people are not in need of a pep talk, a lecture, or a fix-it plan. They need someone to identify with their pain and feel bad with them. Scripture tells us that "when others are happy, be happy with them. If they are sad, share their sorrow" (Romans 12:15). That is what an affirming love does. It impels you to identify with a person's situation, whether happy or sad, and to be there for them.

For years, I (Josh) didn't grasp the truth of an affirming love. Whenever Dottie came to me with a problem she was struggling with, especially one that had caused her hurt, I would try to fix it. I wouldn't address her pain; rather I would address the problem that *caused* the pain. One day Dottie came home from a meeting at school very hurt over what some mothers had said about one of our kids. In the past when she shared a problem like that with me, I would leap on the situation and say something like, "Honey, don't let it get to you. Here's what you need to do." Then I would outline a plan to fix the problem. It may have been a good plan, but it didn't address the pain Dottie felt at the moment. But on this particular occasion, I finally got it right. I simply put my arms around her and said, "Honey, I'm so sorry you had to hear those words, and I hurt for you." That was it—no fix-it plan, no corrective measures outlined, just a heartfelt expression that identified with her pain.

Amazingly, it worked. Dottie felt affirmed and understood, and that was all she needed at the moment. A few days later she came back to me and asked what I thought she could do to address those critical comments about the family member. My fix-it plan was then welcomed.

We don't have to understand exactly what a person is going through in order to give them affirming love. Rather, our love causes us to identify with the one we love who is feeling pain: "What you're going through must be tough, and I want you to know I hurt because you hurt."

Living out an affirming love brings healing to the pain of another and deepens your relationship with that person. Such a demonstration of love also pleases God, and he gives you the joy of being his minister of comfort. Paul tells us that Jesus "is the source of every mercy and the God who comforts us. He comforts us in all our troubles so that we can comfort others. When others are troubled, we will be able to give them the same comfort God has given us" (2 Corinthians 1:3-4).

SUMMARY

Because of Christ's atoning sacrifice, we can be forgiven. Jesus loved us sacrificially, which is why he was willing to come to earth, live with us, and give himself up as our perfect sacrifice. The incarnation—God taking the form of a human—also enabled Jesus to experience what we have experienced and be there for us with an affirming love. Christ demonstrated real love for us, and he wants to love others that way through us. When we accept God's sacrificial and affirming love and in turn love others with this same sacrificial and affirming love, we are living out the truth of Christ's real love.

JESUS ROSE FROM THE DEAD

S he stood a few feet away sobbing as her son hung there, nailed to a rugged cross. John stood beside Mary, trying to comfort her. Moments later Jesus took one last breath and said, "'It is finished!' Then he bowed his head and gave up his spirit" (John 19:30).

Joseph of Arimathea and a few women lowered Jesus' lifeless body from the cross and prepared him for burial. After placing their dead Messiah in the tomb, they rolled a large stone over the entrance to seal him away for good, or so many thought.

Imagine a conversation between two observers of Jesus' ministry immediately after his death.

"I thought this Messiah Movement was going to last," Hamon says dryly.

"Yeah, me too," agrees Benjamin. "I wonder what his disciples are going to do now. Without their Messiah they don't have a message!"

"Sure they do," Hamon argues. "Of course, since Jesus is dead he can't marshal an army to overthrow the Romans, but his disciples can still propagate all his great teachings."

The two men ponder for a moment. Finally Benjamin says thoughtfully, "Yeah, they've lost their charismatic speaker and miracle worker, but they still have a lot of solid teaching, especially if they'll key in on his 'love your neighbor as yourself' theme. That should keep things going. Maybe they'll be just fine."

If Jesus came to earth just to offer a "love your neighbor" message, Hamon and Benjamin might have a good point. But that was not Jesus' primary mission. Far more than the fate of Jesus' teachings or an earthly Messiah Movement hung on the cross that day. The fate of the entire human race hung with him.

If Jesus did not break the power of death over his own body by rising to life, he could not enter the Most Holy Place, offer his blood on our behalf, and cancel our death sentence.

What was the fate of the entire human race? As Paul explains, "Adam's sin brought death, so death spread to everyone" (Romans 5:12). Jesus, as the Holy Lamb of God, was the perfect sacrifice for sin. His death was an atoning necessity if Adam's race was to survive the death that sin imposed on it. No other sacrifice would do.

As we have explained, there was also the need of a holy and blameless High Priest to offer the blood of the Holy Lamb on the altar before God. For if Jesus did not break the power of death over his own body by rising to life, he could not enter the Most Holy Place, offer his blood on our behalf, and cancel our death sentence (see Hebrews 9:11-12). Jesus' bodily resurrection was a historical necessity.

That is why Paul the apostle was so emphatic about the bodily resurrection of Jesus being the foundation of our faith. He said, "If Christ has not been raised, then all our preaching is useless, and your faith is useless" (1 Corinthians 15:14). Jesus' promise to forgive us of our sins and be the atoning sacrifice that would allow us to have a relationship with God was based not only upon his death, but also upon his resurrection.

"But the fact is that Christ has been raised from the dead," said Paul (1 Corinthians 15: 20). It is a historical reality. And because of that, we have new life.

Therefore:

> *We believe the truth that Jesus died on the cross as a sacrifice for our sins and on the third day bodily rose to life again in order to transform our lives and secure our eternal salvation.*

By the resurrection of Christ, God took an apparently disastrous Friday and turned it into Good Friday. The resurrection shows us clearly that death has no power over the righteous Son of the sovereign God. Jesus broke the power of death by rising from the grave, and in doing so he pierced the kingdom of darkness with a penetrating light. What seemed to be the destruction of Christ, throwing the human race into a hopeless situation, proved to be the very means of the hope of eternal life.

Even Gerd Lüdemann, an atheist scholar who has criticized Christianity for its supernatural claims, has admitted, "The resurrection of Jesus is the central point of the Christian religion…Evidently everything quite simply depends on the event of the resurrection of Jesus."[1] Lüdemann is right about that—everything does depend on the event of the resurrection. Christ's sacrificial death for our atonement would have been meaningless without his bodily resurrection.

EVIDENCE THAT JESUS LITERALLY ROSE FROM THE DEAD

It was the apostle Paul who said "our preaching is useless and so is your faith" if Christ has not risen from the dead (1 Corinthians 15:14 NIV). He said this because Jesus would have been less than deity if he could not conquer death. And he would not have been able to present his atoning blood before God without his bodily resurrection. Christ's redemptive act wasn't just in dying. Christ's redemptive act was both dying *and* offering his blood before God in a resurrected bodily form.

If we are not confident Jesus literally rose from the grave to atone for our sins, our faith for salvation is on shaky ground. But the good news is Christ's bodily resurrection is a historical fact. We have ample reason to believe this pivotal event is factually true, and this gives us great confidence in our hope of eternal salvation. As we consider some historical evidences for Christ's resurrection, allow them to solidify and firm up your faith as never before.

THE EMPTY TOMB

It was early in the morning on the first day of the week when several women approached the tomb where Jesus had been buried. Jesus had been placed in the tomb late on Friday, which was the beginning of the Sabbath. Because of strict rules forbidding certain kinds of activities on the Sabbath, the women had not fully completed anointing the body of Jesus. Therefore, they had returned to complete the task.

But as they approached the tomb, they experienced a huge shock. The stone in front of the tomb was rolled away, and after looking inside they discovered Jesus' body was gone. As they gaped, stunned and bewildered, two men appeared dressed in clothes that gleamed like lightning and said:

> "Why are you looking in a tomb for someone who is alive? He isn't here! He has risen from the dead! Don't you remember what he told you back in Galilee, that the Son of Man must be betrayed into the hands of sinful men and be crucified, and that he would rise again the third day?" Then they remembered that he had said this. So they rushed back to tell his eleven disciples—and everyone else—what had happened. The women who went to the tomb were Mary Magdalene, Joanna, Mary the mother of James, and several others. They told the apostles what had happened, but the story sounded like nonsense, so they didn't believe it (Luke 24:5-11).

As much as Jesus' disciples must have wanted to believe the Messiah rose from the dead, they didn't. The women's report was simply too incredible—too good to be true. But soon they would see for themselves. Shortly afterward when the disciples were meeting together, Jesus appeared. "As he spoke, he held out his hands for them to see, and he showed them his side" (John

20:20). But Thomas, one of Jesus' disciples, wasn't at the meeting. When the others told him what they had seen with their own eyes he said, "I won't believe it unless I see the nail wounds in his hands, put my fingers into them, and place my hand into the wound in his side" (verse 25).

Eight days later Jesus showed up again at a meeting of the disciples, and this time Thomas was there. Jesus offered to let the doubting man put his fingers in the wounds in his hand and side and said, "'Don't be faithless any longer. Believe!' 'My Lord and my God!' Thomas exclaimed" (verses 27-28). The evidence was clear even to this man who insisted on empirical evidence— Jesus had risen from the dead!

Neither the friends of Christianity nor its foes could deny the stark fact that three days after Jesus was buried, his tomb was empty. The many who saw him after his resurrection knew why: They had direct, empirical, physical evidence he was alive. It is significant that after the resurrection, these suddenly emboldened disciples of Christ did not go off to Athens or Rome to preach he had been resurrected; they went right back to the city of Jerusalem to proclaim it. That fact is highly significant because if what they were claiming was false, their message could have been easily challenged. It would have been difficult for the story of the resurrection to have been maintained in Jerusalem, the city where Jesus had been killed and buried, if the tomb had not been empty.

Philosopher Stephen Davis observes, "Early Christian proclamation of the resurrection of Jesus in Jerusalem would have been psychologically and apologetically impossible without safe evidence of an empty tomb...the apostles' claims would have been subject to massive falsification by the simple presentation of the body."[2]

One of the most compelling evidences for the truth of the empty tomb story is the fact that it records women as the first witnesses. In first-century Palestine, women had a low status as citizens or legal witnesses. The testimony of a man was considered more reliable and trustworthy than the testimony of a woman. The more important an event, the more likely listeners would rely upon a man's testimony. This raises an interesting question: Why would those who wanted to advance Christianity have contrived a story that embarrassed the disciples—the essential proponents of the new faith? They fled during the crucifixion, and it was the women who courageously approached the tomb and provided the first testimony to its vacancy. It seems far more likely the Gospel writers believed the tomb was actually empty.

The empty tomb of Jesus stands as a clear witness that, as the angel said, "He isn't here! He has risen from the dead" (Luke 24:6).

While the case for the empty tomb is historically solid, various alternative theories have been offered for why it was empty, as well as for the other phenomenal events in the days and weeks after Jesus' death. These theories attempt to explain these events without resorting to Jesus' bodily resurrection as the answer. We will cover five such theories here.*

THE STOLEN-BODY THEORY

The evidence of an empty tomb following the crucifixion and burial of Jesus does not by itself prove he rose from the dead. Yet it does require explanation. One theory offered within hours of the empty tomb's discovery was that the disciples of Jesus had stolen the body (see Matthew 28:11-15).

The possibility that Jesus' tomb was empty because the disciples stole his body may seem plausible at first glance. However, the most cursory consideration will quickly show the stolen-body theory raises some troubling questions. For example:

- It was the Roman guards who were bribed into accusing the disciples of stealing the body. If the guards were sleeping, how could they have known whether the disciples—or anyone—stole the body?

- Roman soldiers were executed for sleeping on guard duty (which explains Matthew's report of the religious leaders promising to protect the guards "if the governor hears about it"). How plausible is it that all the guards at the tomb would have decided to take a nap, knowing it could cost them their lives?

- Even if the Roman guards had slept, consider what it would have

---

* A more exhaustive treatment of Christ's resurrection can be found in our book *Evidence for the Resurrection*, published by Regal Books.

taken for thieves to remove the body from the tomb. The circular stone used to seal the tomb would have weighed between one and two tons! Thieves would have had to sneak past the guards, roll the large stone up a grooved incline, enter the dark tomb, and exit with the body…all without waking a single member of the detachment! How did they do this?

The notion that the disciples stole the body while the Roman guards slept more than strains the bounds of believability.

The Case of the Stolen Body

The detachment of Roman soldiers is not the only problem with the stolen-body theory. It's also difficult to imagine the followers of Jesus as being capable of pulling off such a feat. Consider this:

- It would have taken considerable bravery—even outright daring—to go up against a detachment of Roman soldiers whether they were asleep or awake. The historical record shows that in the days following the death of Jesus the disciples ran away at the first sign of trouble, denied any association with Jesus, and cowered behind locked doors—hardly the picture of a group that would risk arrest to steal their dead teacher's body (see Mark 14:50; Luke 22:54-62; John 20:19).

- One of the first witnesses on the scene of the empty tomb reported that the linen wrappings from Jesus' body were still present, and the grave cloth that had covered his head was neatly folded and arranged on the burial slab (see John 20:5-8). Can you imagine grave robbers taking the time to meticulously unwrap the body and neatly arrange the cloth on the stone slab? On the contrary, if the body had been stolen, the burial wrappings would certainly have been removed with the body.

- According to the historical accounts, the disciples were skeptical when they heard the news of the empty tomb. From all indications, they were not expecting an empty tomb, much less plotting to steal Jesus away.

- Why would a group of men who had run and hidden when Jesus was alive suddenly and courageously decide to steal his body and begin propagating a story that would certainly bring on them the very treatment (arrest, beatings, even death) they had fled just three days earlier?

Yet propagating the story of Jesus' resurrection is exactly what these disciples did. The historical record asserts that mere weeks after the death of Jesus, his followers were publicly preaching the news of his resurrection. During the week of Pentecost, in fact, thousands were "baptized and added to the church" as a result of this preaching (Acts 2:41).

Such preaching must have driven the Jewish leaders to the point of utter consternation. The fact they could not stop the growth of the Christian movement, or disprove the resurrection, further attests to its truth. It seems clear that subscribing to the stolen-body theory means climbing a mountain of implausibilities. In short, while "the difficulties of belief may be great," as noted author George Hanson pointed out in *The Resurrection and the Life,* "the absurdities of unbelief are greater."[3]

But if the disciples did not steal the body of Jesus from his tomb, where did it go?

THE SWOON THEORY

Some people have tried to explain the empty tomb by suggesting Jesus never really died. The swoon theory, as it has come to be called, supposes that Jesus was indeed nailed to the cross and suffered tremendous pain and loss of blood. But when he was removed from the cross, he wasn't quite dead; he was merely in shock.

Some proponents of this view even cite the New Testament record for evidence, showing that even "Pilate couldn't believe that Jesus was already dead" (Mark 15:44). They surmise the disciples—aided by Joseph of Arimathea—took down the still-living Jesus from the cross and laid him in the tomb. (Hugh J. Schonfield, author of the bestseller *The Passover Plot,* even suggested that Jesus *planned* all of this!) Then—so the theory goes—Jesus, aided by the cool air of the tomb, by the reviving effects of the burial spices he was wrapped in, and by the many hours of quiet rest in the tomb, rose from his own burial slab, cast off his shroud, and left the tomb. When he met his disciples, they mistakenly thought he had risen from the dead…when in fact it was nothing more than a surprising resuscitation.

But the swoon theory has several fatal flaws.

The "Death Certificate"

Jesus had undergone a vicious beating. It was typical for Romans to use an instrument known as a *flagrum,* which often ripped the victim's back to shreds. (As a result of this scourging, many prisoners died before they could be executed.) Jesus was then nailed by his hands and feet to a cross.

Then, because the next day was the beginning of the Jewish Passover and Jewish law did not allow them to leave a victim hanging on the cross overnight, the religious leaders asked Pilate to hasten death by ordering that the prisoners' legs be broken (see Deuteronomy 21:22-23; John 19:31). This action usually resulted in death by asphyxiation, as the victim, unable to push up on his feet to relieve the constriction on his lungs and breathing passages caused by the weight of his body, slowly suffocated.

When the crucifixion detail came to break the legs of Jesus, however, they discovered he was already dead. Nonetheless, to be sure, "one of the soldiers…pierced his side with a spear, and blood and water flowed out" (John 19:34). Soon thereafter, when Joseph of Arimathea requested custody of the body, the Roman governor expressed surprise that Jesus was already dead and demanded confirmation. *Only after receiving a firsthand report* did Pilate release the body into the hands of Joseph, thus fully verifying the fact that Jesus was dead before he was buried.

We not only have the scriptural account of Jesus' death by crucifixion, we also have extrabiblical evidence from first-century historians. Biblical scholar John Dominic Crossan writes, "Jesus' death by execution under Pontius Pilate is as sure as anything historical can ever be. For if no follower of Jesus had written anything for one hundred years after his crucifixion, we would still know about him, from two authors not among his supporters. Their names are Flavius Josephus and Cornelius Tacitus."[4] Neither the people most directly involved with Jesus' death nor the writers who reported it believed Jesus merely swooned. They knew he was dead.

The Grave Cloths

Jesus' followers prepared his body according to Jewish burial customs. Nicodemus provided "about seventy-five pounds of embalming ointment made from myrrh and aloes. Together [Nicodemus and Joseph] wrapped Jesus' body in a long linen cloth with the spices" (John 19:39-40).

The custom was to wrap the body tightly from the armpits to the ankles, layering the spices—often of a sticky, gummy consistency—between the wrappings. The spices served the dual purpose of preserving the body and acting as an adhesive for the grave cloths. The head was also wrapped in a turban-style cloth.

The historical records report that when the empty tomb was discovered on the first day of the week, the witnesses on the scene saw "the linen wrappings lying there, while the cloth that had covered Jesus' head was folded up and lying to the side" (John 20:6-7).

Accepting the swoon theory would require us to believe that Jesus, having suffered the unspeakable torture of scourging and crucifixion, awoke in a dark tomb, and with his arms bound to his side within the wrappings, maneuvered himself out of the tightly wound cloths and spices, folded the cloth, laid it on the burial slab, and exited the tomb...naked.

Nineteenth-century theologian David Strauss was one of the most bitter of all opponents of the supernatural elements in the Gospels and a man whose works did much to destroy faith in Christ. Despite all his vicious criticisms and firm denials of anything involving the miraculous, Strauss said this about the theory that Jesus revived from a swoon:

> It is impossible that a being who has been stolen half-dead out of the sepulcher, who crept about weak and ill, wanting medical treatment...could have given to the disciples the impression that he was a Conqueror over death and the grave, the Prince of Life, an impression which lay at the bottom of their future ministry.[5]

The Stone

Not only was Jesus tightly encased in burial cloths and spices, he was also buried in a rock tomb whose entrance was blocked by a stone weighing as much as one to two tons.

Let's assume Jesus had been taken from the cross in a "swoon," and the cold, damp tomb had revived him sometime later. Let's also assume he managed to extricate himself from the hardened encasement of his burial clothes. We must next assume that once free of those constraints, he managed—from the inside of a tomb designed to be opened only from the outside—to roll a two-ton circular stone up the slotted incline (a difficult job for several men) while somehow propping the stone to prevent it from rolling down again and closing the tomb. All this had to be done by a man who, hours before, had been flogged, pierced with a crown of thorns, hanged on a cross by nails through his hands and feet, and stabbed in the ribs with a Roman spear. And it had to be done quietly enough to escape the notice of the soldiers who were guarding the tomb, allowing him to slip away unnoticed.

The Appearances

On the same day that Jesus was supposedly resuscitated in a cold, damp, dark tomb, unwrapped himself from the grave cloths, rolled a two-ton stone uphill, and snuck by Roman sentinels guarding the tomb, he also walked more than seven miles from Jerusalem to Emmaus.

Luke 24 records Jesus' appearance to two of his followers who were on the road to Emmaus. They didn't recognize Jesus until they reached their destination and invited him to eat with them. When he broke the bread in his customary way, "their eyes were opened, and they recognized him" (verse 31). Walking seven miles to Emmaus is hardly the kind of activity you would expect from a man who had been removed from an executioner's cross and had lain in a tomb for more than 36 hours. And somehow the two men he was walking with failed to notice that his skin was punctured, bruised, and shredded.

Yet the appearance of Jesus on the road to Emmaus is only the first in a string of appearances (within days of his brutal experience on the cross) that convinced Jesus' followers he had defeated death and risen from the dead.

The apostle Paul gives us an early and clear account of various appearances of Jesus after the resurrection:

> I passed on to you what was most important…that Christ died for our sins, just as the Scriptures said. He was buried, and he was raised from the dead on the third day, as the Scriptures said. He was seen by Peter and then by the twelve apostles. After that, he was seen by more than five hundred of his followers at one time, most of whom are still alive, though some have died by now. Then he was seen by James and later by all the apostles (1 Corinthians 15:3-7).

New Testament scholars recognize that Paul is passing on a creed to the Corinthians that was earlier passed on to him. A creed is a short statement capturing key Christian beliefs. Here, the creed includes the death, burial, and resurrection of Jesus as well as his appearances to Peter, the Twelve, the 500, James, and then other apostles. If Paul is passing on a creed that predates the letter, and 1 Corinthians was written in the mid-'50s, then Paul is passing on a very early account of the death, resurrection, and appearances of Jesus. Historically speaking, this creed is remarkably early and clear.

The Ascension

If Jesus revived from a deathlike swoon, there is no reason to believe he later ascended into heaven, as Mark and Luke record. But if Christ didn't ascend, where did he go? Is it reasonable to believe Jesus withdrew from his followers to live out the rest of his life in seclusion and die in obscurity?

Such a theory would necessitate the belief that while the young church was preaching the news of Christ's resurrection, Jesus himself lived in some solitary retreat, unknown even to his closest followers, while his absence perpetuated the legend of Christianity. This scenario would make Jesus Christ the greatest deceiver of all time and his resurrection the greatest hoax in history.

That would require believing Jesus knowingly pursued an insane course of action: contriving his own resurrection to gain a renown he would never witness or enjoy.[6]

THE HALLUCINATION THEORY

There are only so many ways to explain the evidence for the resurrection of Jesus. If the body wasn't stolen and hidden away, if Jesus didn't swoon and then resuscitate, what else could possibly have happened? Another popular explanation is the hallucination theory, which suggests that those who "saw" Jesus Christ after his death and burial may have *thought* they saw Jesus alive, but such appearances were the result of hallucination—an internal mental event without an external stimulus.

Hallucinations do occur. People are often mistaken, even deluded, about the things they see or experience. But the hallucination hypothesis does not adequately account for the evidence for Jesus. For one, if the apostles did hallucinate, then the body of Jesus would still be in the tomb. So at best, the hallucination hypothesis can account for part of the evidence but does not account for why the tomb was found empty. Second, the hallucination hypothesis cannot account for the conversion of Paul, who was persecuting Christians before Jesus appeared to him.

But perhaps more troubling is that it is highly unlikely for multiple people to experience the same hallucination. It is as unlikely as people sharing the same exact dream. Recently, I (Sean) interviewed two leading medical doctors on the hallucination hypothesis, Dr. Harold Koenig and Dr. Craig Fowler. Dr. Fowler used one example of the appearances of Jesus to the seven disciples in John 21. Given the individual ages of the disciples (19–30), what are the odds of each of them having the same hallucination of Jesus at the same time? According to Dr. Fowler, this is "basically impossible."[7] And the New Testament reports multiple group appearances of Jesus.

The hallucination theory—like the other theories—doesn't stack up against the historical record. Like the other attempts to explain the resurrection, it seems to require more faith than to believe the testimony of the eyewitnesses: that "during the forty days after his crucifixion, [Jesus] appeared to the apostles from time to time and proved to them in many ways that he was actually alive" (Acts 1:3).[8]

THE SPIRITUAL RESURRECTION THEORY

This theory claims Christ's body decayed in the grave and his real resurrection was spiritual. Jehovah's Witnesses espouse a form of this theory; however, they believe God destroyed the body in the tomb and Jesus rose in an immaterial body. Both of these theories have insurmountable problems.

First, to have any meaning, a resurrection must entail the physical. In the view of Palestinian Judaism, a spiritual resurrection without the physical body would not be a resurrection at all. Rabbi Dan Cohn-Sherbok, a professor of Judaism at the University of Wales, observed:

> Either Jesus was physically resurrected or he wasn't. It's as simple as that. The Gospel account of the empty tomb and the disciples' recognition of the risen Christ point to such a historical conception of the resurrection event. To them it would make no sense that in some spiritual—as opposed to physical sense—Jesus' body was revivified.[9]

British scholar N.T. Wright has demonstrated that although there were various conceptions of the afterlife in first-century Judaism, "resurrection" had a particular meaning. Wright explains:

> However wide that spectrum may have been and however many positions different Jews may have taken upon it, "resurrection" always denotes *one position within* that spectrum. "Resurrection" was not a term for "life after death" in general. It always meant reembodiment.[10]

Wright also demonstrates that "there is no evidence for Jews...using the word *resurrection* to denote something essentially nonconcrete."[11] If Jesus had been raised in an immaterial body, the disciples would not have described it as a *resurrection*.

Jesus himself anticipated and undermined the spiritual resurrection theory. When his startled disciples thought they were seeing a spirit, Jesus admonished them: "See My hands and My feet, that it is I Myself; touch Me and see; for a spirit does not have flesh and bones as you see that I have" (Luke

24:39 NASB). Later, Christ ate fish with his followers, further demonstrating his flesh-and-bone existence. Matthew records that when they met Jesus, they took hold of his feet and worshipped him (see Matthew 28:9). You don't grab the legs of a spirit! Some have argued Jesus temporarily manifested himself in a physical body so the disciples would recognize him. While this is a creative response, there is no evidence to support it, and what is worse, it would involve deception on Jesus' part, which is clearly inconsistent with his character and nature.

Paul also demolishes the spiritual resurrection theory in his discussion of the resurrection body in 1 Corinthians 15:29-58. As a former Pharisee, Paul firmly believed in a physical resurrection. Basing his theology on the resurrection of Christ, Paul argues that we too will be physically raised someday. While resurrected bodies are physically different from our current bodies, the difference involves enhancement; they are nonetheless thoroughly physical.

Some have disagreed with this interpretation of this passage, basing their argument on Paul's claim in 1 Corinthians 15:44 that "it is sown a *natural* body, it is raised a *spiritual* body." "See," they claim, "Paul believed in an immaterial resurrection!" What this objection fails to consider is that the word *spiritual*, in this context, does not connote *immaterial*. We often refer to the Bible as a "spiritual" book, yet we clearly don't mean it is immaterial!

Michael Licona did a fairly exhaustive historical investigation of the Greek terms translated "natural" and "spiritual" in 1 Corinthians 15:44. After searching ancient texts from the eighth century BC through the third century AD he concluded, "Although I did not look at all of the 846 occurrences, I viewed most. I failed to find a single reference where *psuchikon* [the word translated *natural* in 15:44] possessed a meaning of 'physical' or 'material.'"[12] It is simply false to say Paul was contrasting a physical body with a nonphysical body.

Stephen Davis warns:

> We should not be misled by Paul's use of the term "spiritual body." He is not using this term to signify a body "formed out of spirit" or made of "spiritual matter," whatever that might mean, but rather a body that has been glorified or transformed by God and is now fully dominated by the power of the Holy Spirit.[13]

A good example of this is when Paul speaks of "those who are spiritual" in 1 Corinthians 2:15. He clearly did not mean invisible, immaterial people with no physical body; he meant those who are guided by the power of the Holy Spirit.

Others object to a physical resurrection because in 1 Corinthians 15:50 Paul says that "flesh and blood cannot inherit the kingdom of God." "See," they say, "Jesus' body had to be immaterial so he could be in heaven!" Theologian Norman Geisler responded to this assertion: "The phrase, 'flesh and blood,' in this context apparently means *mortal* flesh and blood, that is, a mere human being."[14] His interpretation is supported throughout Scripture. For example, in Matthew 16:17 Jesus says, "Blessed are you, Simon Barjona, because *flesh and blood* did not reveal this to you, but My Father who is in heaven" (NASB).

The spiritual resurrection theory completely ignores our two principles of research. The facts of the case don't even begin to fit the theory, and they are forced into a preconceived conclusion about what happened.[15]

THE MYSTERY-RELIGION THEORY

I (Sean) first encountered this objection in college, and it deeply unsettled me. I heard about the traditions of Osiris, Mithras, Adonis, Dionysus, and other "dying and rising gods" and wondered if the story of Jesus was simply plagiarized from these accounts. But I now consider it one of the weakest objections to the resurrection. In other words, if I were a skeptic, I would definitely choose a different explanation for the origin of Christianity. Why?

Although parallels between Jesus and the mystery religions may appear striking on the surface, they collapse under scrutiny. Osiris, for instance, is considered by many to be a dying and rising god from ancient Egypt. According to the myth, Osiris was killed by Seth and resuscitated by Isis. But rather than returning to the world in a resurrected body, Osiris became king of the underworld—hardly a parallel to the historical resurrection of Jesus. This is one of numerous reasons why Paul Rhodes Eddy and Greg Boyd, authors of *The Jesus Legend,* conclude that "the differences between Christianity and the mystery religions are far more profound than any similarities. While there certainly are parallel *terms* used in early Christianity and the mystery religions, there is little evidence for parallel *concepts*."[16]

Unlike the accounts of the historical Jesus, there is no evidence for the reliability of any of the alleged parallel stories in the mystery religions. Jesus of Nazareth ate, slept, performed miracles, died, and returned to life. These accounts are supported by a reliable historical record. In contrast, the dying and rising gods of the mystery religions were timeless myths repeated annually with the changing seasons. The Christian story finds its roots in Judaism, not paganism. That's why Jesus said, "You search the Scriptures because you think they give you eternal life. But the Scriptures point to me!" (John 5:39 NLT).

THE REALITY OF THE RISEN LORD

The reality of Jesus' resurrection had a profound impact on the disciples. They were transformed from cringing cowards who hid themselves away to bold preachers, most of whom suffered persecution and gave their lives for their risen Lord. This sudden bravery and boldness is an enormous change that demands explanation. Let's examine this transformation more closely and consider its implications.

When the authorities captured Jesus in the Garden of Gethsemane, the Bible tells us that "all the disciples left him and fled" (Matthew 26:56; see Mark 14:50). During Christ's trial, Peter went out and denied three times that he even knew Jesus (see Mark 14:66-72; John 18:15-27). After Christ was crucified, the fearful disciples hid themselves in an upper room and locked the doors (see John 20:19). These disciples were skeptical when they first heard about the empty tomb. One of them refused to believe until he personally touched Jesus' wounds. And two disciples on the road to Emmaus doubted even as they talked personally to Jesus.

But within days something happened to utterly change this group of cowardly followers into a bold band of enthusiasts who were willing to face a life of suffering for the cause of Christ.[17] What was it? What transformed these disappointed followers into true believers? It was the reality of the risen Christ.

That truth is for us as well. Like those early disciples, we can trust the eternal salvation we have in the risen Christ because we have ample evidence to show us that the record of what he did for us is absolutely true.

So, dear brothers and sisters, we can boldly enter heaven's Most Holy Place because of the blood of Jesus. This is the new, life-giving way that Christ has opened up for us through the sacred curtain, by means of his death for us. And since we have a great High Priest who rules over God's people, let us go right into the presence of God, with true hearts fully trusting him (Hebrews 10:19-22).

OVERCOMING THE FEAR OF DEATH

Sixty-five-year-old Thelma Milner and her husband of over 48 years sat in her doctor's examination room. "There is no easy way to say this, Thelma," the doctor said in a serious tone. "The tests confirm you are in the first stages of Alzheimer's disease."

Thelma's hand instinctively went to her mouth as she let out a slight groan. Her husband grimaced as he placed his arm around his stunned wife.

For the next 15 years, Thelma's family watched as her body, mind, and all traces of her memory were ravaged. A once beautiful and vibrant woman was reduced to nothing more than skin and bones. Finally, unable to eat, speak, or respond to the voice and touch of loved ones, Thelma gasped her last breath and was gone, leaving behind a grieving family.

Like the Milner family, all of us will at some point suffer the loss of a loved one. The emptiness and suffering from such a death is real, and at times it feels almost unbearable. Death is an inevitable shadow that robs people of the ones they love.

It is understandable that death is a scary thought, even to many Christians. Job described it as "the king of terrors" (Job 18:14). Most of us avoid talking about death, and even when we do talk about it, we use euphemisms to soften or disguise the harsh reality. We prefer terms such as "pass away," "go to sleep," or "go to be with the Lord."

Why, exactly, do we fear death? There are at least five reasons.

1. *Death is mysterious and unknown.* It is normal to fear the unknown. And death poses the greatest of all unknowns.

2. *We have to face death alone.* If we could join together and face the

mysteries of death in a group, perhaps it would be easier to bear the thought of it. But we cannot. We must travel alone into that dark night.

3. *We are separated from our loved ones.* Death robs us of the ones closest to us. Some may even question whether we will ever meet them again.

4. *Our personal hopes and dreams will not be realized.* When we die, our goals die with us. Death ends the best of our plans.

5. *Death is unavoidable.* Even with today's scientific advances, all of us will die. No one can escape the inevitability of death.[18]

While all of this is true, there is still a significant consolation. As Christians we can experience freedom from the fear of death. The relevance of Jesus' bodily resurrection is not only that our sins are atoned for, but that we will also live again. So will our loved one if he or she has placed their trust in Christ.

FREEDOM FROM FEAR BECAUSE DEATH HAS BEEN CONQUERED

When Jesus' close friends Mary and Martha lost their brother, he told them, "I am the resurrection and the life. Those who believe in me, even though they die like everyone else, will live again. They are given eternal life for believing in me and will never perish" (John 11:25-26). Because Jesus is our resurrected Lord, we will be God's resurrected children. God "has made all of this plain to us by the coming of Christ Jesus, our Savior, who broke the power of death and showed us the way of everlasting life" (2 Timothy 1:10).

Yes, death is inevitable. But death isn't permanent for those who have trusted Christ. "Everyone dies because all of us are related to Adam, the first man. But all who are related to Christ, the other man, will be given new life" (1 Corinthians 15:22).

Not only are we forgiven of our sins and made right with God, but we also inherit a body that will live forever.

Although we are redeemed, justified, sanctified, and adopted as God's children in this life, we have yet to gain the full rights of our adoption. Paul said that "what we suffer now is nothing compared to the glory he will reveal to us later…for we long for our bodies to be released from sin and suffering. We, too, wait with eager hope for the day when God will give us our full rights as his adopted children, including the new bodies he has promised us. We were given this hope when we were saved" (Romans 8:18, 23-24 NLT). That is the added relevance of Christ's resurrection. Not only are we forgiven of our sins and made right with God, but we also inherit a body that will live forever. This means one day we will experience glorification. New bodies. Bodies that won't suffer pain, endure hardships, or wear out. That is our future inheritance.

> Someone may ask, "How will the dead be raised? What kind of bodies will they have?"…Our earthly bodies, which die and decay, will be different when they are resurrected, for they will never die. Our bodies now disappoint us, but when they are raised, they will be full of glory. They are weak now, but when they are raised, they will be full of power. They are natural bodies now, but when they are raised, they will be spiritual bodies…Every human being has an earthly body just like Adam's, but our heavenly bodies will be just like Christ's (1 Corinthians 15:35, 42-44, 48).

That is certainly a truth we can embrace and look forward to. Peter called it our "priceless inheritance": "Now we live with a wonderful expectation because Jesus Christ rose again from the dead. For God has reserved a priceless inheritance for his children. It is kept in heaven for you, pure and undefiled, beyond the reach of change and decay" (1 Peter 1:3-4). This inheritance is a state of being in which each of us will be given "full rights" to a glorified, heavenly body to live where "there will be no more death or sorrow or crying or pain" (Revelation 21:4). This means we will have perfect bodies in a perfect world. Yet for that to come about, Paul said, "our perishable earthly bodies must be transformed into heavenly bodies that will never die" (1 Corinthians 15:53). And that can, and will, happen to the redeemed because Jesus rose from the grave.

This promise is as exciting as anything we read in the Bible. It elates us; it gives us hope; it stimulates the imagination.

Because of Christ's resurrection and the promises he has made to us, our fear of death can be lifted. Because he lives...

- *The mystery of death is revealed.* Yes, death is mysterious and unknown, but after the resurrection of Jesus, we know it is not permanent. Christ went through it, and he blazed a trail we can follow. Thus some of the mystery has been removed.

- *We don't have to face death alone.* Although from our perspective it may seem we have to go through death alone, we now know this is an illusion. Christ has actually stepped into the darkness of death and awaits us there with the light of life to lead us safely through.

- *We are not permanently separated from our loved ones.* Because God has conquered death through Jesus Christ, our loving relationships will continue after death. Death may separate us temporarily from our loved ones, but the resurrection of Christ will bring us back together.

- *Our personal hopes and dreams have a future.* The resurrection also does away with this fear. In fact, it would be accurate to say that in heaven all our hopes and dreams will be fulfilled.

- *Death is unavoidable, yet it is a transition to eternal life.* It's true death is inevitable, and no one can escape it. But because of Christ's resurrection, death is simply the passage to our eternal home in heaven.[19]

While there may not be answers to all our questions, the resurrection of Christ answers the most pressing ones. Above all, this one thing is certain: We are guaranteed a "priceless inheritance" that includes a resurrected spiritual body that will live forever with the Lord and our loved ones. That is possible because Jesus conquered death and rose from the grave.

In the scriptures we have explored in this chapter, God has revealed to us, his adopted children, a taste of what an eternal relationship with him will be like. He has revealed himself through his Spirit and his Word in order that, as Jesus said, "My joy may be in you and that your joy may be complete" (John 15:11 NIV). As a loving father and mother desire to fill their child with anticipation of a vacation or trip to Disney World, so our heavenly Father wants to see our hearts filled with joy of what awaits us. He wants us to sense the joy of what heaven and eternity will be like. He wants us to anticipate living with him eternally in a place where there is no sin or heartache.

One day Jesus will conquer death to bring you and your loved ones into a place of completed joy beyond compare. At that point death will be "swallowed up in victory" (1 Corinthians 15:54). As a Christian, your resurrection is an assured reality. Because of Christ's resurrection, your eternal relationship with God and with your loved ones in heaven is guaranteed. You are destined for an eternal future of bliss. Anticipate what is to come and be excited!

LIVING BODILY ON EARTH
WITH OUR HEARTS IN HEAVEN

If you have trusted in Christ as your Redeemer, your bodily resurrection is assured and you will live forever in God's presence. But how is your anticipation of that future life to affect your life now? Paul says, "Since you have been raised to new life with Christ, set your sights on the realities of heaven, where Christ sits at God's right hand in the place of honor and power. Let heaven fill your thoughts. Do not think only about things down here on earth" (Colossians 3:1-2).

How are we to take this scripture? How are we to fill our thoughts with anticipation of a perfect life in heaven when we have so many things to do, places to go, obligations to fulfill? Your life and ours are consumed with earthly concerns. What am I going to eat today? How am I going to pay all these bills? When am I going to get another raise? Who am I going to marry? How do I keep this marriage together? When are we going to have kids? Who's watching the kids? What are they getting into, anyway?

Our minds are flooded with a million things at once, most of them about earthly things—college, marriage, raising a family, retirement. Yet Jesus said, "Don't worry about everyday life—whether you have enough food, drink, and clothes…Why be like the pagans who are so deeply concerned about these things? Your heavenly Father already knows all your needs, and he will give you all you need from day to day if you live for him and make the Kingdom of God your primary concern" (Matthew 6:25, 32-33).

What does all that really mean? How do we live in anticipation of the resurrection and not make this life such a big priority?

FOCUSING OUR HEARTS IN THE RIGHT PLACE

I (Sean) remember how my thought process and entire life changed after meeting this stunning girl named Stephanie. Yes, I was struck by her beauty, but it was more than that. She was smart and funny and had a great personality. She and I liked a lot of the same things, and I wanted to be with her all the time. When I was at basketball practice, I thought about her. When I was in school, I thought about her. When I was at home, I thought about her. I couldn't get her out of my mind because she had made a place in my heart.

It seemed that every waking moment this woman captivated my thoughts. There was more to it than I could really understand. There was a mystery to this consuming passion of mine. I knew her and yet I didn't, so I wanted to know her more. I wanted to know her on a level I had never really experienced with anyone else before. *Because I was in love!*

After Stephanie and I married, the love affair deepened. In fact, our togetherness created a home of our own for us. While marriage meant we could spend a lot of time together, I still had to be away at times. Stephanie didn't like me being away. She became a little jealous when I was at work or at the seminary too long. At times I had to travel to a speaking engagement. Of course I would e-mail her and call her. But it wasn't the same. She missed me and wanted me home. And I liked it that she did. I missed her too. I missed that place of emotional security and relational intimacy that existed with the person of my dreams.

That is a small picture of what it means to set our "sights on the realities of heaven." It's not a matter of sitting around pining away and hoping for the day we're dead and in heaven. It means our priorities, our interests, and our devotion are placed in another world with another person—Jesus. And when we get too focused on earthly things, he gets jealous.

The disciple James wrote, "If your aim is to enjoy this world, you can't be a friend of God. What do you think the Scriptures mean when they say that the Holy Spirit, whom God has placed within us, jealously longs for us to be faithful?" (James 4:4-5). Jesus said, "No one can serve two masters. For you will hate the one and love the other, or be devoted to one and despise the other" (Matthew 6:24). When we give our devotion, our undivided heart to earthly things, Jesus gets jealous.

Isn't it humbling to think that Jesus is jealous if our hearts and thoughts are on earthly things rather than on him and our home with him? He wants "heaven to fill our thoughts." He wants us to keep him as our priority. He wants us to long for him as we long for our earthly lover and our home with them.

Living for our future home with a new body in the presence of Jesus isn't a matter of just daydreaming day in and day out. It's about what kind of treasures we are building and where our priorities are in this life. Paul talked about those whose "god is their appetite"—their earthly pleasures—"and all they think about is this life here on earth" (Philippians 3:19). But we who are spiritually resurrected in Christ are not about building earthly kingdoms and living for the pleasures this world can give. Rather, "we are citizens of heaven," Paul says, "where the Lord Jesus Christ lives. And we are eagerly waiting for him to return as our Savior. He will take these weak mortal bodies of ours and change them into glorious bodies like his own, using the same mighty power that he will use to conquer everything, everywhere" (Philippians 3:20-21). Our focus on our future doesn't take us out of this world; it simply keeps our attention where it belongs while we are here.

Jesus prayed for his disciples by saying to his Father, "I'm not asking you to take them out of the world, but to keep them safe from the evil one. They are not part of this world any more than I am. Make them pure and holy by teaching them your words of truth" (John 17:15-17). Living in this world with our hearts in the next does involve our being engaged in the business and activities going on around us. Yet the fact that our hearts are properly focused on the next enables us to be more effective in God's business right here and now—living out his truth and building up his kingdom. C.S. Lewis said it well:

If you read history, you will find that the Christians who did most for the present world were just those who thought most about the next. The apostles themselves, who set on foot the conversion of the Roman Empire, the great men who built up the Middle Ages, the English Evangelicals who abolished the Slave Trade, all left their mark on Earth, precisely because their minds were occupied with heaven. It is since Christians have largely ceased to think of the other world that they have become so ineffective in this. Aim at heaven and you will get earth "thrown in": Aim at earth and you will get neither.[20]

A MATTER OF FAITH

Living in this world with our heart in the next doesn't happen naturally. To "set your sights on the realities of heaven" and keep them there requires that we live by faith. "What is faith?" the writer of Hebrews asks. "It is the confident assurance that what we hope for is going to happen. It is the evidence of things we cannot yet see" (11:1). To maintain a kingdom of heaven mentality requires a "confident assurance" God is in control and his promises are real and will be fulfilled. When we have an intelligent faith that knows why we believe, we are confident God's promises are true.

The saints of old had an intelligent faith that gave them confidence. "It was by faith that Abel brought a more acceptable offering to God than Cain…It was by faith that Enoch was taken up to heaven without dying…It was by faith that Noah built an ark to save his family…It was by faith that Abraham obeyed when God called him to leave home and go to another land…All these faithful ones died without receiving what God had promised them, but they saw it all from a distance and welcomed the promises of God" (Hebrews 11:4-5, 7-8, 13). These faithful followers of God lived in the world, but they were not of this world. "They were no more than foreigners and nomads here on earth…They were looking for a better place, a heavenly homeland. That is why God is not ashamed to be called their God, for he has prepared a heavenly city for them" (11:13, 16).

It is by an intelligent faith that we endure hardship, trials, and difficulties here on earth. It is by this kind of faith that we set our eyes and hearts on a future of joy after death. It is only by faith we can have joy in the face of tragedy. Because faith is trusting what the eyes can't see.

To live in this world with our heart in the next requires a faith that fixes our spiritual eyes on Jesus.

Max Lucado speaks of what faith sees in his book *When God Whispers Your Name*:

> Eyes see the prowling lion. Faith sees Daniel's angel.
> Eyes see storms. Faith sees Noah's rainbow.
> Eyes see giants. Faith sees Canaan.
> Your eyes see your faults. Your faith sees your Savior.
> Your eyes see your guilt. Your faith sees his blood.
> Your eyes see your grave. Your faith sees a city
> whose builder and maker is God.[21]

We are surrounded by a world that clamors for our attention and attempts to draw our hearts in its direction. Our task is to see yet another world invisible to the eye. It can only be seen by faith. The writer of Hebrews wraps up his great chapter that lists example after example of people who longed for another country and saw it by faith by saying: "Therefore, since we are surrounded by such a huge crowd of witnesses to the life of faith, let us strip off every weight that slows us down, especially the sin that so easily hinders our progress. And let us run with endurance the race that God has set before us. We do this by keeping our eyes on Jesus, on whom our faith depends from start to finish" (12:1-2).

Deepening Our Longing for God

"Keeping our eyes on Jesus." That's the key. To live in this world with our heart in the next requires a faith that fixes our spiritual eyes on Jesus. He longs for us to long after him. He wants us to be homesick for him. He wants us to thirst after him. He wants us to be like King David who prayed, "As the deer pants for streams of water, so I long for you, O God. I thirst for God, the living God. When can I come and stand before him?" (Psalm 42:1-2). David goes on to pray, "O God, you are my God; I earnestly search for you. My soul thirsts for you; my whole body longs for you in this parched and weary land where there is no water" (63:1).

Take time to cultivate your longing and thirst for God and the home he is preparing for you. The more you spend time focused on him, the more life in this temporal world takes on an eternal perspective. The things that are real and lasting come into focus. When we keep our hearts in the next world, we can experience true peace when this earthly world all around us is in turmoil.

Pastor and theologian Calvin Miller captured the secret to the true peace we can have when we see God through the power of his Holy Spirit:

> God becomes visible to those who look for him in the right place. Therefore, no eye—no literal eye—can see him! No ear can hear him! No mind can conceive him! He hides his vastness only in the deepest dimensions of our inner existence...
>
> First Corinthians 2:10 contains one little word that lunges at us with challenge: "...God has revealed it to us by his Spirit. The Spirit searches all things, even the *deep* things of God" (NIV).
>
> *Deep* is the dwelling place of God. *Deep* is the character of the ocean...Deep is where the noisy, trashy surface of the ocean gets quiet and serene. No sound breaks the awesome silence of the ocean's heart. Most Christians, however, spend their lives being whipped tumultuously through the surface circumstances of their days. Their frothy lifestyles mark the surface nature of their lives. Yet those who plumb the deep things of God discover true peace for the first time.[22]

Take time out of your busy schedule to "plumb the deep things of God." Spend time with his Word. Meditate on him and cultivate your longing for him. Let him know you hunger to know him more deeply than ever. See him by faith in your new home of the future. Praise him in advance for the new body he will give you because of his resurrection. As you do you will gain a new perspective on this life and the things that really matter, just as the biblical writers did:

> I have seen you in your sanctuary and gazed
>> upon your power and glory.
> Your unfailing love is better to me than life itself;
>> how I praise you!
> I will honor you as long as I live, lifting up
>> my hands to you in prayer (Psalm 63:2-4).

Now we see things imperfectly as in a poor mirror, but then we will see everything with perfect clarity. All that I know now is partial and incomplete, but then I will know everything completely, just as God knows me now (1 Corinthians 13:12).

Yes, dear friends, we are already God's children, and we can't even imagine what we will be like when Christ returns. But we do know that when he comes we will be like him, for we will see him as he really is. And all who believe this will keep themselves pure, just as Christ is pure (1 John 3:2-3).

WE ARE JUSTIFIED THROUGH FAITH

The crowd was silent. You could have heard a pin drop. I (Josh) had walked down into the audience and asked one of the deacons of the church sitting near the front this question: "How are you saved—how have you gained a relationship with Christ?" He answered without hesitation, "By faith—I am saved by faith."

I looked at the entire congregation and then to him and said, "No, you're not. No one is ever saved by faith!" That is when the crowd went deathly silent and a chill swept over the auditorium. I went on to explain my statement before the crowd branded me with a capital "H" for heretic.

The truth is, none of us is saved by faith. If we could be saved by faith, then Jesus didn't have to die for us. We could have saved ourselves simply by an exercise of faith.

Here's the question: Does faith and faith alone have any power? An entire generation is growing up today believing so. Many think their choice to believe something has, in fact, the power to make that belief into their own truth. They seem to think if you believe something hard enough and sincerely enough, it will be the truth that will work for you.

But when it comes to salvation, there is only one power that can change your separated and lost status before God. Namely, Jesus Christ—because Jesus, Son of the Almighty God, is the one who died for you and rose again to purchase your salvation. "It is by grace you have been saved, through faith—and this is not from yourselves, it is the gift of God" (Ephesians 2:8 NIV).

In Scripture, faith is never presented as the power that justifies or makes us right with God; rather, faith is the arm that reaches out to receive the saving grace of God. Jesus and Jesus only has the power to forgive and raise us from death to life. That is why we are not saved *for* believing, but *through* believing in Jesus. If Jesus is not the Messiah, the Son of God who died on the cross for your sins, then your faith is absolutely "worthless."

THE ABSOLUTE NECESSITY OF BEING JUSTIFIED

Born dead spiritually, we can do nothing to gain favor with God. As we stated earlier, it is sin that continues to enslave all of us to a "life of death." But through faith in Christ we can be set free. Yet we still have a problem. We are still human beings tainted by sin. How can a holy God be in relationship with unholy and imperfect humans? God had a solution. Redemption (purchasing us out of a life of slavery) also includes justification (being declared righteous before God).

As Paul explained it, "No one can ever be made right in God's sight by doing what his law commands, for the more we know God's law, the clearer it becomes that we aren't obeying it. But now God has shown us a different way of being right in his sight...We are made right in God's sight when we trust in Jesus Christ [place our faith in him] to take away our sins...God in his gracious kindness [grace] declares us not guilty" (Romans 3:20-22, 24). So by placing our faith in Jesus we are redeemed—purchased out of slavery; and justified—declared righteous before God.

When God declares we are right before him, he is establishing us as his people; he sets us apart from a life of continual sin. This set-apart life is called *sanctification.* Paul began his letter to the church in Corinth by addressing it "to those sanctified in Christ Jesus and called to be holy" (1 Corinthians 1:2 NIV). While being justified is a "declared righteous" state that comes into being instantly, sanctification is the process of continually being conformed to Christlikeness, as some churches teach. Other churches emphasize sanctification as a separate instantaneous work followed by continued growth in holiness. Whichever emphasis you or your church makes, we are in right standing before God due to being redeemed, justified, and sanctified.

King David had sinned and sought forgiveness before God. He prayed,

"Purify me from my sins, and I will be clean; wash me, and I will be whiter than snow" (Psalm 51:7). David was praying for an unobstructed relationship with a holy God. But how could David enjoy a redeemed, justified, and sanctified relationship with God prior to Christ's death? Jesus had not even been born into the world yet.

The answer is that the power of Christ's death and resurrection not only reaches forward in time to free us from sin today, it also reaches back in time to cover all those born prior to Jesus' sacrificial death (see Romans 3:25-26). Our righteousness before God is made possible through our trust in Jesus, because he solves our sin problem past, present, and future. Because of Christ's atoning death, we too can claim the promise God made to Israel: "No matter how deep the stain of your sins, I can remove it. I can make you as clean as freshly fallen snow" (Isaiah 1:18).

So is there nothing we can say to God or do for God that would merit our redemption? Is there nothing we can do to earn our justification? Is there nothing we can leverage to acquire sanctification? Paul asked and answered those questions when he wrote, "Can we boast then, that we have done anything to be accepted by God? No, because our acquittal is not based on our good deeds. It is based on our faith [in Jesus]. So we are made right with God through faith and not by obeying the law" (Romans 3:27-28).

Performance-based people who want to earn what they get may find salvation by grace through faith hard to accept. But there is no human requirement to obtain God's offer of a relationship except to freely accept it. It is a gift based upon the requirements fulfilled by Jesus. That is why, when speaking of salvation, Paul said, "It does not depend on the man who wills or the man who runs, but on God who has mercy" (Romans 9:16 NASB).

Therefore:

> *We believe the truth that being justified*
> *before God and cleansed of our sins*
> *is a result of God's grace through faith*
> *alone in Jesus as our sacrifice for sin.*

Christ atoned for our sin by his death on the cross. When we place our faith in him as our substitute, we are redeemed and justified before God. We are set apart as his holy people. Not by what we have done, but because of what Christ has done. "Abraham believed God, and God counted him as righteous because of his faith. When people work, their wages are not a gift, but something they have earned. But people are counted as righteous not because of their work, but because of their faith in God who forgives sinners" (Romans 4:3-4).

EVIDENCE THAT CHRIST HAS
THE POWER TO SAVE US

Her brother had been dead for four days. So Martha pointed out the obvious when her friend told the men to open up the tomb. "'Lord, by now the smell will be terrible...' Jesus responded, 'Didn't I tell you that you will see God's glory if you believe?'" (John 11:39-40).

Is the implication here that if Martha believed hard enough her brother, Lazarus, would be raised from the dead? Does believing have that kind of power? Not at all. There is no power in the act of believing in and of itself. The power of our faith resides in the object of what is believed. Unless Jesus was truly the Son of God, all the believing in the world could not have raised Lazarus from the dead, and no amount of faith in Christ will save us. We cannot be redeemed and justified before God, given the gift of eternal life, unless Jesus is who he claimed to be. It is important therefore to our confidence in salvation that we know with certainty that Jesus is indeed God in the flesh.

Jesus clearly intended his miracles to be understood as a validation of his identity as God's Son.

We have already discussed two reasons why we can have such a confident faith that Jesus is the Christ: He was virgin born, and he fulfilled all the messianic prophecies. But there is yet another piece of evidence. Jesus himself pointed out that his actions, like his miracle to raise Lazarus from the dead, were evidences that he is God's Son.

THE MIRACLES OF CHRIST

The following verses give us examples of how Jesus himself asserted that his miracles provided proof of his identity as the Son of God:

> I have a greater witness than John [the Baptist]—my teachings and my miracles. They have been assigned to me by the Father, and they testify that the Father has sent me (John 5:36).

> The miracles I do in my Father's name speak for me (John 10:25 NIV).

> Even though you do not believe me, believe the miracles, that you may know and understand that the Father is in me, and I in the Father (John 10:38 NIV).

After his ascension his followers also pointed to his miracles as proofs of his identity. As the apostle Peter said on the Day of Pentecost, "God publicly endorsed Jesus of Nazareth by doing wonderful miracles, wonders, and signs through him, as you well know" (Acts 2:22). The apostle John, pointing to Christ's identity as God, reports Jesus did many other "miraculous signs" that weren't even recorded for us (John 20:30).

The most important miracle Jesus performed was rising from the dead, as we just saw in chapter 6. For if he had not conquered death, "your faith is useless, and you are still under condemnation for your sins" (1 Corinthians 15:17).

Imagine Walking with Jesus

Imagine being one of Jesus' disciples walking along beside him on a sunny Sabbath afternoon. You have just exited the temple, where religious leaders have accused Jesus of being possessed by a demon. They were so angry that they had come close to stoning him before you made your escape.

Walking briskly, you pass a blind beggar sitting cross-legged on the street. You proceed some distance before you realize Jesus has not kept pace with you and his other disciples. You look back and see the Master gazing at the man, who is somewhat of a fixture in the area because he frequently begs at this spot. Though few know the beggar's name, most know his circumstances: He has been blind since birth.

You turn with the disciples and tentatively approach the pair, wondering why Jesus has stopped here. One of Jesus' companions, always impetuous and eager to please, blurts out a question. "Teacher, why was this man born blind? Was it a result of his own sins or those of his parents?" (John 9:2).

Jesus, with characteristic kindness, plants his knees in the dirt beside the man and answers, more to him than to the questioner, "It was not because of his sins or his parents' sins…He was born blind so the power of God could be seen in him" (verse 3).

The strangeness of Jesus' words echoes off the stone walls of the buildings that surround the scene. He explains that this man's eyes—which have never seen his mother's smile, never beheld the dazzling white marble of Herod's Temple reflecting the rays of the sun, never watched waves of wind wafting through the golden grain of a wheat field, never gazed on the face of a blushing young girl in love—have been dark all these years so the power of God can be seen in them today!

You and the others watch, your attention riveted on the man who has lived in darkness and the man who has called himself the light of the world. Jesus spits in the dust, not once but several times. No one speaks as he forms a mud pack in his carpenter's hands and patiently, tenderly, spreads the mud over the blind man's eyes.

Jesus speaks, "Go and wash in the pool of Siloam" (John 9:7). What happens next defies natural explanation; it even exceeds the comprehension of twenty-first-century medical science. When the man obeys Jesus and washes the mud from his eyes, he can see!

In an instant of time, one of the most complex organs in the human body is mended. Without a scalpel to gingerly remove the probable cause—a congenital cataract that had clouded the man's lenses—without a tiny suction tube to clear the clouded, jellylike orbs of vitreous humor, the man's eyes are healed. There was no laser surgery to reattach the retinas. There was no highly sophisticated serum applied to the complex layer of light-sensing cells at the back of the eyes that allowed 7 million cones and 125 million rods to send their coded messages of light once more to the brain via the millions of fibers that comprise the optic nerve. And there was no prescribed therapy for the permanent amblyopia inside the man's eyes—the underdevelopment of the visual system resulting from decades of disuse.[1]

Twenty centuries later, such congenital blindness is still often irreparable, even if the surgery is performed by the most skilled surgeon in the most advanced operating room of the best hospital in the world. But Jesus, the Galilean carpenter, performed it in an instant, using mud and his own saliva as his only tools.

As fascinating as this healing is—and it's just one among the many miracles Jesus performed—it should not be surprising. Though the task of removing cataracts, reattaching retinas, and reconstructing the ultrasensitive machinery of the human eye is a highly specialized and still-evolving field of modern medicine, it was no great feat for Jesus of Nazareth—because he is Creator God, the architect of the human eye.

"I BELIEVE!"

The healing of the man who had been born blind was more than simply miraculous to those who first heard about it—to some, it was disturbing. When the news got to the Pharisees, it caused a stir: "Some of the Pharisees said, 'This man Jesus is not from God, for he is working on the Sabbath.' Others said, 'But how could an ordinary sinner do such miraculous signs?' So there was a deep division of opinion among them" (John 9:16).

The healing of the man born blind was mind-boggling to Jesus' critics. Many of the Pharisees had already rejected him as the Messiah. He had not measured up to their political and religious expectations. The kingdom he was proclaiming called for humility, repentance, servanthood, and devotion to God. They expected the Messiah to insist on devotion to a body of rabbinical rules and regulations in order to purify the people for their national destiny. So they wanted nothing to do with Jesus' relational brand of religion. Yet his miracles presented them with a major dilemma. How could they accept a man who did not share their nationalistic ambitions; yet how could they reject a man who exhibited such astounding powers?

First, the Pharisees decided to investigate. They called for the healed man to come before them to explain what had happened. Then they called for his parents to confirm that he in fact had been born blind. Finally, they brought the man back again for cross-examination, hoping to resolve the dilemma.

The truth is, their investigation was not really open and objective, because they could not bring themselves to believe what the miracle clearly indicated: that Jesus was more than a man. And yet, they could not explain how a mere man—a man they presumed to be a sinner like themselves—could perform such a miracle (see John 9:17-22). To their questions, the formerly blind man replied, "I don't know whether he is a sinner...But I know this: I was blind, and now I can see!...Never since the world began has anyone been able to open the eyes of someone born blind. If this man were not from God, he couldn't do it" (verses 25, 32-33).

John's account concludes the story:

> When Jesus heard what had happened, he found the man and said, "Do you believe in the Son of Man?"
>
> The man answered, "Who is he, sir, because I would like to." [Remember, this man had no idea what Jesus looked like; he had never seen him before.]
>
> "You have seen him," Jesus said, "and he is speaking to you!"
>
> "Yes, Lord," the man said, "I believe!" And he worshiped Jesus (verses 35-38).

The man who had been born blind had no trouble seeing the truth because the Truth was standing before him. This man who could work miracles was more than merely human. His power simply reflected his identity.

Who else but God has the mastery Jesus demonstrated over the human body? Who else but God's Son could do these things?[2]

- calm a storm (see Matthew 8)
- make a mute person speak (see Matthew 9)
- feed 5000 people with five loaves and two fish (see Matthew 14)

- cast out demons (see Mark 5)

- walk on water (see Mark 6)

- bring sight to the blind (see Mark 10)

- heal a paralyzed man (see Luke 5)

- raise a boy from the dead (see Luke 7)

- heal incurable hemorrhaging (see Luke 8)

- cleanse lepers (see Luke 17)

- turn water into wine (see John 2)

- make the lame walk (see John 5)

- forgive sin (see John 8)

- raise a man from the dead (see John 11)

The miracles of Jesus provide convincing evidences that he was the perfect Lamb of God who sacrificed himself so you and I might be redeemed and justified before God. Jesus said, "Believe that I am in the Father and the Father is in me. Or at least believe because of what you have seen me do" (John 14:11). When we place our faith in Jesus, we can be confident that he is the One who God accepts as a sacrifice on our behalf: "There is no condemnation for those who belong to Christ Jesus. For the power of the life-giving Spirit has freed you through Christ Jesus from the power of sin that leads to death" (Romans 8:1-2). Your death sentence has been commuted, and you are a child of God!

THE JOY OF SALVATION

Imagine being transported to a great courtroom. Almighty God sits as Judge behind a towering desk; the prosecution table is to his left, and the defense table is on his right. You identify Satan standing at the prosecution table, while a frightened-looking man sits alone at the defense table. The court clerk proclaims loudly, "Case #8032666." The Great Judge responds, "Proceed."

"Your...*Honor,*" Satan sneers at the judge as he motions toward the cowering defendant. "I know I don't have to tell you all the sins the accused has committed. His sins of adultery alone are enough to convict him, not to mention his heritage from Adam. Exhibit A details the times and dates the accused lusted after women—65,243 times. To make matters worse, the lines marked in red on the chart show the occasions when the man's lust led him to actual adultery. For example, in July of last year—"

"All right, all right," the man interrupts. "That's enough."

"How do you plead?" the Judge asks.

"Not guilty, Your Honor, because I do have a defense."

"Proceed," the Judge says with a nod.

"It really wasn't my fault," the man begins. "My secretary was a lonely woman, and what I did was out of compassion. You see, she was abused by her husband, and someone had to comfort her. I was there, and—"

"Immaterial!" Satan shouts. "It doesn't matter why, Your Honor. The simple fact that he committed the deed is all that counts. His so-called reasons are mere excuses. This man's a sinner." He lifts a ream of paper into the air and shakes it. "And your law says, 'The soul who sins will die'" (Ezekiel 18:4 NASB).

"I...I may be a sinner, but...I have another defense, Your Honor," the accused stammers.

"Proceed," the Judge states.

"I know you are fair and just," he replies. "So I offer here all the good I have done throughout my life as a defense." Three men enter, carrying large notebooks filled with paper. "I have compiled my noble deeds: how I helped my fellow humans, gave some of my time and considerable sums of money to ease the suffering of others. Furthermore, I faithfully loved my second wife." The man smiles proudly. "So, you see, my good deeds are many while my adulteries—by comparison, at least—are few. Clearly the good far outweighs what little bad I've done."

"Immaterial!" Satan shouts. He faces the man. "It doesn't matter how much good you've done, you're still a sinner. That's all this court needs to know." He points to the man. "Good deeds can't erase your sin, Mister, and nothing you can do will commute your death sentence!"

Satan turns to the Judge, an expression of smug satisfaction on his face.

"I rest my case, Your Honor. You have no alternative but to administer justice and hand down a sentence of death."

"So it is written," the Great Judge states, certainty and sadness mingling in his voice. "The wages of sin is death" (Romans 6:23). He bangs the gavel on his desk, and two demon guards enter and drag the man from the courtroom, slumped and sobbing bitterly. Satan follows, hissing at him all the way.

Suddenly you are ushered to the defense table, and you lower your head in shame at what you fear will be revealed.

The Judge reads from a sheet in front of him. "Case number 2308777." He looks at you and says, "How do *you* plead?"

"Not guilty, Your Honor," you answer.

"So entered," says the Great Judge. "The prosecution may make its case."

Satan strides forward again, cocky, arrogant, his pitiless countenance exuding contempt and disdain. "So you think you're innocent," he sneers. "I happen to know otherwise. I have a long record of all your sins, and they are legion." Satan proceeds to list your sins, one after the other—pride, envy, lust, greed, bursts of uncontrolled anger, hatred, selfishness—giving example after example of your worst sins. You hang your head in shame as the list goes on and on. Finally he stops, looks at the Great Judge, and says, "And Your Honor, these are things the defendant did in only one year." Turning to you he says, "Shall I continue, or do you want to change your plea?"

"I stand by my plea," you say.

Satan cackles in derision. "What kind of fool are you? You have no defense! According to the law, your birth as a sinner warrants your death. And to top that off, your list of sins would sink a battleship. You may as well quit wasting the court's time. You have no possible defense, and it's an outrage you even pretend to be innocent."

You stand and reply, "It's true, I have no right to plead innocent. I would stand before this holy court condemned by my very nature and guilty in thought and deed. Except for one thing."

"And just what could that possibly be?" replies Satan, his voice dripping with contempt.

You swallow hard, drop to your knees, gaze up at the Judge, and cry out, "Mercy, Your Honor." At that moment a figure you had failed to notice stands up beside the Great Judge and makes his way toward you. He gives you a nod and a smile, indicating you should continue. You clear your throat, stand to your feet, and continue. "I have sinned. I have been a slave to sin and death."

"Now you're talking my language," Satan chimes in.

"And there is no question I deserve death," you continue. "But I claim the blood of my dear Savior Jesus Christ, which has cleansed me from my sins and wiped all guilt away." By this time the figure from behind the Judge's bench has made his way to your side. He speaks.

"It is true—this human is guilty of death." At that point Satan breaks out in applause. The Great Judge raises his hand. "Silence!" he demands.

"Death is the payment for sin," the figure at your side continues. "And I have made that payment myself."

"Objection!" Satan screams out.

"Overruled!" The word booms out in the mighty voice of the Great Judge. You feel a hand gently squeeze your shoulder. You look up and see it is Jesus who stands beside you.

"It is true," Jesus states, his voice strong and confident. "I, God the Son, have paid the debt of sin on this human's behalf." Then Jesus looks at you as he continues. "And you, my child, have placed your complete trust in me as your defense."

"Preposterous!" Satan screams at the Great Judge. "You can't allow this kind of double-talk. Who's in charge here anyway? The law must rule—'The soul who sins will die.'" Satan turns toward Jesus and glares. "The defendant sinned. Thus it is the human who is deserving of death, not you." Satan jabs his pointing finger at Jesus. "So it's the defendant who must die."

Jesus addresses the Great Judge, saying, "The prosecution is making my case for me, Your Honor. He is absolutely right—I was not deserving of death, and thus I was a perfect substitute for my client."

"This is crazy…outrageous! Unfair! It's…it's not legal," Satan bellows.

"Apparently the prosecution has forgotten your infallible words, Your Honor," Jesus responds. "If the court please, I will refresh his memory by asking my client to read from your holy writings." Jesus hands you God's holy words and points to a passage. He smiles assurance at you and whispers, "Read it loud and with confidence." You clear your throat again and read. "'God put into effect a different plan to save me. He sent his own Son in a human body like mine, except that mine is sinful. God destroyed sin's control over me by giving his Son as a sacrifice for my sins'" (Romans 8:3 paraphrased).

"No. No. No!" Satan yells out beating the table with his fist. "That's not fair. That's mercy, and I can't stand mercy. Besides, that's not what this court is about. Your Honor, you are a just Judge, and I know you will insist on justice. In fact, I demand justice!"

Jesus looks up at the Great Judge and says, "Justice has been done, Your Honor. Sin was committed, and my death as God the Son paid the penalty for it. Now that justice has been served, this court has every right to extend mercy and exonerate this human. My dear friend here is legally innocent because I have taken all sins committed upon myself and suffered the penalty. Is that not true, Father?"

"It is written in my eternal Word," the Judge began. He looks straight at you as he continues. "'You are made right in my sight when you trust in my Son, Jesus Christ, to take away your sins'" (see Romans 3:22). "And your testimony here is that you have done that, correct?"

"Right!" you say without hesitation.

"No! No! No!" Satan screams. "This wretch is a sinner through and through. I've shown you the evidence. The human has fallen short of your standards of rightness. Far short! I insist payment of the wage—eternal death for this child of Adam."

The Judge lifts his hand and says, "Silence in my court! The payment of death has been made. The sins of this human are abolished; they are cast as far as the east is from the west. And this child of Adam is now a child of God. It is written, 'Yet, now, I in my gracious kindness declare you,' he looks directly into your eyes, 'not guilty. I have done this through Christ Jesus, who has freed you by taking away your sins'" (see Romans 3:24).

You feel the arm of your defender wrap around your shoulder as he pulls you to him. You look into his face. He smiles and gives you a wink of assurance.

The Great Judge continues to read. "'I sent Jesus to take the punishment for your sins and to satisfy my anger against you. You are made right with me when you believe that Jesus shed his blood, sacrificing his life for you'" (see Romans 3:25).

"Not fair or just! Not fair or just!" Satan screeches.

The Judge raises his hand to bring silence again and says, "'I am entirely fair and just in this present time when I declare this sinner to be right in my sight because this child of mine believes in Jesus'" (see Romans 3:26).

With that the Great Judge pounds his gavel thunderously on the great judgment desk and declares, "This person is justified by my grace through faith in Jesus. Case dismissed!"

The essence of this fictional illustration is absolutely true. The telling passages from Romans, while personalized within the context of our story, are not fiction at all, but direct scriptural quotes. The majority of people may believe their good deeds will persuade God to give them a place in heaven. The reality is, your death sentence is commuted and you are redeemed and justified before God through your faith alone in Christ. And because of Christ's sacrifice and your faith in him, your status as a son or daughter of Adam has changed. You are now a child of God.

YOUR JOY MADE COMPLETE

"Long ago, even before he made the world, God loved us and chose us in Christ to be holy and without fault in his eyes. His unchanging plan has always been to adopt us into his own family by bringing us to himself through Jesus Christ. And this gave him great pleasure" (Ephesians 1:4-5). You were born dead. You were alone, abandoned, and without love because of sin. But now, if you have trusted in Jesus, you have a real family. The apostle Paul said that "God has sent the Spirit of his Son into our hearts prompting us to call out, 'Abba, Father [or Daddy]'" (Galatians 4:6).

We have been freed from sin, received peace of mind and heart, released from guilt, given a reason for living, and provided hope of eternal life with him.

As a result of being justified before God, his Holy Spirit enters our lives and we are adopted into his family. We not only receive his eternal life and can call God our Daddy, but "since we are his children, we will share his treasures—for everything God gives to his Son, Christ, is ours too" (Romans 8:17). Chosen, redeemed, justified, sanctified, adopted into a family, given eternal life, and willed an eternal inheritance! What more could we ask?

King David spoke of this, describing the happiness of an undeserving sinner who is declared to be righteous:

> Oh, what joy for those whose disobedience is forgiven, whose sins are put out of sight. Yes, what joy for those whose sin is no longer counted against them by the Lord (Romans 4:6-8).

In effect Jesus is saying to you, "I have come to earth, demonstrated my love by giving my life for you, and I ask you to trust in me as your only solution to life, 'so that my joy may be in you and that your joy may be complete'" (John 15:11 NIV). "He [Christ] himself gives life and breath to everything, and he satisfies every need there is" (Acts 17:25).

Your completion, your total joy and happiness, is found in a relationship with God as your Daddy. He didn't have to save you. But by his grace he grants you an adoptive relationship—and all of us who have placed our faith in Jesus. We have been freed from sin, received peace of mind and heart, released from guilt, given a reason for living, and provided hope of eternal life with him. "We've been given a brand-new life and have everything to live for, including a future in heaven—and the future starts now!" (1 Peter 1:3-4 MSG).

ONE OF THE GREATEST JOYS OF MY LIFE

From the age of 11, when I (Josh) left that corn bin feeling abandoned, alone, and angry, I was determined to find happiness. I have explained how my quest to find it took me through religion, education, and prestige, only to be disappointed at each turn. But God was faithful to me. I didn't love him, but he loved me. I could sense Jesus at the door of my heart pleading, "Look, I have been standing at your door and constantly knocking. If you hear me calling and will open the door I will come in" (paraphrased from Revelation 3:20).

I was in my second year at the university, and I was keeping that door shut and bolted. I didn't care if Jesus did walk on water or turn water into wine. I didn't want any party pooper spoiling my fun. I couldn't think of any faster way to ruin my good times.

I called them good times, but I was really miserable. I was a walking battlefield. My mind was telling me Christianity was true, but my will was resisting it with all the energy it could muster.

Then there was the pride problem. At that time the thought of becoming a Christian shattered my ego. I had just proved all my previous thinking had been wrong and my friends had been right. Every time I got around those enthusiastic Christians, the inner conflict would boil over. If you've ever been in the company of happy people when you are miserable, you know how their joy can get under your skin. Sometimes I would literally get up, leave the group, and run right out of the student union. It came to the point where I would go to bed at ten o'clock at night but wouldn't get to sleep until four in the morning. I couldn't let go of the problem. I had to do something before it drove me out of my mind.

It was at that point I took a step of intelligent faith. I turned my back on my old life and placed my trust in Jesus as my sacrifice for sin—my Savior. And I can say with Paul, "How differently I think about him [Jesus] now! What this means is that those who become Christians become new persons. They are not the same anymore, for the old life is gone. A new life has begun!" (2 Corinthians 5:16-17).

For me, one aspect of this new life was peace—the relief from my restlessness. Before I trusted Christ, I always had to be occupied. I had to be over at my girlfriend's place, at a party, at the student union, or running around with friends. I'd walk across the campus with my mind in a whirlwind of conflicts. I was always bouncing off the walls. I'd sit down and try to study but couldn't do it. But after I turned my life over to Jesus, a kind of mental peace settled over me. Don't misunderstand; I don't mean all conflicts ceased. What I found in this relationship with Jesus wasn't so much the absence of conflict as the ability to cope with it. I wouldn't trade that for anything in the world.

Another area that began to change for the better was related to my bad temper. I used to blow my stack if anyone just looked at me cross-eyed. I still have the scars from a fight in which I almost killed a man in my first year at the university. My temper was such a part of me that I didn't consciously seek to change it. But one day I encountered a crisis that should have set me off, only to find that I stayed calm and collected. My temper was gone! It wasn't my doing; Jesus had given me a new life. That doesn't mean I was perfect. I went 14 years without losing my temper, but when I did blow it, I'm afraid I made up for all those times I didn't.

Jesus changed me in another way. My old life consisted of hatred. I had a heavy load of hatred weighing me down. It sapped the joy out of my life. It didn't show outwardly, but it kept grinding away inwardly and made life miserable. I was ticked off with people, with things, with issues. I was insecure. Every time I met anyone different from me, that person became a threat.

But I hated one man more than anyone else in the world…and that was my father. I was mortified that he was the town alcoholic. If you're from a small town and one of your parents is an alcoholic, you know what I mean. Everybody knows. My high school friends would make jokes about my father's drinking. They didn't think it bothered me because I fell in with the joking and laughed with them. I was laughing on the outside, but let me tell you, I was crying on the inside. I would go to the barn and find my mother beaten so badly by my father that she couldn't get up, lying in the manure behind the cows. That tore me up as a kid. When we had friends over, I would take my drunken father out to the barn, tie him up, and park his car behind the silo. I was ashamed of anyone seeing him that way. We would tell our guests he'd had to go somewhere. I don't think anyone could hate a person more than I hated my father.

About five months after I placed my faith in Christ, a love from God entered my life so powerfully that it took that hatred, turned it upside down, and emptied it out. In its place God gave me love and joy. I was able to look my father squarely in the eyes and say, "Dad, I love you." And I really meant it. After some of the things I'd done to him, that really shook him up.

After I transferred to a private university, a serious car accident put me in the hospital. When I was moved home to recover, my father came to visit me. Remarkably, he was sober that day. But he seemed uneasy, pacing about the room. Then he blurted out, "Son, how can you love a father like me?" I answered, "Dad, six months ago I despised you." Then I shared with him the story of my research and conclusions about Jesus Christ. I told him, "I have placed my trust in Christ, received God's forgiveness, invited him into my life, and he has changed me. I can't explain it all, Dad, but God has taken away my hatred and replaced it with the capacity to love. I love you and accept you just the way you are."

We talked for almost an hour, and then I received one of the greatest joys of my life. This man who was my father, this man who knew me too well for me to pull the wool over his eyes, looked at me and said, "Son, if God can do in my life what I've seen him do in yours, then I want to give him the opportunity. I want to trust him as my Savior and Lord."

Usually after a person places their trust in Christ, the changes in his or her life occur over a period of days, weeks, months, or even years. In my own life the change took about six to eighteen months, and there are still changes taking place. But the life of my father changed right before my eyes. It was as if God reached down and flipped on the light switch. Never before or since have I seen such a dramatic change. My father touched an alcoholic beverage only once after that day. He got it as far as his lips before thrusting it away. Forever. I can come to only one conclusion: A relationship with Jesus Christ changes lives, and that makes our joy complete.[3]

EXPLAINING HOW TO HAVE
A RELATIONSHIP WITH GOD

God went to extraordinary lengths to form a relationship with you. He left heaven, died a torturous death, and rose again to raise you to new life in him. Again, he did all this because "he is a God who is passionate about his relationship with you" (Exodus 34:14).

If you do not have that relationship and want to find it, what steps should you take? Here is a simple presentation of the gospel story you can use as a guide to establish a relationship with God—or to lead someone you know into that relationship.

1. Can you really know God personally?

- God does *love* you. "This is real love. It is not that we loved God, but that he loved us" (1 John 4:10).

- God has a *plan* for you to know him personally. "Now this is eternal life: that they may know you, the only true God, and Jesus Christ, whom you have sent" (John 17:3 NIV).

- God has a *future* for you. "You can claim the promise God made to the children of Israel when he said, 'I know the plans I have for you,' declares the LORD, 'plans for welfare and not for calamity to give you a future and a hope'" (Jeremiah 29:11 NASB).

2. What prevents us from knowing God personally?

- Humans are *sinful*. "All have sinned and fall short of the glory of God" (Romans 3:23 NIV). Although we were created to have a relationship with God, we choose to go our own independent way in disobedience to him because of our self-centeredness. This self-will, characterized by an attitude of active rebellion or passive indifference, is an evidence of what the Bible calls sin.

- Humans are *separated*. "The wages of sin is death" (Romans 6:23). The death Paul speaks of here is not mere physical death, but spiritual separation from God. It means that "those who do not know God and do not obey the gospel of our Lord Jesus…will be punished with everlasting destruction and shut out from the presence of the Lord" (2 Thessalonians 1:8-9 NIV).

This sin, which is manifested in each of our individual lives, separates us from experiencing God's love and from an intimate relationship with him. Such separation brings both earthly turmoil and eternal consequences.

3. God provided a way to bridge this separation.

Jesus Christ, God's Son, is God's *only* provision for our sin. Through him alone we can know God personally and experience his love.

- *Christ died in our place.* "God sent Jesus to take the punishment for our sins and to satisfy God's anger against us" (Romans 3:25).

- *Christ rose from the dead.* "Christ died for our sins…He was buried, and he was raised from the dead on the third day, as the Scriptures said. He was seen by Peter and then by the twelve apostles. After that, he was seen by more than five hundred" (1 Corinthians 15:3-6).

- *Christ is the only way to God.* Jesus said, "I am the way, the truth, and the life. No one can come to the Father except through me" (John 14:6).

But…

4. It is not enough just to know these truths.

- We must individually *receive* Jesus Christ as Savior and Lord; then we can know God personally and experience his love. "To all who received him, to those who believed in his name, he gave the right to become children of God" (John 1:12 NIV).

- We receive Christ through faith, placing our trust in him, his power and authority. "It is by grace you have been saved, through faith—and this not from yourselves, it is the gift of God—not by works, so that no one can boast" (Ephesians 2:8-9 NIV).

- We receive Christ by accepting his personal invitation. He says, "Look! Here I stand at the door and knock. If you hear me calling and open the door, I will come in" (Revelation 3:20).

And…

5. When we receive Christ, we are changed.

- When we receive him by faith, as an act of our will, we experience a new life. "He died for everyone so that those who receive his new life will no longer live to please themselves. Instead, they will live to please Christ" (2 Corinthians 5:15).

Just to agree intellectually Jesus Christ is the Son of God and he died on the cross for our sins does not qualify as faith. Faith requires a serious renouncing of one's previous ways and a trust in God to direct the future. Mere intellectual belief is not adequate to have Christ come into your life. Nor is it enough to have an emotional religious experience. Receiving Christ involves turning to God from self (repentance) and trusting Christ to come into our lives to forgive us of our sins and to make us what he wants us to be.

6. The Bible promises eternal life to all who receive Christ.

- When we receive him, we are assured of eternal life in heaven and joy here on earth. "God has given us eternal life, and this life is in his Son. He who has the Son has life; he who does not have the Son of God does not have life. I write these things to you who believe in the name of the Son of God so that you may know that you have eternal life" (1 John 5:11-13 NIV).

If you have not yet trusted in Christ by faith, you can do so right now. The words of the following prayer are not magical; they are simply a suggestion to enable you to express a sincere desire to turn from self to God:

> *Lord Jesus, I believe you are who you claim to be, and I want to know you personally. Thank you for dying on the cross for my sins. I accept your forgiveness and place my trust in you as my Savior and Lord. Come into my heart and make me the person you created me to be. In your name. Amen.*

A NEW BEGINNING

If you just now placed your trust in Jesus, or if you have just led someone to trust him for salvation, you or your acquaintance has embarked on a new beginning. "Those who become Christians become new persons. They are not the same anymore, for the old life is gone. A new life has begun!" (2 Corinthians 5:17). What does this mean?

- You have *recognized* that you had a problem. You had sinned against God and had gone your own way.

- You have *realized* Jesus is your only solution. You asked God to forgive you of your sins. You turned away from your old life and turned to Jesus as your only hope of a relationship with God.

- You have *responded* to Jesus in faith, placing your trust in him as your Savior—the One who took your place.

- You have *relied* upon Jesus to raise you from death to life. In faith you reached out and received his gift of eternal life, and you now have an adopted relationship in God's family.*

What's next? As a transformed follower of Christ, God does have a plan for your life and mine. The remaining truths in this book explain your purpose and mission.

LEADING A PERSON TO JESUS

One of the keys to leading a person to Christ or nurturing someone to spiritual health is developing a relationship with that person. Since you will have established a relationship with the person to whom you present the gospel message, you will find it's good to have another effective tool in your arsenal. There is no better way to show an example of what it means to be a Christian than your own testimony. A testimony is a simple sharing of what Christ has done in your life. It's not difficult to develop your own story in a way that can be concisely and effectively shared. Here are some guidelines.

How to Prepare Your Personal Testimony

Before you begin, ask God to give you wisdom and guidance. Then you can use the following three-point outline as a framework for putting together your own personal story.

---

* Hundreds of thousands of people have been led to a personal relationship with God through the simple presentation of the gospel given to you above. This presentation is drawn from a booklet titled *Would You Like to Know God Personally?* published by CruPress, the publishing ministry of Cru. You can order quantities of that booklet by going online to crustore.org.

1. My life before knowing Christ.

   a. Make your first sentence interesting and attention-getting.

   b. Include the good elements of your life before Christ (for example, good person, athlete, achievements, moral, generous, church attender).

   c. Identify one key problem (for example, lack of joy, lack of purpose, pride, wrong priorities) that characterized your life before you became a Christ-follower.

   d. Show how this problem affected your life.

   OR if you had a childhood conversion, describe your "early years."

   e. Tell of how you were provided for as a child (for example, physical needs of food and shelter were provided for by your parents or guardians).

   f. Tell of how your need for a personal relationship with God was made evident (for example, "at the age of _____ I became aware of my spiritual need to know God").

2. How I came to Christ.

   a. Be specific.

   b. Avoid confusing statements (for example, "I went forward," "I marked a card"). Also avoid "Christianese" (for example, "I was redeemed by the substitutionary death of the Lamb").

   c. Talk about Christ and his work (that is, actually give a gospel presentation within your testimony).

3. My life since I trusted Christ.

   a. Describe how life has changed since you accepted Christ (for example, what problem he has helped you with, how he has affected your actions and attitudes).

b. Tell how Christ dealt with your problem or, if yours was a childhood conversion, give one positive benefit of following Christ (for example, joy, peace, hope of eternal life, no fear of death, forgiveness of sin, purposeful life).

c. Be honest, positive, and realistic (for example, "Not all of my problems in this life have been eliminated").

d. Include an appeal to know God personally.

e. Close with a strong, compelling conclusion.

Avoid:

- Clichés that are meaningless to the non-Christian, such as "blessings," "born again," "praise God," "conversion," "glorious," and so on.

- Vague generalities about what has happened in your life. Be specific.

- Being critical of any churches, denominations, or individuals.

- Employing too many overused catchwords such as "fantastic," "exciting," "awesome," and so on.

- Preaching. Just share your experience.

To further help develop your testimony we have provided two examples of what a testimony might sound like.

Testimony example #1: *Childhood conversion.*

(*My life before Christ*) I had parents who genuinely loved me and cared for me as a child. Even though they were never rich, they always provided for my most basic needs of food, clothing, shelter, and love. Along with providing for my physical needs, my parents made me aware of my need for a spiritual life.

(*How I met Christ*) When I was six years old, my father and I attended a funeral service. As we were walking through the cemetery grounds, I asked him a basic question I think we all ask at some time or another: "Where do you go when you die?" My father answered that question by using the Bible and showing me there are two possible destinations for us after death...heaven and hell. He also explained the Bible was written that we might know for certain we can have eternal life...or heaven (1 John 5:13). Dad told me heaven was the benefit given by God for those who would become Christ-followers. He said that following Christ was as simple as depending on Christ to guide my life instead of myself.

(Since I met Christ) Since I've become a Christ-follower, I have never feared death because Christ has promised that as his follower I will live forever with him in heaven. Don't get me wrong, my life isn't perfect; I still face many of the same problems you do. But the assurance of eternal life gives me a peace and confidence in which to face these problems.

If you don't mind, I would like to share with you how you, too, can have a personal relationship with God and have the certainty of eternal life.

Testimony example #2: *Later-life conversion.*

(My life before Christ) At age 20 I realized I was putting up a front—looking good on the outside but hitting a lot of peaks and valleys on the inside. I spent a lot of time searching for a personal relationship that would last, but I was disappointed time after time until I found it in friendship with Jesus.

(How I met Christ) When I gave my life to Jesus, I began to understand that true, meaningful relationships begin with a relationship with God. I didn't know how to find that relationship until a friend explained it to me. He said God loved me and sent His Son to pay the penalty for my sin so I could have a personal relationship with God. Because my friend cared enough for me to tell me the truth, I asked Jesus Christ into my life.

(Since I met Christ) My Christian faith has helped me put my priorities in order. Since I made God number one and keep his priorities in my life, I have found a new understanding of what it means to have a friend who cares about you. Jesus has become my best friend, and that has helped me be a better friend to others.

Testimonies are powerful tools to help draw people to Christ. Just remember, salvation is not by our works or anything we've done but is purely a free gift of grace we receive by faith. We are saved by God's grace, not by our efforts to be moral. But when we're truly saved, God does begin working in our hearts and changing our lives and affections. Let's explore that transformation in the next chapter.

CHRISTIANS ARE A TRANSFORMED PEOPLE

C arl is hungry all the time. He is obsessed with eating. He thinks of nothing except keeping his stomach full. You see, Carl is a caterpillar, and as a caterpillar he will shed his skin four or five times in order to make room for the steady supply of leaves his insatiable appetite demands. In fact, he will increase his weight ten-thousand-fold in less than 20 days. His gluttonous appetite will cause tremendous damage to crops and the economy of humans. There is nothing of lasting value or worth to say about Carl the caterpillar.

But something marvelous is about to happen to Carl. Deep inside something calls him to stop eating and yield to a process of being fully encapsulated by a mysterious substance that hardens around him.

Many days pass, and then it happens. Carl bursts out of his cocoon. He has undergone a radical change called metamorphosis. He is now a new creature with new habits and a whole new look...because Carl the caterpillar, obsessed only with fulfilling his gluttonous appetite, has been transformed into a beautiful butterfly. He no longer crawls about with a ravenous appetite that destroys crops. He now soars through the air, flying from plant to plant, pollinating flowers to enhance the beauty of his world.[1]

OUR METAMORPHOSIS TO BE LIKE CHRIST

"Those who live only to satisfy their own sinful desires," Paul the apostle says, "will harvest the consequences of decay and death" (Galatians 6:8). Like Carl the caterpillar, "their god is their appetite, they brag about shameful things, and all they think about is this life here on earth" (Philippians 3:19).

But deep within our souls a voice is heard. It is the voice of God that calls us out of sin and death so a miraculous metamorphosis can take place. For "those who become Christians become new persons. They are not the same anymore, for the old life is gone. A new life has begun! All this newness of life is from God, who brought us back to himself through what Christ did" (2 Corinthians 5:17-18).

Our transformation changes us from self-seeking creatures to godlike beings. "God knew his people in advance," Paul declared, "and he chose them to become like his Son" (Romans 8:29). Even though sin broke our relationship with God and we crawled about fulfilling our own sinful appetites, because of Christ "we...are being transformed into his likeness with ever-increasing glory, which comes from the Lord, who is the Spirit" (2 Corinthians 3:18 NIV).

"You must display a new nature," Scripture says, "because you are a new person, created in God's likeness—righteous, holy, and true" (Ephesians 4:23). As redeemed, justified, sanctified, and adopted children of God, "his divine power gives us everything we need for living a godly life...And by that same mighty power...he has promised...that you will share in his divine nature" (2 Peter 1:3-4). When God raises us to new life he imparts his DNA to us so we can be a living replica of Christ. That is the root meaning of Christian— "Little Christ."

"God loved us and chose us in Christ to be holy and without fault in his eyes. His unchanging plan has always been to adopt us into his own family by bringing us to himself through Jesus Christ. And this gave him great pleasure" (Ephesians 1:4-5). Just as we humans take pleasure in our children looking and acting like us, so our heavenly Father exults to see each of us transformed into a new person who is becoming more and more like his Son.

I (Sean) will never forget the birth of our first child. It had been a long day, and when Stephanie told me it was time to take her to the hospital I was both excited and a little scared. I would be a father. That was going to be a new and frightening experience all rolled into one.

Then little Scottie was delivered. And I was a proud father. I have to admit that as I looked at him, I searched for any resemblance he might have to Stephanie or me. Did he have my nose or Stephanie's eyes? Did he have my color hair, or was the shape of his face like Stephanie's? For some reason I wanted my offspring to have a resemblance to me and his mother.

By the time Scottie was one year old, it was clear. He was the physical image of his father at that age. In fact, when I pulled out both my baby pictures and those of Josh, my dad, we found that little Scottie resembled two generations of McDowells! In the future when our ancestors look at these photos of the three of us at that age, it will be difficult to distinguish who was who because we three looked so alike.

There was something about having a child who looked like me that felt honoring. And it filled me with joy. So it is with God. He is honored when we live in relationship with him and begin to look and act like him. When God said, "Let us make people in our image, to be like ourselves" (Genesis 1:26), he was designing each of us to live and enjoy life as he did. God in effect was saying, "Become intimate with me, and through our close relationship you will bear the fruit of my nature—love, joy, peace, patience, kindness, goodness, faithfulness, gentleness and self-control—and that will make me proud and give me honor" (see Galatians 5:22-23). It pleases God to see us resemble him. In fact, that defines our purpose in life.

WHY ARE WE HERE?

God created us to bring glory to himself. And we glorify God—reflect honorably upon him—as we live in devoted love of him, desiring to please him. "Whatever you eat or drink or whatever you do," Paul said, "you must do all for the glory of God" (1 Corinthians 10:31).

You and I begin to fulfill our purpose when we begin to live out the Godlike life he designed for us. He created us to relate to him and enjoy all the blessings that come from being godly. As we said before, acting according to God's ways brings blessing because all that is defined as perfectly right and good is derived from his nature (see James 1:17).

Therefore:

> *We believe the truth that followers of Christ are meant to live in relationship with God and be transformed into the likeness of Christ, which defines our very purpose for living—to honor and glorify God.*

We were created to live contented lives of joy. We were made to know the gratifying joy of being accepted, approved of, and appreciated, with the ability to freely love and be loved. We were designed to experience fulfillment and satisfaction beyond measure, and contentment and peace beyond understanding. And that kind of meaningful life comes only from living in fellowship with God and being conformed to his image. When we come into relationship with God, it begins a process of change that allows his divine nature to permeate our lives. And as we live out that Godlike nature we fulfill the very reason we are here.

EVIDENCES OF A CHANGED LIFE

"Hypocrites—the church is full of hypocrites." You have probably heard more than one person say that. Today perhaps more than ever, one of the justifiable criticisms of Christianity is that those who call themselves Christians don't live much differently than non-Christians. People may wear the name and want the benefits, but many have not submitted to God for the process of transformation.

How can we tell the difference? How can we know who is really Christian and who is not? Jesus gives us a simple measure by which we can identify false prophets or false Christians: "You can detect them by the way they act, just as you can identify a tree by its fruit" (Matthew 7:16). The same criteria can be used to identify authentic Christians as well. One who has submitted to God's redeeming love will inevitably show evidence of a changed life. My (Josh's) life is a testimony to the fact that God changes lives. My father is living proof a drunk can be transformed into a godly person.

Countless lives over the course of history speak out as a testimony to the God who changes lives. There are not enough books to hold the stories. If you have placed your faith in Christ, you are living proof a "metamorphosis" has taken place—you have been redeemed and are being continually transformed into the image of Christ. Use your testimony as a way to honor God and give him pleasure. Whenever you have an opportunity to tell others how God has changed you, take it. The more you display his godly nature and tell others of God's love and mercy, the more it honors him and fills him with joy.

Following are just a few stories of people who are living proof that God changes lives.

AN ADDICT AND ALCOHOLIC

Rich was an angry man with a violent temper, addicted to drugs and alcohol. He shares his own story:

> I grew up on the west side of Cleveland. I was thirteen when I first joined a gang. That's when I started to drink and take drugs. By the time I was 14 I had graduated to more serious drugs. Stealing, fighting, dealing drugs, and taking them myself was all I knew.
>
> That summer a buddy of mine gave me a book entitled *Run Baby Run* by Nicky Cruz. It was about how Cruz, a member of a New York street gang, became a Christian. His story had a real impact on me, but it would be 15 years before the message of Jesus took root. Drugs, alcohol, and my stormy temper would haunt me into my forties.
>
> I wasn't good at relationships. I was in my late twenties and already into my second marriage. The new marriage wasn't going too well. Laura, my second wife, was also into drinking and drugs. She had two twin boys, Tim and Tom, who were around eight years old when I married Laura. I wasn't a very good dad to those kids. I was away from home most of the time—at work or drinking— and when I was home I yelled a lot.

While driving home from a night of drinking and doing drugs, I came to the end of my rope. Life had no meaning. I couldn't keep a love relationship; I wasn't a good father; drugs and drinking brought no satisfaction anymore. So what was the point of even living?

The Nicky Cruz story came back to me, and I started praying. When I got home I began reading the Bible. The twins had been attending church, and that had an impact on me. I went to Laura and said, "Why don't we stop going to the bars, start going to church like the boys are, and try to turn our lives around?" Laura said she'd be willing to try.

I'm not really sure why I wanted to go to church, because all I got from church people was condemnation and Scripture verses thrown at me. My life was already going up in flames. And when your house is in flames you don't want someone on your front lawn quoting scriptures; you want a fireman with a water hose. I guess I was hoping that somewhere out there I might find a church with a hose that gushed with love and acceptance. Maybe in the back of my mind I figured that was probably too much to ask, but I was going to give it a try anyway.

When I walked into church I was greeted sweetly by a lady with a smile that stretched from ear to ear. We chatted for a minute. She was so bubbly and happy, I figured this must be some kind of cult. I thought no one could be that happy at a regular church.

She then introduced me to her husband and said, "Tom will take you to the Stoner's class." Stoner's class!

As it turned out, Stoner was the last name of the small group leader. I was a long-haired, skinny, burned-out addict. And they could see that. Yet these people accepted me for who I was.

In the past, most people had told me that my problem was drugs and alcohol. But the reality was that these things were my "solution."

These church people knew that too. They saw that my problem was being alone and disconnected. I was looking for a sense of meaning and belonging. I was trying to solve things by joining a gang and getting into drugs and alcohol. But I didn't find what I was really looking for. Those things were an attempt to drown out the hurt and aloneness of my miserable existence. My solution wasn't a solution at all.

For the first time in my life I met real people who loved me for being me. *I* didn't even love me, and so I was sort of shocked that these people could really care about me. And they were so doggone happy it almost bugged me. They loved life; it had meaning to them, and I began to really crave what these people had.

Over time I learned who Jesus really was, what he did for me, and how he was the real solution to my messed-up life. Laura struggled. She said she couldn't make it without her old life. And one day she up and moved out without warning. The marriage I hoped could be salvaged was permanently broken. The twins were now stuck with me, their stepdad.

Two years later the pastor introduced me to Pam, a Christian woman. I guess he believed I had a shot at making a relationship work since Christ would be the head of it. I fell in love with Pam, and while it's not all been a bed of roses, life after finding Christ has been more than I could ever have dreamed. The twins went off to college, and we adopted three children. A broken and shattered life was transformed into a loving marriage, a loving home, and a family that is reaching out to give hope and light to others.

Today, Rich Bucha is a leader in his church. He leads a recovery group that guides men and women with a dependency into recovery. He has written a book, is a happy father, and is still married to Pam. She also is an active leader in the church, participating in small group discipleship and outreach events.[2]

A MEDICAL SCIENTIST

Dr. Francis Collins is one of this country's leading geneticists and former head of the Human Genome Project. During his medical residency, this budding medical professional was shocked by the serenity of some of his mortally ill patients. As an agnostic, he would listen intently while someone with an incurable brain tumor would calmly say, "Well, I guess it won't be long before I see my husband and my dear Savior." He would observe others in dreadful pain say things like, "I know this hurts a lot, but when I think how much more Jesus suffered for me, I can't really complain."

Time after time he saw patients and families of patients face tragedy with a sense of gratitude, courage, and optimism. It was the display of God's grace in the lives of those facing death that drew Dr. Collins to search for the source of such peace. Someone gave him the book *Mere Christianity* by C.S. Lewis. And he began to read it.

The argument Lewis made for God on the evidence of the moral law had a profound impact on Collins. That evidence convinced his mind there was a God. But it was the eternal hope of the suffering believers that attracted his heart. As a result this brilliant scientist gave his heart and mind to Jesus Christ.[3]

A "SUPER SPIRITUAL" CHURCHGOER

Pastor Jeff Bogue shares how, as a seminary student, his "super spirituality" was exposed as fake:

> During summer break from seminary I got a job in the inner city of Philadelphia. The job involved working with physically, sexually, and emotionally abused kids that had been removed from their homes. They were now living in a group home environment. I drove out to Philadelphia and settled into my new job, interacting with several other college students who, like me, were there working for the summer.
>
> I met this guy named Steve. To put it mildly, Steve was a freak of nature. When I first looked at him, I could not believe what I saw. Both ears were pierced, and he had rings hanging from them.

Tattoos covered his arms, and his hair hung past his shoulders—all things I had been taught were sure signs of a *liberal*. I, on the other hand, considered myself a super spiritual person. My hair was short, there were no unnecessary holes in my body, and my skin was never marred with anything other than an occasional sunburn.

So Jeff the "super spiritual" and Steve "the liberal" had to work together. I knew it would be hard, but somehow I had to find a way to get along with this freak, because we would be working side by side all summer. I tried to make polite conversation, but I was convinced that Steve and I really had nothing in common. This was going to be a tough summer.

One day, Steve invited me to go to a Bible study with him. I must tell you I had about as much interest in studying the Bible with Steve as I had in hanging out with him—none. However, also working at the center was a really attractive blonde girl that I wanted to impress. I had learned that girls like her were impressed if you were spiritual enough to attend Bible studies and prayer meetings. So I agreed to go to the Bible study with Steve. It was to take place in someone's apartment.

I walked into the Bible study, and all the participants were like Steve: long-haired, ear-pierced, tattooed freaks! I was definitely the odd man out. But that night I experienced something radical. All of these long-haired, ear-pierced, tattooed freaks loved Jesus. They actually read the Bible to get to know its author.

When they sang worship songs, they seemed to be singing directly to God; I sang them because they were in style. When they read the Bible and meditated on it, they seemed to be doing it to get to know God intimately; I memorized it to take tests and to impress people with my knowledge. When they prayed aloud they seemed to be talking to their dearest friend; when I prayed aloud I was making a point to the people around me.

I remember thinking, *With these guys it's not about following a certain set of rules, it's about loving a certain person.* I started meeting with them more and more. There was something about them that I sensed was authentic and real, and I was drawn to them. Instead of just going to church, they were about being the church. Instead of focusing on being "super spiritual," they focused on a loving relationship with Jesus that affected every aspect of their lives.

I started to change my view about Steve and his friends. I had intense conversations with them that lasted until the wee hours of the morning. I found their authenticity and openness to God so appealing. The God they talked about seemed different than the God I believed in. They were passionately pursuing an intimate relationship with him—a closeness I never knew was possible.

I had just enough spiritual intuition to know that I couldn't fake what Steve and his friends had. But it wasn't as simple as yielding to God and admitting I didn't have what it took to be a spiritual person. To do this would be like exposing me as a spiritual infant who needed God and others to mature. To me that felt like starting at the bottom. And to think of being led by a group of freakish people that my church and college considered totally unacceptable was out of the question. But these guys had turned my world upside down. I was having a crisis of faith. I didn't quite know how to cope with this new reality of what being spiritual really meant. I was in a quandary because these guys had a connection with God that was so real, and mine seemed so fake.

Then came a moment of clarity. I was walking around a soccer field one evening where I often went to run and exercise. I had my Bible with me, and as the summer sun was setting I sat down in the soccer field and prayed. "God, I want what those guys have. I don't even really know what it is. I want it but I'm also afraid of how it is going to affect my life. Would you show yourself to me so I can know you for who you really are?"

I opened my Bible and began to read the story of Jesus walking on the water. Then it happened. Somehow, God interacted with me on a deep level. I began to realize that either Jesus walked on the water or he didn't. Either this whole religion thing is real, or it is all fake. I thought, only God could overcome and suspend the laws of nature to perform such a miracle. So either Jesus is who he claimed to be or he isn't. Either he is the God of the universe and the One I should submit to and trust in as my Savior, or the whole thing is one big lie.

That night I sensed God speaking to me, saying, "Jeff, you have to choose. Trust in me for who I am and let me take your ordinary life and transform it into an extraordinary life, or forsake the God of your mother and father and walk away from me forever." I saw the gravity and the far-reaching impact of that choice. It was an either/or decision.

The verse I was taught came to me: "If we confess our sins to him, he is faithful and just to forgive us and to cleanse us from every wrong" (1 John 1:9). That night I made a choice to trust in Christ and know him for who he is, and it changed my life forever.[4]

AN IMPRISONED THIEF

Pacing back and forth in his prison cell, Leo D'Arcangelo was deeply disturbed—who wouldn't be, facing what was ahead of him?

As a boy of 11, he had snatched a lady's handbag. That was the start. Five years of stealing followed, before his first arrest at 16 in a Philadelphia department store. After being put on probation, he started mainlining heroin. Then began the seemingly endless set of arrests and finally jail time.

As he paced his jail cell, he noticed these few lines crudely scrawled on the wall:

When you come to the end of your journey and this trouble is racked in your mind, and there seems no other way out than by just mourning, turn to Jesus, for it is Him that you must find.

The words started him thinking. *This is the end of my journey. What have I got to show for it? Nothing except a lousy past and a worse future.* He cried out, "Jesus, I need your help. I've made a mess of my life, and this is the end of the journey. Jesus, if you can change my life please do it. Help me make tomorrow different."

For the first time Leo felt something besides despair. He felt free even though he was imprisoned.

Released two years later, Leo earned his high school diploma and then went on to graduate from West Chester State College and the Reformed Episcopal Seminary in Philadelphia. Leo had changed. He became active in prison work, leading others to the same spiritual freedom he had found in Christ.

These personal stories help illustrate important biblical truths:

> They overcame him [Satan] by the blood of the Lamb and by the word of their testimony (Revelation 12:11 NIV).

> We put no confidence in human effort. Instead, we boast about what Christ Jesus has done for us (Philippians 3:3).

> I am not ashamed of this Good News about Christ. It is the power of God at work, saving everyone who believes (Romans 1:16).

SEEING YOURSELF AS GOD SEES YOU

Even though God imparts his new nature to us, we need others around us to administer grace sometimes to help us in the process of correcting our unhealthy patterns—or you might say, help us unravel our grave clothes...

The man approached the grave of his dead friend. He had missed the funeral that was conducted four days prior. The body was actually entombed in a cave with a massive stone rolled across its entrance.

"Roll the stone aside," the man commanded to those with him. He then raised his head toward heaven, said a prayer, and shouted, "Lazarus, come out!" At that moment his dead friend came to life, raised at the call of Jesus of Nazareth.

Lazarus had been wrapped in a linen burial shroud soaked in spices to help preserve his corpse. With the spices now dried, the linen was hardened.

At Jesus' word, new life went right through the hardened grave clothes and into the body, and Lazarus hobbled out of the tomb wrapped like a mummy.

Outside the tomb, Lazarus no longer needed his grave clothes. So Jesus told Lazarus' family and friends, "Unwrap him and let him go!" (John 11:44).

INSTANT NEW LIFE, YET A PROCESS TO LIVE IT

Notice the grave clothes did not fall off Lazarus the moment Jesus called out to him. There was a *process* involved in getting him unwrapped after he had come to life again.

When we become Christians, it is as if Christ calls to us, "Come out! Come out of your old, dead existence. Come out and enjoy the new life I have given you." Christ is the initiator of the new life. And it is his power that activates the transformation process of becoming more and more like him. "You have stripped off your old evil nature and all its wicked deeds," Paul says. "In its place you have clothed yourselves with a brand-new nature." But notice how Paul refers to the process. He concludes that your brand-new nature "is continually being renewed as you learn more and more about Christ, who created this new nature within you" (Colossians 3:9-10).

Like Lazarus, we emerge from the tomb of our past shrouded in grave clothes. We may be bound by the negative influences of our family of origin, our old friends, and the old life we used to live. Christ's invitation to new life penetrates the grave clothes—the things that bind us—and new life begins. But we may still be hobbled by the wrappings. We may instantly be alive with Christ's nature within us, but it takes a process of time and spiritual growth for that nature to be lived out to maturity. Paul talked about being built up so "we will be mature and full grown in the Lord, measuring up to the full stature of Christ…becoming more and more in every way like Christ" (Ephesians 4:13, 15).

The work has begun in us, but it must be continued day in and day out as God's nature is unleashed through our attitudes and actions.

Jesus could have chosen to have Lazarus burst out of his grave clothes in a display of power. But he didn't. He chose to involve the people in Lazarus' life. It was as if Jesus said to Lazarus' friends and family, "You be part of the process of releasing him from the grave clothes! You help him in the transformation process!" Jesus does the same with us. He continues the process of transformation by bringing others into our lives who love us enough to extend grace to us, teach us, and mentor us in the process of becoming more and more like him.

Paul said, "I'm sure that God, who began the good work within you, will continue his work until it is finally finished on that day when Christ Jesus comes back again" (Philippians 1:6). The work has begun in us, but it must be continued day in and day out as God's nature is unleashed through our attitudes and actions. Peter said, "As we know Jesus better, his divine power gives us everything we need for living a godly life" (2 Peter 1:3).

There is a very important principle here about the transformation process. As new followers of Christ we *do* live differently from our old lives. But the doing isn't what continually transforms us. It is living in relationship with Christ and his nature, which is being imparted and empowered by the Holy Spirit.

DISCOVER WHO YOU ALREADY ARE

The transformation process isn't about becoming a new person by just doing right. A lot of new Christians are urged to start immediately *doing* things in order to activate the process of becoming like Christ: study the Bible, memorize verses, attend church as often as possible, witness to others, and replace old, sinful habits with patterns of godly living. These are all important in order to be rooted in the faith. In fact, we can't actually discover who Christ is and the power of God's truth without prayer and the study of God's Word. But we must realize that spiritual or studious activity isn't what continually transforms us.

Living a Christlike life is about *discovering the new person we already are in relationship with Christ and acting accordingly.* It's about interacting with and relating to Christ so that the grace and power of God's Spirit is appropriated within us. Studying the Bible, attending church, and sharing our faith do not cause God to regard us as more redeemed, justified, sanctified, or adopted.

He *already* sees us in these ways because they define who we really are. So we don't *do* our way into becoming God's adopted children. We are not changed from the outside in; we are changed from the inside out. As we live in relationship with Christ, we can start behaving according to our new nature and do those things that God's children do—act like Christ.

I (Josh) have a good friend who became a Christian in his early twenties. Well-meaning Christian leaders got him involved in personal Bible study right away to help him start growing in his faith. They loaded him down with materials that challenged him to scrutinize portions of Scripture in order to discover promises to claim, sins to avoid, and commands to obey. It was a very thorough study project, and he dived into it wholeheartedly, spending hours and hours each week digging through the Bible.

But after only a few weeks he told me he was worn out. He was so busy digging out verses in order to "grow" that he had missed the whole point of his exercise. So he changed his focus. He turned his attention to getting to know the God of the Bible personally, the God who had so marvelously saved him. His pursuit led him back into the Word, but his motivation was completely different. Instead of diving into its pages to *become* someone, he scoured the Word to find the heart of the One who had *made* him someone and sought a deeper relationship with him.

Today my friend is one of the most knowledgeable men of the Word I know. More importantly, he is more intimately in touch with the God of the Word than most Christian leaders. He learned early that living like Christ is primarily a matter of getting to know Jesus better because "his divine power has given us everything we need for living a godly life" (2 Peter 1:3). We should read, memorize, and meditate on the Bible primarily to get in touch with God's heart. The more we know God's heart, the more we know who we are in him, which will naturally result in acting like him.

HOW THE MOST IMPORTANT
PERSON IN YOUR LIFE SEES YOU

The truest statements about your transformed relationship with God are what God says about you in his Word. The Bible is where God opens his heart about who you are and how he sees you. If what you think or feel about yourself does not line up with how the Bible describes you, you are making yourself the victim of a case of mistaken identity.

It has been said that our self-concept is largely determined by what we believe the most important person in our lives thinks about us. If my (Josh's) wife tells me I'm a loving husband, I'll tend to believe her, because she is the most important woman in my life. If my (Sean's) father tells me I'm a caring son, I'll tend to believe him, because he is the most important man in my life.

So when God tells you there are certain things about you that are true, what should you do? If he is the most important person in your life, then how you think and feel about yourself will conform to his view. The ongoing change of your life in Christ is inextricably linked to how confidently you believe the truth of what God says about you.

Thirty-four-year-old Scott became a Christian in college, but he has lived under a dark cloud of guilt over his past sins ever since. As a teenager, Scott was involved in sexual immorality. After he trusted Christ, he changed his lifestyle because he knew immorality was wrong according to Scripture. But Scott could not escape the sense that God still condemned him for his past sin. He felt like a second-class Christian; he felt God would never trust him with an important ministry because of his teenage promiscuity. As a result he felt defeated most of the time.

Scripture declares that "now there is no condemnation for those who belong to Christ Jesus" (Romans 8:1). Who has the accurate picture of Scott's true identity: Scott, who sees himself as condemned and of little value? Or God, who has forgiven Scott for his sin and no longer condemns him? God, of course! We see God's heart concerning Scott's sin in Romans 8:1. Scott is forgiven, cleansed. Scott's inaccurate sense of himself began to change only as he believed the truth of what God said of him in that Scripture passage.

Apart from the Word of God, we will have great difficulty understanding how God sees us. It is like the man who had a friend who loved jigsaw puzzles. When the friend's birthday came around, the man bought two large puzzles as gifts. But as a joke, he switched the box tops on the two puzzles. The fellow who received the gift became totally frustrated as he tried to put the first puzzle together. Using the picture on the box top as a guide, he could not make any sense of the pieces inside. He found the second puzzle just as difficult, until his friend revealed the prank.

We experience similar frustration in understanding our position in Christ when we look at the wrong "box top." If you regard your feelings, judgments, and personal experiences as the criteria for determining who we are, you will struggle to put together your true identity in Christ. Our picture to go by is the Word of God. The more you are in tune with God's picture, the easier the pieces of your life will fit together to resemble that picture.

There are certain things true of you from the moment you trust Christ as Savior and Lord. The first two chapters of Ephesians provide a concentrated look at your attributes as a new creation in Christ. Remember, these statements from God's Word are *already* true of you because you are in Christ. They are part of your basic identity apart from how you might perform from time to time. This list shows how the most important person in your life sees you. The list is written in the first person so you can read the blessings as your own. We suggest you reread this list from Ephesians often to help you see yourself clearly as God sees you.

- I am blessed with every spiritual blessing (1:3).

- I was chosen before the creation of the world to be holy and blameless in God's sight (1:4).

- I was chosen to be adopted as his child through Christ (1:5).

- I have redemption through his blood (1:7).

- I am forgiven (1:7).

- I have received an eternal inheritance from God (1:11).

- I am identified as God's own by receiving the Holy Spirit (1:13).

- I am alive in Christ (2:5).

- I am seated with Christ in the heavenly realms (2:6).

- I am an example of God's grace (2:7).

- I am saved by his grace (2:8).

- I am God's masterpiece (2:10).

- I belong to Christ (2:13).

- I have direct access to God through the Spirit (2:18).

In addition to this concentrated dose in Ephesians 1 and 2, God's Word abounds with many other descriptions of how God sees you. (You can find a broader list of statements in Neil Anderson's book *Victory Over the Darkness*.)

Can you see more clearly what it means to be a new creation in Christ? One of the keys to your transformed relationship with God is to acknowledge that something very good happened to you when you trusted Christ. In Paul's words, you have "clothed yourselves with a brand-new nature" (Colossians 3:10). You are not primarily what your parents, spouse, or friends say you are, even though many of them may be Christians. You are not what your negative emotions or condemned feelings may say you are. And you are certainly not what the godless culture says you are. You are who God says you are—nothing more, nothing less. The more you review, recite, and internalize the verbal picture God paints of you in Scripture, the better positioned you are to grow like that picture.[5]

LIVING OUT A CHANGED LIFE

Prior to mechanically powered tractors, plowing the land for farming was done with horses or oxen. But harnessing two oxen separately made it nearly impossible to plow a straight furrow because the oxen would not pull in unison. So a yoke was employed. A yoke was usually made of wood and consisted of a strong crossbar that spanned the backs of both animals. Extending downward from the bar were two U-shaped loops that fit around each ox's neck. The yoke actually bonded them together so they would walk side by side in step and pull the plow in unison.

Prior to receiving God's divine nature, we could not walk in step with Christ. We were not yoked with him, and we could not accomplish God's purpose. As Paul the apostle said, "No matter which way I turn, I can't make myself do right...When I want to do good, I don't. And when I try not to do wrong, I do it anyway" (Romans 7:18-19). What he needed, as all of us need, was God's imparted nature as a yoke enabling him to walk in unison with Christ.

Jesus extends this invitation to each of us: "Take my yoke upon you. Let me teach you, because I am humble and gentle, and you will find rest for your souls. For my yoke fits perfectly, and the burden I give you is light" (Matthew 11:29-30). When we are harnessed in Christ's yoke, he will teach us how to be motivated like him, think like him, and act like him. He wants us to know what his true nature is like and live it out yoked with him. But if we don't really know the characteristics of his nature and how it is to be acted out, it will be difficult for us to reflect it.

THE NATURE OF GOD DEFINED

Moses had gotten his instructions. While he was on Mount Sinai, God had provided exacting details for how sacrifices were to be offered. God's instructions were to be carried out to the letter.

On the first day of presenting the sin offering, burnt offering, and peace offering, Aaron's sons, who were the priests officiating at the sacrifices, put coals of fire in their incense burners in a way that directly contradicted God's commands. "So fire blazed forth from the LORD's presence and burned them up…Then Moses said to Aaron, 'This is what the LORD meant when he said, "I will show myself holy among those who are near me. I will be glorified before all the people"'" (Leviticus 10:2-3).

God's holiness could not tolerate sin, and he consumed the offenders with fire. Holiness is the fundamental descriptor of who God is. He is holy, and anything or anyone who is out of character with him is impure and unholy.

Some people have trouble grasping the concept of holiness. What does it really mean to say God is holy? To be holy is to be set apart from the unclean and impure things of life. God's holiness is reflected in his absolute perfection of goodness and righteousness. There is no imperfection of character or motive in God; he is the holiest of the holy, the purest of the pure.

No one compares to God's absolute holiness. When God spoke of himself as "I AM WHO I AM" (Exodus 3:14) he was defining himself by himself. He separated himself from all others because there was no other purer being he could compare himself to. Yet God said to his people, "You must be holy because I, the LORD your God, am holy" (Leviticus 19:2). Paul the apostle wrote, "God has called us to be holy, not to live impure lives" (1 Thessalonians 4:7). The very essence of God's nature is holy, and humans created in his likeness are designed to be holy too. We obviously cannot be holy in the absolute sense as God is, yet he does require us to be holy. So the question is, what exactly does holiness look like in the lives of fallen people who cannot be perfectly pure as God is perfectly pure?

If you were to crystallize the essence of what holiness looked like in a person's life it could be summed up in perhaps two words: "Godlike love." John, a disciple of Jesus, wrote, "God is love, and all who live in love live in God, and God lives in them. And as we live in God, our love grows more perfect. So we will not be afraid on the day of judgment, but we can face him with confidence because we are like Christ here in this world" (1 John 4:16-17).

John was very conscious of God's holy judgment when he wrote this. God is holy, and his holiness will ultimately consume everything that is unholy. But he said that when love lives in us and we live in love, we don't need to fear judgment "because we are like Christ here in this world." The divine nature of God's holiness is imputed to us. That is, since we as sinners lack holiness on our own, he shares his holiness with us when we submit to him. By that sharing he sets us apart and consecrates us as his holy people (Ephesians 3).

When we receive his holy nature we receive this pure love. That enables us to live his love out in relationship to others. So, one of the clear expressions of God's holiness in our lives is loving as God loves.

DEFINING GODLIKE LOVE

A lot of people know God is love and we are to love others as he does, but they lack a concise definition as to what Godlike love is. In 1 Corinthians 13, Paul gives a good description of what love does and does not do. "Love is patient and kind. Love is *not jealous* or *boastful* or *proud* or *rude*. Love does not demand its own way. Love is not irritable, and it keeps no record of when it has been wronged. It is never glad about injustice but rejoices whenever the truth wins out" (verses 4-6).

Paul also wrote that "love does no wrong to anyone" (Romans 13:10). Instead, we are to treat all people as we would like to be treated. Remember the Golden Rule? "Do for others what you would like them to do for you" (Matthew 7:12). Paul put it this way: "Each of you should look not only to your own interests, but also to the interests of others" (Philippians 2:4 NIV).

When Jesus was asked to identify the most important commandment, he said it was to love God and "love your neighbor as yourself" (Matthew 22:39). Paul gave us a specific application of this principle when he told husbands "to love their wives as they love their own bodies…No one hates his own body but lovingly cares for it" (Ephesians 5:28-29).

Drawing from these verses and others similar, we can derive a concise definition of pure Godlike love. *Love is making the security, happiness, and welfare of another person as important as your own.* Godlike love is giving and trusting, unselfish and sacrificial, secure and safe, loyal and forever. Its priority is to protect and provide for the loved one.

WHAT GODLIKE LOVE LOOKS LIKE

His time on earth was coming to an end. Jesus had spent the last few years pouring his life and teachings into his followers. Just hours before his death he met with them to celebrate Passover, and Scripture says, "He now showed the disciples the full extent of his love…He got up from the table, took off his robe, wrapped a towel around his waist, and…began to wash the disciples' feet" (John 13:1, 4-5).

Jesus had just taken on the role of a servant to wash the feet of his followers. And within that context he issues a new commandment: "A new command I give you: Love one another. As I have loved you, so you must love one another. By this all men will know that you are my disciples, if you love one another" (verses 34-35 NIV).

This was huge. God had written out Ten Commandments on tablets of stone for all to read and follow. Now Jesus was dictating the eleventh commandment to his disciples. You can't get much bigger than a commandment coming straight from the mouth of God. And this one command would be the mark of a true Christian. This "love one another as I have loved you" would be the universal identifier—the distinguishing brand—of Jesus' disciples. Loving as Christ loved would be a clear expression of God's holiness.

If Jesus had done nothing more than simply pronounce the command, these disciples might have raised the question, *Well, if we are to love each other like he loves us, just how has he loved us? What does that look like?* Jesus illustrated the command with a demonstration so they would see, firsthand, that to love another is to serve him. A few hours later, they would see love stretched out on the cross, dying in their stead.

Following Jesus' death and resurrection, God inspired the disciples and apostles to write out specific instructions to show what Christlike love looks like in our lives. Many of these instructions appear in the "one another" passages of Scripture. At least 35 times in the New Testament, we see a recurring word pattern—an action verb followed by the words "one another." These admonitions give us a much clearer picture of how Christ wants us to live out his divine nature of love in our lives. Consider the following list in light of *"love is making the security, happiness, and welfare of another person as important as your own."*

The "One Anothers" of Scripture

1. Love one another (John 13:34).

2. Accept one another (Romans 15:7).

3. Forgive one another (Ephesians 4:32; Colossians 3:13).

4. Be gentle to one another (Ephesians 4:2).

5. Be clothed in humility toward one another (1 Peter 5:5).

6. Weep with one another (Romans 12:15).

7. Live in harmony with one another (Romans 12:16).

8. Don't judge one another (Romans 14:13).

9. Be patient with one another (Ephesians 4:2).

10. Admonish one another (Colossians 3:16).

11. Greet one another (Romans 16:16).

12. Wait for one another (1 Corinthians 11:33).

13. Care for one another (1 Corinthians 12:25).

14. Serve one another (Galatians 5:13).

15. Be kind to one another (Ephesians 4:32).

16. Be devoted to one another (Romans 12:10).

17. Be compassionate toward one another (Ephesians 4:32).

18. Encourage one another (1 Thessalonians 5:11).

19. Submit to one another (Ephesians 5:21).

20. Make allowances for one another (Colossians 3:13).

21. Stimulate love in one another (Hebrews 10:24).

22. Offer hospitality to one another (1 Peter 4:9).

23. Minister gifts to one another (1 Peter 4:10).

24. Rejoice with one another (Romans 12:15; 1 Corinthians 12:26).

25. Don't slander one another (James 4:11).

26. Don't grumble against one another (James 5:9).

27. Confess your sins to one another (James 5:16).

28. Pray for one another (James 5:16).

29. Fellowship with one another (1 John 1:7).

30. Don't be puffed up against one another (1 Corinthians 4:6).

31. Carry one another's burdens (Galatians 6:2).

32. Honor one another (Romans 12:10).

33. Depend on one another (Romans 12:5 AMP).

34. Prefer one another (Romans 12:10).

35. Comfort one another (2 Corinthians 1:4).

Living Out the "One Anothers"

For me (Josh), living out Christ's holiness through loving others was not easy. I still needed to shed some of those grave clothes that clung to me after my conversion.

Because I grew up in the home of an alcoholic, I developed a pattern of behavior that made me what psychologists call a "rescuer." Each time I saw my father try to hurt my mom, I would step in and try to prevent her from being hurt. This became a lifelong pattern—I always tried to rescue hurting, struggling people. When I became a Christian I continued this unhealthy pattern, but I didn't realize it was unhealthy. I thought it was compassion. I thought I was exhibiting Godlike love.

Take the "one another" scripture that says we are to "bear one another's burdens, and thereby fulfill the law of Christ" (Galatians 6:2 NASB). Because of my rescuer compulsion I felt emotionally responsible to solve the person's problem by removing whatever burden they had. Through wise and spiritual counsel, I learned bearing another person's burden doesn't mean taking responsibility for that person's problem or hurt. It means being responsible *to* them—to comfort, encourage, and support them in their pain or difficulties.

It was God's Word that ultimately brought me around. The key to my turnaround was the passage I discovered just three more verses down the page. Galatians 6:5 declares, "Each one will bear his own load" (NASB).

Now, this may sound confusing at first, but it comes together when you consider that there is an important difference between a "burden" and a "load." The Greek word for "burden" is a word that means "boulder," a large rock that is too heavy to carry alone. We all face situations that bear down heavily on us, and we need someone to come alongside and share our burden. The situation causing the burden could be an injury, an illness, the death of a loved one, or the loss of a job, for example.

The Greek word for "load" is different, however; it refers to a military knapsack, the supply pack a soldier would carry into the field. It represents something each of us is responsible for carrying. It's yours, it's assigned to you, and bearing it is your responsibility alone. It's the idea Paul was conveying when he said, "Each of us will have to give a personal account to God" (Romans 14:12).

We all have personal responsibilities, and when we fail in our responsibilities—by using poor judgment, making wrong choices, or harboring bad attitudes—we must face up to the consequences. To step in and remove the natural and corrective consequences of people's irresponsible behavior may rob them of valuable lessons—lessons that may be critical for their continued growth and maturity.

I can't possibly express how valuable this revelation from God's Word has been to me. When I realized that loving others as Christ loved didn't mean I was responsible *for* other people, then I was set free to be responsible *to* others—and particularly to those who were hurting. I then began looking for opportunities to allow his comfort, encouragement, and support to flow through me to others because I knew that in doing this I was loving others as Christ loves me.

Take time this week to *do* one or more "one anothers" of Scripture. With a servant's heart and in a spirit of sacrifice, make someone's security, happiness, and welfare as important as your own. As you do this you will be expressing your transformed, Christlike nature.

We close with Paul's admonition:

> Since God chose you to be the holy people whom he loves, you must clothe yourselves with tenderhearted mercy, kindness, humility, gentleness, and patience...And the most important piece of clothing you must wear is love. Love is what binds us all together in perfect harmony. And let the peace that comes from Christ rule in your hearts. For as members of one body you are all called to live in peace (Colossians 3:12, 14-15).

WE WORSHIP ONE GOD IN THREE PERSONS

The Jordan River water was cold. John, now waist deep, reached out his hand to yet another penitent waiting to be baptized. As soon as the man faced him, John recoiled. *No, this isn't going to work,* he thought. Looking his cousin straight in the eyes he said, "'I am the one who needs to be baptized by you…so why are you coming to me?' But Jesus said, 'It should be done, for we must carry out all that God requires.' So John agreed to baptize him" (Matthew 3:14-15).

John had baptized many people in his short ministry, but what happened next was like nothing that had ever happened before. The moment Jesus, the Son of God, "came up out of the water, the heavens were opened and he saw the Spirit of God descending like a dove and settling on him. And a voice from heaven said, 'This is my dearly loved Son, who brings me great joy'" (verses 16-17).

There it was—an earthshaking phenomenon for all to see and hear. Three distinct persons of the Godhead made their presence known: God the Son being baptized, God the Father voicing pleasure in his Son, and God the Holy Spirit settling, like a dove, on the Son. Thus we are introduced to the three persons of God we call the Trinity.

The Trinity has existed eternally. Scripture records that all three of the persons of God were involved in creation. "In the beginning God created the heavens and the earth...And the Spirit of God was hovering over its surface" (Genesis 1:1-2). "In the beginning the Word already existed. He was with God, and he was God...He created everything there is. Nothing exists that he didn't make...So the Word became human and lived here on earth among us" (John 1:1-3, 14). "Then God said, 'Let us make people in our image'" (Genesis 1:26).

The question naturally arises, "Does the existence of the Trinity mean there are three different Gods? Or, is there one God who shows himself in three different roles or relationships—sometimes as a father, sometimes as a son, and at other times as a representative agent?" The Trinity is something altogether different. God is neither three separate, independent beings nor one being manifested in three different roles. God exists as three persons, yet one being. Christians have taught this doctrine of the Trinity from the first century on because Scripture clearly asserts our God is a triune Godhead—one God in three persons.

THERE IS BUT ONE GOD

Moses commanded, "Hear, O Israel: The LORD our God, the LORD is one" (Deuteronomy 6:4 NIV). Isaiah the prophet declared that God said, "Believe in me and understand that I alone am God. There is no other God; there never has been and never will be. I am the LORD, and there is no other Savior" (Isaiah 43:10-11). Over and over Moses and the prophets declared there was only one Almighty God of the universe.

God Is Father, Son, and Holy Spirit

Scripture also tells us that he coexists as three divine persons.

Jesus is the divine Son of God. This does not mean Jesus was created by God. In fact, Scripture tells us plainly he has always coexisted with God (see John 1:1-3). Paul the apostle declared Jesus to be deity: "Christ himself was a Jew as far as his human nature is concerned. And he is God, who rules over everything and is worthy of eternal praise!" (Romans 9:5). The writer of Hebrews says, "The Son reflects God's own glory, and everything about him represents God exactly" (Hebrews 1:3).

Therefore, God the Father coexists with God the Son. "Christ is the visible image of the invisible God. He existed before God made anything at all and is supreme over all creation. Christ is the one through whom God created everything in heaven and earth…He existed before everything else began, and he holds all creation together" (Colossians 1:15-17). The apostle Paul refers to both the Father and Jesus as God. "It is by the command of God our Savior that I have been trusted to do this work for him…May God the Father and Christ Jesus our Savior give you grace and peace" (Titus 1:3-4).

God the Father is deity. God the Son is deity. God the Holy Spirit is also deity.

The apostle Peter recognized this when he pointed out the wrongdoing of a man in the Jerusalem church (Acts 5:3-4). The Spirit has eternally coexisted with the Father and the Son and was present at creation (see Genesis 1:2). Jesus said, "I will ask the Father, and he will give you another Counselor…He is the Holy Spirit, who leads into all truth…When the Father sends the Counselor as my representative—and by the Counselor I mean the Holy Spirit—he will teach you everything" (John 14:16, 26). Jesus called his coexisting Spirit "holy" because he is the Spirit of the Holy God. The Holy Spirit is the third person of the triune Godhead.

God Is Three Distinct Persons

The Scriptures quoted above tell us clearly that God is not merely one God with three different roles or relationships. He is one God in three persons interacting both with each other and with us. God the Father is a distinct person. God the Son is a distinct person. And God the Holy Spirit is a distinct person.

We have clear evidence that Jesus, God's Son, is a distinct person because he took on a human form while God the Father did not. But Jesus referred many times to his Father God as a person. He said he was with a person—his Father—before he was born a man (John 8:38). He said this person—his Father—sent him into the world (17:18). He said there were many rooms in his Father's house (14:2). He prayed to his Father (17:1).

Jesus also referred to the Holy Spirit as a person many times. He used the pronoun "he" when referring to him. Jesus said, "When the Spirit of truth comes, he will guide you into all truth. He will not speak on his own, but will tell you what he has heard. He will tell you about the future. He will bring me glory by telling you whatever he receives from me. All that belongs to the Father is mine; this is why I said, 'The Spirit will tell you whatever he receives from me'" (John 16:13-15). Jesus also referred to all three persons of the Trinity when he told his followers to make disciples, "baptizing them in the name of the Father and the Son and the Holy Spirit" (Matthew 28:19).

Some people believe the Holy Spirit is simply the influence of good and not a separate entity. This assertion seems to fly in the face of the fact that Jesus certainly referred to him as a person. Paul the apostle indicates the Holy Spirit has a mind, saying, "He who searches our hearts knows the mind of the Spirit" (Romans 8:27 NIV). Scripture also tells us he can feel. We are not to "bring sorrow to God's Holy Spirit by the way you live" (Ephesians 4:30). The Holy Spirit makes choices as to who will receive what spiritual gifts. "It is the one and only Holy Spirit who distributes these gifts" (1 Corinthians 12:11). Also, Peter told Ananias, "You lied to the Holy Spirit" (Acts 5:3). Ananias wasn't lying to an influence; he was lying to a person. Peter said to him, "You weren't lying to us but to God" (Acts 5:4).

THE ONENESS OF THE TRINITY

God exists as three distinct persons, yet he is one being. Each person—the Father, the Son, and the Holy Spirit—has a separate identity while enjoying the same essence of nature as the others, not merely similar natures in different roles. The Trinity is one God who eternally coexists as three persons. God is, was, and always will be. He is almighty, perfect, holy, light, and love. The Father, Son, and Holy Spirit as three distinct persons share this one substance and essence of being God.

There is no perfect analogy that captures the Trinity, which shouldn't surprise us since God is utterly unique in his character. One of the most popular illustrations is water, which has a common substance but three states—solid, liquid, and gas. If you put an ice cube in a beaker and heat it, you will see a solid melting into liquid and then rising into a gas. As this operation is in process, you will have all three states of the H_2O chemical coexisting.

Like all illustrations, this helps to a degree, but it ultimately falls short. How so? In this example, the same water goes through three different states.

If we apply this to the Trinity, it would be like God being one person who goes through the "state" of being the Father, then the "state" of being the Son, and then the final "state" of being the Holy Spirit. Clearly this is not what Scripture teaches about God's character, because such transformation denies the distinctions in personhood between the Father, Son, and Holy Spirit.

Other popular illustrations include a three-leaf clover, a cube with three dimensions, and a person who is (for example) a father, teacher, and coach. Each of these may help us understand part of the Trinity, but none capture what the Bible teaches—there is one God in being who eternally exists as three persons. While, again, there is no analogy that perfectly captures the Trinity, this does not mean the biblical view contradicts. If the view was that there was one God and three Gods, then it would contradict. If the view was that there was one person and three persons, it would contradict. But the biblical view maintains there is one being (unity) and three persons (distinction). While there may be a mysterious element to the Trinity, there is no contradiction.

The Eternal Relationship of Love

God, consisting as he does of three persons, shows us that intimate relationship has existed eternally. God didn't create humans because he needed a relationship; he already had relationship. He exists in relationship. The Father has always infinitely loved the Son. The Son has always infinitely loved the Father. The Holy Spirit has always infinitely loved both the Father and the Son. A continuous cycle of perfect relationships is ever being experienced within the Godhead. Just as God *is* holy and righteous, God is also relationship. While we are unable to comprehend such a perfect and continuing relationship fully, all of us long to experience this kind of relationship ourselves.

God's unity in the Trinity is the secret to unlocking how relationship is meant to work.

As individuals without relationship we stand alone, incomplete in the darkness of seclusion. This is not how we were meant to exist, and that is why God said, "It is not good for the man to be alone" (Genesis 2:18). He had made humans in his image, and that image was reflective of the perfect relationship of the three persons of the Godhead—a relationship so infinitely loving that it produced an intimate oneness, a bonding, a togetherness, and a connectedness unparalleled in the universe. What he desired for his human creation was a oneness similar to his. So instead of leaving his newly created man alone, he made another human by drawing substance from the man's side. God then said, "This explains why a man leaves his father and mother and is joined to his wife, and the two are united into one" (Genesis 2:24).

Just as God is one in relationship by his very being, so he created us to be in relationship with him and others. The oneness of the Trinity serves as more than our master model for such oneness. God's unity in the Trinity is the secret to unlocking how relationship is meant to work. While we may never comprehend God's oneness in relationship in an absolute sense, we can gain enough insight into this mystery to experience the true meaning of relationship. Exploring the mystery of the Trinity is like peering into the very heart of God.

Listen to Jesus talk about his Father. First he says, "I assure you, the Son can do nothing by himself. He does only what he sees the Father doing" (John 5:19). "I do nothing on my own, but I speak what the Father taught me" (8:28). Jesus is God, yet he doesn't speak or act on his own; in fact, Jesus declares, "The words I say are not my own, but my Father who lives in me does his work through me" (14:10).

The strange thing is that in spite of the fact that Jesus insists he cannot do anything by himself, he goes on to say, "The Father leaves all judgment to his Son" (5:22). "For you [the Father] have given him [the Son] authority over everyone in all the earth" (17:2). God the Father gave his Son all the authority and power to do anything he wanted. Jesus even had power over his own life. He said, "I lay down my life voluntarily. For I have the right to lay it down when I want to and also the power to take it again" (10:18).

Jesus is God, the actual creator of the universe and the one who sustains it (see Hebrews 1:2-3). Yet he says he can't do anything on his own. Why? Does Jesus feel somehow restricted by God his Father? Is he so rigidly under the Father's authority that he dares not do anything without his Father's permission? Not at all. The relationship is one in which the Father is pleased to give everything to the Son because he loves his Son. The Son is pleased to give everything to the Father because he loves his Father. Jesus prayed, "Father, the time has come. Glorify your Son so he can give glory back to you...And I give myself entirely to you" (John 17:1, 19). "The one who sent me is with me," Jesus said. "He has not deserted me. For I always do those things that are pleasing to him" (8:29).

Incomprehensible Unity

It is this infinite love in perfect relationship that produces a oneness beyond our comprehension. It is not a relationship with a leverage of power and authority. It is not some hierarchical chain of command. It is a circle of relationships that looks out for the best in each other because of a deep abiding love for one another. In their infinite love, the three persons of the Trinity are so intent on pleasing one another that the very essence of their beings is indistinguishable. Speaking in math terms, they are one to the infinite power.

Jesus said, "The Father and I are one" (John 10:30). He goes on to help us understand what this infinite love does to their relationship. "I am in the Father and the Father is in me" (14:11). He's talking about a perfect oneness, a bonded relationship that actually fuses them together to the point that Jesus can accurately say, "Anyone who has seen me has seen the Father" (14:9).

Let's ponder that statement for a moment. Jesus is saying his relationship with his Father is so intimate that if you see him, if you talk to him, if you trust him, if you please him, you are seeing, talking, trusting, and pleasing the Father (see John 12:44). That is oneness!

In our love relationships, we as humans try to share the joy and pain of those we love. Yet we do that imperfectly. We try to anticipate the needs of our children and meet them, yet we do that imperfectly. We try and understand the dreams and expectations of our spouses, yet we do that imperfectly. But within the Godhead, the Father perfectly anticipates the needs of the Son. The Son perfectly understands the expectations of the Father. The Holy Spirit perfectly shares the joys and pain of the Father and the Son.

It is hard to grasp, but this loving relationship between the Father, the Son, and the Holy Spirit is such an intimate oneness that they feel the same, give the same, love the same, and so on. We know, for example, God so loved the world that "he gave his only son" to die for us. Yet Jesus said, "I lay down my life voluntarily" (John 10:18). So which is it? Did the Father give his Son to die or did the Son decide on his own to give his life? To us it seems the two options are mutually exclusive. Both cannot be true. The difficulty resides in the fact that we think as individuals rather than as a coexistence in perfect harmony with another. The answer is that both the Father took the initiative to give out of his love and the Son took the initiative to give out of his love, because the two are of one nature. We suggest the incomprehensible oneness of the Godhead is not so much a result of God's awesome power as it is the divine love shared within the Trinity.

Consider this—Paul said we can know the secret things of God "because God revealed them to us by his Spirit, and his Spirit searches out everything and shows us even God's deep secrets" (1 Corinthians 2:10). He goes on to say, "But we can understand these things...for we have the mind of Christ" (1 Corinthians 2:15-16). So which of the Godhead shows us the secrets of God?

Paul understood that when we have God's mind and his wisdom, we have the mind and wisdom of God the Father, God the Son, and God the Holy Spirit—because all three are in perfect relationship. So when you experience one, you experience all three. This isn't the same as saying all three members of the Godhead are simply interchangeable. Each person is distinct, yet they are in such perfect harmony and oneness of relationship that to know one, his nature and being, is to know the others.

Paul said to the church at Ephesus, "I fall to my knees and pray to the Father...I pray that from his glorious, unlimited resources he will give you mighty inner strength through his Holy Spirit. And I pray that Christ will be more and more at home in your hearts as you trust in him" (Ephesians 3:14, 16-17). Then he goes on to say, "May your roots go down deep into the soil of God's marvelous love...Then you will be filled with the fullness of life and power that comes from God" (verses 17-19). So whose love are we experiencing? Paul makes it clear that it is the love of God—who is Father, Son, and Holy Spirit.

Granted, it is impossible for us to fully comprehend the Trinity. We can't muster up enough imagination to grasp such a perfect union of love and relationship. We tend to think of relationships in terms of position, hierarchy, authority, and who is responsible to fulfill what roles. But in God we see three persons in perfect relationship and harmony because their nature is one. The Father so loved the world that he gave his Son. The Son so loved his Father that he gave his life. The Holy Spirit so loved the Father and the Son that he gave us his Spirit (see Romans 5:5). And together they—one God—demonstrate a perfect love toward us.

Paul said, "May you experience the love of Christ, though it is so great you will never fully understand it" (Ephesians 3:19). We will "never fully understand it," yet the triune nature of God has been manifested to us. We see God's handiwork of creation; he revealed himself in the flesh for our salvation; and we experience his empowering presence through his Spirit.

Therefore:

> *We believe the truth that there is one God who is eternally coexisting as the Father, Son, and Holy Spirit in a perfect relationship of oneness.*

"'I am the Alpha and Omega—the beginning and the end,' says the Lord God. 'I am the one who is, who always was, and who is still to come, the Almighty One'" (Revelation 1:8). Such an almighty, awesome, and powerful God is too frightening to look upon, for God said, "no one may see me and live" (Exodus 33:20). Yet the miracle of the Trinity gives us access to this amazing God. Remember, Jesus said, "Anyone who has seen me has seen the Father!" (John 14:9). And because the Father has sent the Holy Spirit, we can know the entire Godhead on a personal basis.

Previously we have provided evidence for the Almighty God of the universe and also for Jesus, the Son of God. Next we will provide evidences for God the Holy Spirit, for it is the Holy Spirit who enables us to experience God. Keep in mind that the Holy Spirit, just like the Father and the Son, is a divine person. The Holy Spirit is not a force but the *third* person of the Trinity.

EVIDENCE THAT THE HOLY SPIRIT EXISTS

Amazed. Confused. Not understanding. Uncomprehending. This is how the disciples must have been conflicted as Jesus spent his last moments with them after his resurrection. When he said he was going back to his Father, it must have saddened them. Yet in spite of the fact that he was leaving, he also said, "Be sure of this: I am with you always, even to the end of the age" (Matthew 28:20).

What an apparent contradiction! But because of the mystery and perfect relationship of the Trinity, Jesus would be with them through the presence of the third person of the Trinity, the Holy Spirit. "And now I will send the Holy Spirit," Jesus said, "just as my Father promised" (Luke 24:49).

Ten days later, as the disciples and others (about 120 believers) were gathered in prayer, something extraordinary happened. It is a matter of historical record. The book of Acts explains that "there was a sound from heaven like the roaring of a mighty windstorm in the skies above them, and it filled the house where they were meeting. Then what looked like flames or tongues of fire appeared and settled on each of them. And everyone present was filled with the Holy Spirit and began speaking in other languages, as the Holy Spirit gave them this ability" (2:2-4).

Jews from many nations had gathered in Jerusalem for the annual festival of Shavuot (*Pentecost* in Greek), and they came running out to see what all the commotion was about. To their surprise, they heard "their own language being spoken by the believers" (verse 6). Then Peter stepped forward and said, "What you see this morning was predicted centuries ago by the prophet Joel: 'In the last days, God said, I will pour out my Spirit upon all people. Your sons and daughters will prophesy, your young men will see visions, and your old men will dream dreams'" (verses 16-17). Peter continued with a message about Jesus dying and being raised to life again for the forgiveness of sin. And that day about 3000 people became followers of Christ.

Later, Peter and John went to the temple for afternoon prayers and saw a crippled man begging for money. Peter told him, "I don't have any money for you. But I'll give you what I have. In the name of Jesus Christ of Nazareth, get up and walk" (3:6). Amazingly, the lame man leaped up and began praising God. The disciples went throughout the city preaching and doing many miracles in the name of Jesus through the power of the Holy Spirit.

GOD AT WORK THROUGH HIS SPIRIT

What started as a band of 120 followers of Jesus grew to thousands within weeks. The message of Jesus spread beyond Jerusalem like wildfire. It was happening exactly as Jesus had said it would. "When the Holy Spirit has come upon you, you will receive power and will tell people about me everywhere—in Jerusalem, throughout Judea, in Samaria, and to the ends of the earth" (Acts 1:8).

Transformed lives, answers to prayers, miracles performed in Jesus' name are all a result of the workings of the third person of the Trinity—the Holy Spirit.

Previously frightened disciples had become bold preachers of Jesus and his message. They performed signs and wonders. The message they proclaimed resulted in millions of lives being transformed. This was not a result of a vague, undefined influence of good, or some mystical force. It was God the Holy Spirit at work. And by the third century over 20 million people had made claim to the transforming power of Christ through the Holy Spirit.[1] All this enormous growth in Christianity is evidence of God sending his promised Comforter. And for over 2000 years every true believer of Jesus has been a testimony to the living proof that the Holy Spirit is a real person who is active in the lives of people. Transformed lives, answers to prayers, miracles performed in Jesus' name are all a result of the workings of the third person of the Trinity—the Holy Spirit.

Jesus himself said he would never leave us, but he clearly sits at God's right hand in heaven after his ascension (see Acts 1–2). Yet we know he is in our hearts through the power of his Holy Spirit. In fact, Jesus said, "When I am raised to life again, you will know that I am in my Father, and you are in me, and I am in you" (John 14:20). That means the one God in his fullness dwells within us and us within him through the power of the Holy Spirit.

We might say that after Jesus ascended into heaven to sit at the Father's right hand, God the Holy Spirit became the interactive agent of God to us.

Jesus said, "The Father sends the Counselor [Holy Spirit] as my representative" (John 14:26). But he is more than just a being for us to know about intellectually. Someone has suggested that when the Holy Spirit was poured out, the word *God* was not only a noun—it also became a verb. Rather than just learning who God is or following the teaching of Jesus impersonally, the Holy Spirit brings God actually into our lives. He is the active, moving nature of God that impels us to action. God the Holy Spirit is about living, loving, responding, enjoying, embracing, comforting, supporting, accepting, encouraging, respecting, disciplining, growing, empowering, and myriad other such verbs. He demonstrates himself even in our capacity to love as God loves. "If we love each other," John said, "God lives in us, and his love has been brought to full expression through us. And God has given us his Spirit as proof that we live in him and he in us" (1 John 4:12-13).

The Holy Spirit is real. He evidenced himself powerfully on the Day of Pentecost two millennia ago. And his Spirit is additional proof that we live in him, for the "Holy Spirit speaks to us deep in our hearts and tells us that we are God's children" (Romans 8:16).

Because of these things we can confidently know the truth that God the Holy Spirit exists. And because he is the active and interactive person of the Trinity that dwells within us, he is infinitely relevant to our lives.

THE PURPOSE OF THE HOLY SPIRIT IN OUR LIVES

All of us have experienced imperfect relationships to some degree or another. It's hard to imagine relationships that aren't to some extent skewed by focusing too heavily on performance, control, rules, obedience, expectations, obligations, and so on. Too often relationships consist of little more than people trying to get their needs met by one another. Much of the way we approach relationships has been programmed from early childhood. Sadly, what many of us have experienced isn't God's idea of what an intimate relationship is all about.

God's idea of an intimate relationship is about giving, yielding, trusting, and regarding another's concerns to be as significant as our own. It's about finding joy in pleasing others, and first and foremost, about pleasing the one who died for us. "Those who are dominated by the sin nature think about sinful things, but those who are controlled by the Holy Spirit think about things that please the Spirit" (Romans 8:5).

When God redeemed us he intended more than just to save us from eternal death. He plans to restore us to live as we were meant to live—in an intimate relationship with him and with one another. And that restoration begins at the moment of conversion.

But for us to live out God's idea of intimate relationships, many of us will need to be reprogrammed with the true meaning of relationships. We are by birth self-reliant, self-centered, and self-condemning. On top of inborn tendencies, many of our childhood models have programmed us with patterns that work against forming relationships based on giving, trust, yielding, and so on.

So how does God go about reprogramming our hearts and minds to live out his kind of relationships? Jesus could have just said, "Read about how I lived my life and then go live yours the same way." He could have given us a 12-step plan to intimate relationships. Or he could have told us to "practice, practice, practice." Instead, he sent himself in the person of the Holy Spirit so we could become an intimate part of God's relational unity. And the more we participate in the Triune relationship the more we are empowered to live and love and relate like he does.

The indwelling presence of the Holy Spirit is given to us to accomplish at least five relevant things in our lives.

1. To Make Us One with God

"When you believed in Christ, he identified you as his own by giving you the Holy Spirit, whom he promised long ago" (Ephesians 1:13). The purpose of that relationship isn't just to give you a home in heaven; the Holy Spirit is there to form a relationship of intimate oneness between you and God.

Jesus prayed to his Father for his disciples and for you "that they will be one, just as you and I are one Father—that just as you are in me and I am in you, so they will be in us...I in them and you in me, all being perfected into one" (John 17:21, 23). The Holy Spirit takes up residence in your life with the intent to create a miraculous oneness like that which exists in the Trinity.

The Holy Spirit hasn't come just to live in you, however. You are to also live in him. Jesus said, "They [each follower of Christ] will be in us." "God has given us his Spirit as proof," the apostle John said, "that we live in him and he in us" (1 John 4:13). You are invited to become an integral part of the perfect cycle of relationship enjoyed within the Trinity. It is then that this mutual giving of selves will result in an intimacy between you and God that makes living in his image as natural as breathing.

A woman named Martha struggled with the idea of giving of herself to God. She wanted to prepare a big dinner for Jesus, her special guest. Her sister, Mary, was supposed to be helping with the meal, but instead she was sitting at the feet of Jesus listening to what he had to say. So Martha marched in and said to Jesus, "'Lord, doesn't it seem unfair to you that my sister just sits here while I do all the work? Tell her to come and help me.' But the Lord said to her, 'My dear Martha, you are so upset over all these details! There is really only one thing worth being concerned about. Mary has discovered it—and I won't take it away from her'" (Luke 10:40-42).

What had Mary discovered that Martha didn't? She discovered there was just one priority in life worth being concerned about, and that was giving herself to Jesus. The Master was saying to Martha, "It's not your detailed endeavors I'm after; it's your personal devotion. If you give yourself to me, I'll show you how to live life as it was meant to be lived." Jesus may not be here in the flesh to teach us that, but he has given us his Spirit to lead us to a oneness—an intimate relationship that will instruct us how to reorder our lives to be pleasing to him. He is in us that our joy may be complete, and as we yield and give ourselves to him, we give him joy.

Living to give each other joy in a relationship is what intimacy is all about.

2. To Make Us Christlike

Our goal as a Christ-follower shouldn't be focused so much on acting like Jesus as on *being* in him and with him. It's about being in relationship with him through the Holy Spirit, which naturally results in acting like him. The Holy Spirit is in us to be with us and so we may be connected to God. Then we begin to see as Jesus sees, hear as Jesus hears, think like Jesus thinks, and ultimately act like Jesus acts. As we live in the power of the Holy Spirit, he exercises his power to live through us. He is our power source.

During my junior year in college, I (Sean) took a hike with some friends that is forever etched into my memory. I was the resident assistant for my college dorm and decided to take 18 of my floormates up to the mountains of San Diego. This would be a weekend retreat of bonding and fun. For a good challenge, we decided to hike the three miles to the top of Stonewall Mountain.

I had been living near the city lights of Los Angeles for only a couple of years, but already I had forgotten how dark a starry night can be in the mountains. Although we brought enough food, water, and other supplies for the trip to the top, we forgot to bring enough flashlights for a safe trek down. The sun set, dark clouds moved in, and by the time we gathered all our goods and set out for the trail, the night had become pitch black. When we pulled out the two flashlights we did bring, we found out *neither* of them worked!

Imagine 19 college men trying to climb down a dark, windy mountainside without the light needed to see what lay ahead. We began to feel a bit of panic, but we realized that if we were to make it down safely, we would have to work together. Since some of the path could be dangerous, all 19 of us held hands and inched our way down the mountain. Without the power of the flashlight, we were left to grope haltingly down the darkness of the mountain, feeling our way around boulders and crevasses. If we'd had good batteries, our trip would have been much less frustrating and dangerous. In fact, it would have been easy.[2]

When we give ourselves over to the Holy Spirit, he provides the power and light for us to walk in his ways. "When the Holy Spirit controls our lives, he will produce this kind of fruit in us: love, joy, peace, patience, kindness, goodness, faithfulness, gentleness, and self-control" (Galatians 5:22-23). The Holy Spirit living his life through us is the power source for our lives.

3. To Illuminate the Truth of Scripture

God's Word, through the power of his Spirit, "is useful to teach us what is true and to make us realize what is wrong in our lives. It straightens us out and teaches us to do what is right. It is God's way of preparing us in every way, fully equipped for every good thing God wants us to do" (2 Timothy 3:16-17). God's Word contains guidelines and insights that teach us to cultivate a deeper oneness with God. It also gives us principles that outline what

Christlikeness looks like in our lives. And it is the Holy Spirit who translates this truth into our lives.

"No one can know God's thoughts," Paul says, "except God's own Spirit. And God has actually given us his Spirit (not the world's spirit) so we can know the wonderful things God has freely given us" (1 Corinthians 2:11-12). As this passage tells us, another function of the Holy Spirit in our lives is to show us himself and his truth. He helps us understand who he wants us to be and how he wants us to love and live. The only way for us to know God's heart is for him to reveal it. And it is the Holy Spirit who makes that revelation come alive in our hearts.

The presence of the Holy Spirit in our lives does not mean pastors and teachers of the Word are not necessary. Some cite John 14:26 as support that we don't need Scripture, because the Holy Spirit will teach us everything. But the context of this passage reveals Jesus meant these words for his disciples, not necessarily for all subsequent believers. If the Holy Spirit were our sole guide to truth, then we wouldn't need the Scriptures, let alone books like *12 Crucial Truths*. We must not simply disregard all study or the wisdom of good teachers and rely solely on the internal leading of the Spirit. Because we are fallen, we are subject to being fooled by voices we think may be from God but are actually from darker sources. Paul warned the church at Corinth of false teachers who disguise themselves as apostles of Christ. "Even Satan can disguise himself as an angel of light" (2 Corinthians 11:13-14).

That is why it is crucial for us to heed the challenge of Paul to "be diligent [in] accurately handling the word of truth" (2 Timothy 2:15 NASB). God involves the wise and godly teachings of men and women around us to lead us into all truth. The Holy Spirit takes the truth of Scripture and ingrains it into our lives. Nonbelievers can often grasp the truth of the Bible, but it's only through the power of the Holy Spirit that the truth can take hold of our lives and transform our character.

4. To Empower Us for Service

"When the Holy Spirit has come upon you," Jesus said, "you will receive power and will tell people about me everywhere" (Acts 1:8). In fact, Jesus said that when the Holy Spirit came, his followers "will do the same works I have done, and even greater works, because I am going to be with the Father" (John 14:12). The Holy Spirit is our empowerment to do God's work.

"There are different ways God works in our lives," Paul said, "but it is the same God who does the work through all of us. A spiritual gift is given to each of us as a means of helping the entire church" (1 Corinthians 12:6-7). It is the Holy Spirit who distributes these gifts and then empowers us to use them—serving others, spreading the gospel message and, in short, doing extraordinary things for God's glory.

The writer of Hebrews tells us those who lived by faith and had God's Spirit on them "shut the mouths of lions, quenched the flames of fire, and escaped death by the edge of the sword. Their weakness was turned to strength. They became strong in battle and put whole armies to flight. Women received their loved ones back again from death" (11:33-35). He also points out that others "were tortured, preferring to die rather than turn from God and be free" (verse 35).

Whether God's Spirit empowers us to perform miracles, to die courageously as a martyr, or to live until we die a natural death, he is there in our lives to reflect his light to this darkened and needy world. Jesus said, "Don't hide your light under a basket! Instead, put it on a stand and let it shine for all. In the same way, let your good deeds shine out for all to see, so that everyone will praise your heavenly Father" (Matthew 5:15-16). Our focus on God's infilling of his Spirit in us does not center on the power to perform, but on praising the person of God. The Holy Spirit empowers us to give glory and honor and praise to the Father, Son, and Holy Spirit.

5. To Bring Meaning to Our Lives

We were made in God's image, and when we become intimate with God through his Holy Spirit we begin to live as God intended and be the person God designed. Paul said, "It's in Christ that we find out who we are and what we are living for" (Ephesians 1:11 MSG). "He [Christ] gives life and breath to everything, and he satisfies every need there is" (Acts 17:25). The Holy Spirit puts us on a journey to fulfill our purpose in life. Because when "his Holy Spirit speaks to us deep in our hearts and tells us we are God's children" (Romans 8:16), he is actually completing us. We were meant to live in an intimate relationship with God as his child. When we do this, through the power of the Holy Spirit, we find our true meaning and purpose.

Jesus told his disciples to obey his father's commands "so that my joy may be in you" and their joy would "be complete" (John 15:11 NIV). Jesus was saying he was the great "completer." His life completes ours; he gives us meaning; he provides us the fulfillment and joy in living; all because the Holy Spirit is God's agent for a continuous relationship between God and ourselves.

The relevance of the Holy Spirit to our lives is this: He creates in us an intimacy with God, transforms us into Christlikeness, leads us into all truth, empowers us for service, and brings true meaning and completion to life. That's the "what," but what about the "how"? The apostle Paul said to "let the Holy Spirit fill and control you" (Ephesians 5:18). But how do we do that so we can daily walk in the power of God's Spirit? What should be the attitude of our heart so we can reflect God's character and live a life pleasing to him? That is the subject of the next section.

HOW TO LIVE IN THE POWER OF THE HOLY SPIRIT

"Bob! Weave! Feint!" the trainer yelled. "Now duck!"

It was too late. Jim's sparring partner landed a left cross that put him on the canvas.

"You've got to block that punch," the trainer said as Jim slowly got off the mat. "Let's go at it again. You can win the fight next week if you master the techniques."

For weeks Jim had gone through a rigorous training regimen. Push-ups. Weightlifting. Sit-ups. Running. Punching bags. Sparring. Good diet. Jim was giving his all to win the Golden Gloves—the big prize of amateur boxing.

The big night came. It was 60 seconds into the fourth round. Jim bobbed and weaved and feinted. The left cross came flying at him, and he blocked it. With his opponent wide open, Jim responded with a left uppercut followed by a thunderous right hand. His opponent went down with a thud. The crowd cheered. Jim bounced back and forth waiting for the reeling boxer to get up. But he couldn't.

The referee waved his hands to signal the fight was over. And Jim leaped onto the ropes with his hands held high. He was victorious.

The power for Jim to overcome his opponent came from what he did—the push-ups, the running, the footwork, eating right, and consistent hard practice. Because in most endeavors, this kind of training and discipline is the way to achieve your goal. So many people think it's also the way to achieve an effective Christian life. But achieving an empowered, effective Christlike life requires an altogether different approach—even what some might call an upside-down approach. The power for living a Christlike life doesn't depend as much on what we do as it does on what we *don't* do.

The apostle Paul wrote to the Christians in Galatia, who were confused about what it took to live the Spirit-filled, or Spirit-empowered, life: "After starting your Christian lives in the Spirit, why are you now trying to become perfect by your own human effort?...I ask you again, does God give you the Holy Spirit and work miracles among you because you obey the law of Moses?" (Galatians 3:3, 5). Paul was explaining that performance and doing good didn't unleash God's power in their lives.

Yet on the other hand, Paul told Timothy to "spend your time and energy in training yourself for spiritual fitness. Physical exercise has some value, but spiritual exercise is much more important, for it promises a reward in both this life and the next" (1 Timothy 4:7-8). Here Paul seems to be saying that training and effort is required for living a Christlike life, just as it was required of the boxer Jim to win the Golden Gloves. So is the Christian life a matter of effort or merely a matter of plugging in the power of the Holy Spirit and sitting back to let him do the work? The answer is that certain efforts are needed and certain efforts are not. That leaves us with the question, which efforts are required and which ones are not?

We know our efforts or good works are useless to gain our salvation (Ephesians 2:8-9), yet there *is* something we must do. Paul explains: "The Spirit gives us desires that are opposite from what the sinful nature desires. These two forces are constantly fighting each other, and your choices are never free from this conflict" (Galatians 5:17). We fallen humans must contend with an entrenched sin nature that will plague us until we die. By receiving God's Holy Spirit, we have his new nature within us, but we still must contend with that sin nature, which is resistant to and in conflict with the Holy Spirit. That is why we must train ourselves in spiritual discipline and work hard at living godly. But this is not enough. No matter how rigorous our spiritual exercise and training, we will never gain the spiritual muscle to overcome the sin nature by our own power. So while spiritual discipline is necessary to keep us focused on God's will for our lives, effective godly living takes something more.

GIVING UP IS THE KEY

That is why Paul says, "Give your bodies to God. Let them be a living and holy sacrifice—the kind he will accept" (Romans 12:1). Instead of exercising our spiritual muscles in futile hopes of overpowering sin, Paul says to sacrifice yourself. He goes on to say, "Those who belong to Christ Jesus have nailed the passions and desires of their sinful nature to his cross and crucified them there" (Galatians 5:24). This means we are to nail even our "good work efforts" and self-reliance to the cross. Then we can say with Paul, "I have been crucified with Christ. I myself no longer live, but Christ lives in me. So I live my life in this earthly body by trusting in the Son of God, who loved me and gave himself for me" (Galatians 2:19-20).

It is when we are yielding to God that he can unleash his Holy Spirit in and through our lives.

We are to bring all our ambitions, desires, hopes, and dreams, however noble they may be, and sacrifice them to God. This means we give up on our own abilities, talents, goodness, and self-help efforts and consider them useless. We are then to place our trust in his goodness and in his strength. When we let God know we want to see him honored, not us, he sees and responds powerfully. It is when we are yielding to God that he can unleash his Holy Spirit in and through our lives.

After I (Josh) trusted Christ, I transferred from a state college to Wheaton College, a Christian school. But I really wanted to be in law school. I remember a visiting speaker telling us during a chapel service how we as students needed to bring all our gifts and talents before God and sacrifice them to him so we could be of service. He used Romans 12:1 as his text.

Many from the student body began going forward. I didn't. In fact, I ran out of the auditorium. I told God I'd be open to giving him my gifts and talents if I had any, but I didn't. I still struggled with my stuttering; I was terrible at English; I really questioned what, if anything, I could offer God that was of value. Then the thought passed through my mind: *What if you gave God all your limitations?*

One day I left class in frustration and started walking. A block away from the seminary campus, I heard a bell ring. It was exactly 11:45 a.m.—lunchtime at the local junior high. The sound of the bell startled me, and I stopped. The doors of the school burst open, and young people came flooding out. I backed up against a telephone pole on the sidewalk as kids rushed past me in every direction. I felt momentarily paralyzed. It was as if time had stopped for me and I was watching a sea of young people move in slow motion. In that moment, my mind went to the book of Isaiah, when God asked the prophet, "Whom shall I send? And who will go for us?" (Isaiah 6:8 NIV). In my mind, those words possessed a new context. It was as if God said to me, "These young people are in crisis; they are a hurting generation, and you have what I need to help them. So, 'whom shall I send, and who will go for us?'"

At that point I prayed, "God, all I sense that I have are my limitations. But if that is what you need, I'll give my all to you to reach this generation." Instantly, my struggle to have my own career in law ended. My sense of inadequacy ended. I felt the empowering presence of the Holy Spirit fill my life.

What I *didn't* do is promise God I'd get advanced youth leader training, practice my speaking, build a youth leader network, or hire a public relations firm in order to do great ministry for him. What I did do was give up trying on my own and sacrifice whatever I had to God, which wasn't much. And God in effect said back to me what he said to Paul, "My gracious favor is all you need. My power works best in your weakness" (2 Corinthians 12:9).

When we turn our backs on our self-reliance, our self-centeredness, or our self-condemnation and simply say, "I need you and I want to please you," God responds by living his life through us. He wants our obedience, of course, but first and foremost, he wants *us*. That is why we are told to "follow the Holy Spirit's leading in every part of our lives" (Galatians 5:25); "give yourselves completely to God" (Romans 6:13); "put aside your selfish ambitions" (Luke 9:23); and "[trust] Christ to give the victory" (1 John 5:4). It is our yielding and submitting to the Holy Spirit that allow his power and presence to be seen through our lives. Paul said, "This light and power that now shine within us—is held in perishable containers, that is, in our weak bodies. So everyone can see that our glorious power is from God and is not our own" (2 Corinthians 4:7). When we seek to honor him and not ourselves, he is pleased to exhibit his power and life through us.

Once we give up and sacrifice ourselves to him, the Holy Spirit empowers us. And that is when spiritual exercise and discipline comes into play. We cultivate good spiritual fitness by consistently studying God's Word, going to him in constant prayer, worshipping with fellow believers, and fulfilling all the "one anothers" of Scripture. But we are never to feel we are strong in ourselves. We must always remember the true source of our spiritual power.

King David struggled with his pride, his lust, and his self-centeredness. Yet in spite of all David's weakness, God said David was a man after his own heart. Why? Because David understood that God didn't want his self-serving works; he wanted his honesty and transparency. David wrote, "You would not be pleased with sacrifices, or I would bring them. If I brought you a burnt offering, you would not accept it. The sacrifice you want is a broken spirit. A broken and repentant heart, O God, you will not despise" (Psalm 51:16-17).

Because we are human and struggle with our sin nature, it means we must continually repent when we do wrong, turn from our wrongdoing (confess), and seek God's forgiveness. That is why James said, "Humble yourselves before God. Resist the Devil, and he will flee from you. Draw close to God, and God will draw close to you...Let there be tears for the wrong things you have done. Let there be sorrow and deep grief...When you bow down before the Lord and admit your dependence on him, he will lift you up and give you honor" (James 4:7-10).

When we give ourselves to God with all our faults, failures, and weaknesses, God gives himself to us in return. And with him in our lives in the person of the Holy Spirit, we are an empowered follower of Christ.

DISCOVERING THE SPIRIT-FILLED LIFE

Dr. Bill Bright, founder of Campus Crusade for Christ International, was one of the most Spirit-filled and empowered persons we have ever known. He developed a booklet that hundreds of thousands of believers around the world have used to understand the Spirit-filled life.* In the following pages we are including a replica of that booklet as we finish out this chapter.[3]

If you have yet to experience the Spirit-filled life, we invite you to trust in God, surrender to the Holy Spirit right now, and ask him to take control of your life. If you feel you have more to learn before you are ready to do this, we pray that reading the following booklet will lead you to open your life to him.

---

* The booklet is published by CruPress and is available in bulk at crustore.org.

Every day can be an exciting adventure for the Christian who knows the reality of being filled with the Holy Spirit and who lives constantly, moment by moment, under His gracious direction.

The Bible tells us that there are three kinds of people:

1. NATURAL PERSON

(One who has not received Christ)

"A natural man does not accept the things of the Spirit of God; for they are foolishness to him, and he cannot understand them, because they are spiritually appraised" (1 Corinthians 2:14).

Self-Directed Life
S – Self is on the throne
✝ – Christ is outside the life
● – Interests are directed by self, often resulting in discord and frustration

2. SPIRITUAL PERSON

(One who is directed and empowered by the Holy Spirit)

"He who is spiritual appraises all things... We have the mind of Christ" (1 Corinthians 2:15,16).

Christ-Directed Life
✝ – Christ is in the life and on the throne
S – Self is yielding to Christ
● – Interests are directed by Christ, resulting in harmony with God's plan

3. WORLDLY (CARNAL) PERSON

(One who has received Christ, but who lives in defeat because he is trying to live the Christian life in his own strength)

Self-Directed Life
S – Self is on the throne
✝ – Christ dethroned and not allowed to direct the life
● – Interests are directed by self, often resulting in discord and frustration

"Brothers, I could not address you as spiritual but as worldly—mere infants in Christ. I gave you milk, not solid food, for you were not yet ready for it. Indeed, you are still not ready. You are still worldly. For since there is jealousy and quarreling among you, are you not worldly? Are you not acting like mere men?" (1 Corinthians 3:1–3, NIV).

The following are four principles for living the Spirit-filled life.

God has provided for us an abundant and fruitful Christian life.

Jesus said, "I have come that they may have life, and that they may have it more abundantly" (John 10:10, NKJ).

"I am the vine, you are the branches. He who abides in Me, and I in him, bears much fruit; for without Me you can do nothing" (John 15:5, NKJ).

"The fruit of the Spirit is love, joy, peace, patience, kindness, goodness, faithfulness, gentleness, self-control; against such things there is no law" (Galatians 5:22,23).

"You shall receive power when the Holy Spirit has come upon you; and you shall be My witnesses both in Jerusalem, and in all Judea and Samaria, and even to the remotest part of the earth" (Acts 1:8).

The following are some personal traits of the **spiritual person** that result from trusting God:

- Love
- Joy
- Peace
- Patience
- Kindness
- Faithfulness
- Goodness

- Life is Christ-centered
- Empowered by Holy Spirit
- Introduces others to Christ
- Has effective prayer life
- Understands God's Word
- Trusts God
- Obeys God

The degree to which these traits are manifested in the life depends on the extent to which the Christian trusts the Lord with every detail of his life, and on his maturity in Christ. One who is only beginning to understand the ministry of the Holy Spirit should not be discouraged if he is not as fruitful as more mature Christians who have known and experienced this truth for a longer period.

Why is it that most Christians are not experiencing the abundant life?

Worldly Christians cannot experience the abundant and fruitful Christian life.

The worldly (carnal) person trusts in his own efforts to live the Christian life:

◆ He is either uninformed about, or has forgotten, God's love, forgiveness, and power (Romans 5:8–10; Hebrews 10:1–25; 1 John 1; 2:1–3; 2 Peter 1:9; Acts 1:8).

◆ He has an up-and-down spiritual experience.

◆ He cannot understand himself—he wants to do what is right, but cannot.

◆ He fails to draw on the power of the Holy Spirit to live the Christian life (1 Corinthians 3:1–3; Romans 7:15–24; 8:7; Galatians 5:16–18).

Some or all of the following traits may characterize the **worldly person**—the Christian who does not fully trust God:

• Legalistic attitude	• Fear
• Impure thoughts	• Ignorance of his spiritual
• Jealousy	heritage
• Guilt	• Unbelief
• Worry	• Disobedience
• Discouragement	• Loss of love for God and
• Critical spirit	for others
• Frustration	• Poor prayer life
• Aimlessness	• No desire for Bible study

(The individual who professes to be a Christian but who continues to practice sin should realize that he may not be a Christian at all, according to 1 John 2:3; 3:6–9; Ephesians 5:5.)

The third truth gives us the only solution to this problem . . .

Jesus promised the abundant and fruitful life as the result of being filled (directed and empowered) by the Holy Spirit.

The Spirit-filled life is the Christ-directed life by which Christ lives His life in and through us in the power of the Holy Spirit (John 15).

◆ One becomes a Christian through the ministry of the Holy Spirit, according to John 3:1–8. From the moment of spiritual birth, the Christian is indwelt by the Holy Spirit at all times (John 1:12; Colossians 2:9,10; John 14:16,17).

◆ *Though all Christians are indwelt by the Holy Spirit, not all Christians are filled (directed and empowered) by the Holy Spirit on an ongoing basis.*

◆ The Holy Spirit is the source of the overflowing life (John 7:37–39).

◆ The Holy Spirit came to glorify Christ (John 16:1–15). When one is filled with the Holy Spirit, he is a true disciple of Christ.

◆ In His last command before His ascension, Christ promised the power of the Holy Spirit to enable us to be witnesses for Him (Acts 1:1–9).

How, then, can one be filled with the Holy Spirit?

We are filled with the Holy Spirit by faith; then we can experience the abundant and fruitful life that Christ promised.

You can appropriate the filling of the Holy Spirit **right now** if you:

◆ Sincerely desire to be directed and empowered by the Holy Spirit (Matthew 5:6; John 7:37–39).

◆ Confess your sins. By **faith**, thank God that He **has** forgiven all of your sins—past, present, and future— because Christ died for you (Colossians 2:13–15; 1 John 1; 2:1–3; Hebrews 10:1–17).

◆ Present every area of your life to God (Romans 12:1,2).

◆ By **faith** claim the fullness of the Holy Spirit, according to:

His command: Be filled with the Spirit.

"Do not get drunk on wine, which leads to debauchery. Instead, be filled with the Spirit" (Ephesians 5:18, NIV).

His promise: He will always answer when we pray according to His will.

"This is the confidence we have in approaching God: that if we ask anything according to his will, he hears us. And if we know that he hears us—whatever we ask—we know that we have what we asked of him" (1 John 5:14,15, NIV).

Faith can be expressed through prayer . . .

How to Pray in Faith to Be Filled with the Holy Spirit

We are filled with the Holy Spirit by **faith** alone. However, true prayer is one way of expressing our faith. The following is a suggested prayer:

> Dear Father, I need You. I acknowledge that I have sinned against You by directing my own life. I thank You that You have forgiven my sins through Christ's death on the cross for me. I now invite Christ to again take His place on the throne of my life. Fill me with the Holy Spirit as You **commanded** me to be filled, and as You **promised** in Your Word that You would do if I asked in faith. I pray this in the name of Jesus. As an expression of my faith, I now thank You for directing my life and for filling me with the Holy Spirit.

Does this prayer express the desire of your heart? If so, bow in prayer and trust God to fill you with the Holy Spirit **right now**.

How to Know That You Are Filled (Directed and Empowered) by the Holy Spirit

Did you ask God to fill you with the Holy Spirit? Do you know that you are now filled with the Holy Spirit? On what authority? (On the trustworthiness of God Himself and His Word: Hebrews 11:6; John 17:17.)

Do not depend on feelings. The promise of God's Word, not our feelings, is our authority. The Christian lives by faith (trust) in the trustworthiness of God Himself and His Word. This train diagram illustrates the relationship among **fact** (God and His Word), **faith** (our trust in God and His Word), and **feeling** (the result of our faith and obedience) (John 14:21).

The train will run with or without the caboose. However, it would be futile to  attempt to pull the train by the caboose. In the same way, we as Christians do not depend on feelings or emotions, but we place our faith (trust) in the trustworthiness of God and the promises of His Word.

How to Walk in the Spirit

Faith (trust in God and His promises) is the only way a Christian can live the Spirit-directed life. As you continue to trust Christ moment by moment:

◆ Your life will demonstrate more and more of the fruit of the Spirit (Galatians 5:22,23) and will be more and more conformed to the image of Christ (Romans 12:2; 2 Corinthians 3:18).

◆ Your prayer life and study of God's Word will become more meaningful.

◆ You will experience His power in witnessing (Acts 1:8).

◆ You will be prepared for spiritual conflict against the world (1 John 2:15–17); against the flesh (Galatians 5:16,17); and against Satan (1 Peter 5:7–9; Ephesians 6:10–13).

◆ You will experience His power to resist temptation and sin (1 Corinthians 10:13; Philippians 4:13; Ephesians 1:19–23; 2 Timothy 1:7; Romans 6:1–16).

Spiritual Breathing

If you become aware of an area of your life (an attitude or an action) that is displeasing to the Lord, even though you are walking with Him and sincerely desiring to serve Him, simply thank God that He has forgiven your sins—past, present, and future—on the basis of Christ's death on the cross. Claim His love and forgiveness by faith and continue to have fellowship with Him.

If you retake the throne of your life through sin—a definite act of disobedience—breathe spiritually. Spiritual breathing (exhaling the impure and inhaling the pure) is an exercise in faith that enables you to experience God's love and forgiveness.

1. *Exhale:* Confess your sin—agree with God concerning your sin and thank Him for His forgiveness of it, according to 1 John 1:9 and Hebrews 10:1–25. Confession involves repentance—a change in attitude and action.

2. *Inhale:* Surrender the control of your life to Christ, and receive the fullness of the Holy Spirit by faith. Trust that He now directs and empowers you, according to the **command** of Ephesians 5:18 and the **promise** of 1 John 5:14,15.

GOD'S KINGDOM IS AT HAND

I t was a strange time for the Judean people living under the rule of the Roman Empire—a time of great religious fervor, and yet a time of extreme cultural despair. Religion flourished among the leaders, who proclaimed the Scriptures with zeal. Many of the Jewish people followed their teachings to the letter. Most claimed to believe in God. Yet religion seemed confined within the walls of their place of worship and had little visible effect on the culture at large. Poverty was rampant among tenant families and the disenfranchised slaves and servants. The Jewish religious leaders were doing little to help the poor—widows, orphans, beggars, social outcasts, those who were heavily taxed. In fact, the moral and ethical lives of the religious elite were not significantly different from the Roman culture in which they lived.

Within this sea of societal despair, a little band of men and women saw a ray of hope. It was their Messiah, the Christ they followed in the hope that he would lead their nation out of tyranny into a new kingdom of rightness and glory. These followers of Jesus saw him and his coming kingdom as a solution to every problem they faced. They stayed with him as he taught the people, healed them, fed them, and ministered to their needs. But all the while they looked forward to the glorious day when he would assemble an army, defeat the Roman oppressors, and establish a new kingdom of prosperity and freedom.

But to their utter horror, their Master was arrested, put through a mockery of a trial, and crucified. Their hope for freedom from Roman bondage was cruelly dashed and, in hiding, they despaired. But then on the first day of the following week their emotions soared again when the seemingly impossible happened: Jesus arose from the dead. The little band was now back on top, wild with the hope that their long-promised kingdom was about to be established at last. What better drawing card for an enthusiastic army than to be led by a man who had defeated death! They were ready; they were excited; they could hardly wait.

They met with Jesus many times after his resurrection, and he talked often about the kingdom. Finally they asked, "Lord, are you going to free Israel now and restore our kingdom?" (Acts 1:6). He replied that his Father set such dates as those, and it was not for them to know. Furthermore, he announced he was about to leave them again. But he promised to send his Holy Spirit, who would empower them to spread his kingdom "in Jerusalem, throughout Judea, in Samaria, and to the ends of the earth" (verse 8).

No doubt such answers confused these followers even more. Why wouldn't Jesus move to establish himself as ruler of his kingdom now? Why would he leave them in his moment of greatest triumph? And how could they establish the kingdom without its leader? Then Jesus actually ascended before their very eyes and disappeared into the clouds. We can only imagine their emotional turmoil as they turned and slowly descended the Mount of Olives and plodded dejectedly toward Jerusalem.

For a long while they must have walked silently, each nursing his own deep disappointment. Picture Philip finally breaking the heavy silence. "I just don't get it, Peter," he said. "I thought he was going to restore our kingdom."

"I don't get it either," Peter replied, shaking his head in despair. "Practically everything he taught us was about the kingdom, and I ate up every word. I mean, I was ready to leave my fishing business completely and follow him because I felt called to help make it all happen."

"Me too," James chimed in. "I never saw anyone put a finger on our problems like he did. He healed people, he loved them, he preached radical change, he fed the hungry. And my, how he took those religious leaders to task...They are exactly what he said they were, 'white sepulchers with dead men's bones inside.' He was our hope. I thought he was going to be the leader of a movement that would change everything."[1]

SPIRITUAL KINGDOMS AT WAR

Jesus was in fact the leader of a kingdom movement that would change everything. But Jesus' idea of the kingdom was considerably different than that of his disciples and the rest of the world. What was this "kingdom" Jesus talked about?

The Roman governor, Pontius Pilate, was trying to get some clarity on that issue when Jesus was brought before him. He asked Jesus if he was the king of the Jews. The governor was trying to determine Jesus' political ambition. "Then Jesus answered, 'I am not an earthly king. If I were, my followers would have fought when I was arrested by the Jewish leaders. But my Kingdom is not of this world'" (John 18:36).

This further confused Pilate. Jesus was not an earthly king? *What other kind of king is there?* the governor probably wondered.

Jesus' kingdom idea was not about toppling the Roman Empire. His opposition wasn't the Romans or even the Jewish leaders. His opposition was Lucifer, his archenemy. You see, once Adam and Eve sinned it was Satan that moved in and made this present world his kingdom, the kingdom of darkness.

When we live out Jesus' kingdom worldview, we are engaging in a mighty spiritual conflict to overthrow Satan's kingdom, the kingdom of this world, and establish Christ's kingdom in its place.

In effect, Satan snatched the kingdom of this world away from God's children. Two kingdoms now exist—the kingdom of this world, with Satan as its king, and the kingdom of heaven with God as its King. That means we are presently in the midst of a mighty conflict between two kingdoms warring against each other.

The war is between God and his ways and Satan and his ways. And we as followers of Jesus are to be fighting this war alongside Christ. "For we are not fighting against people made of flesh and blood," the apostle Paul told us, "but against the evil rulers and authorities of the unseen world, against those mighty powers of darkness who rule this world, and against wicked spirits in the heavenly realms" (Ephesians 6:12). When we live out Jesus' kingdom worldview, we are engaging in a mighty spiritual conflict to overthrow Satan's kingdom and establish Christ's kingdom in its place.

What God did when he entered human history 2000 years ago was to put Satan on notice that the kingdom of this world was going to be rescued and conquered by the kingdom of heaven. Jesus saw this world as a stolen kingdom temporarily under the dominion of an enemy whose rule would one day come to an end. As C.S. Lewis put it, Christians on the earth live in "enemy occupied territory."[2] But their loyalty is to their commander, Jesus, who is the leader of a spiritual resistance movement to free them from the rule of the usurper.

DIFFERING WORLDVIEWS

There will be a day when Jesus as conquering King will return to earth to establish his kingdom (our inheritance) as an eternal kingdom in heaven and on earth. But until that day comes, we continue to battle in the power of the Holy Spirit.

It is a spiritual war between two ruling concepts or worldviews. Just before his crucifixion Jesus made clear to Pilate that he had a kingdom to rule. "I was born for that purpose," Jesus said. "And I came to bring truth to the world" (John 18:37).

That truth is in stark contrast to the basic assumptions of this present world. On the first day of Jesus' public ministry he "began to preach, 'Turn from your sins and turn to God, because the Kingdom of Heaven is near,'" and from that point on "Jesus traveled throughout Galilee teaching in the synagogues, preaching everywhere the Good News about the Kingdom" (Matthew 4:17, 23).

The kingdom truth Jesus proclaimed wasn't about power and politics, earthly authority and thrones, or a permanent homeland and occupied territories. His truth message was about the heart and the sin nature, attitudes and actions, love and relationships. His message called for a complete transformation of a person's life. And that life-change was radical.

The people of that time hadn't heard anything like it. The Jewish law commanded them not to murder. Yet Jesus said that to hate a person is the same as murder. The Jewish law said not to commit adultery. Jesus said if you lust after a woman you are already an adulterer in your heart. The Jewish leaders taught to "love your neighbor and hate your enemy." Jesus said love your enemy. Jesus said you must die to live, give in order to get, bow down in order to rise up, be last in order to be first. It didn't make sense to a lot of people then, and it doesn't make sense to a lot of people today. That's the thing about Jesus' kingdom: It is a whole new way to see God, ourselves, life, and relationships. It is a worldview defined by God and his Word. And it only makes sense to those who have been spiritually transformed and are living an empowered life in loving relationship with God.

The apostle Paul said, "God has actually given us his Spirit (not the world's spirit) so we can know the wonderful things God has freely given us...We speak words given to us by the Spirit, using the Spirit's words to explain spiritual truths. But people who aren't Christians can't understand these truths from God's Spirit. It all sounds foolish to them" (1 Corinthians 2:12-14). Jesus' worldview accurately sees what sin and separation from God have done to humans and the natural world. The dilemma of the Judean people at the time of Christ and ours today isn't primarily a material, political, or physical problem that can be solved by material, political, or physical solutions. Yes, there are real physical, economic, social, moral, ethical, and environmental problems. Yet Jesus proclaimed that all our problems require a spiritual solution.

That spiritual solution didn't make sense to Jesus' disciples at that time, because their priorities were upside down. They had not yet embraced the kingdom-of-heaven worldview. But when the Holy Spirit filled them, they viewed life and death through a new lens. They saw that Jesus had in fact established his kingdom in the hearts of those who trusted in him. And now, instead of the one person of Jesus spreading the kingdom movement, there would be multiplied thousands of Christians—"little Christs"—proclaiming the message through how they lived. Because of Christ's death, resurrection, and the indwelling presence of the Holy Spirit, the leader of the kingdom movement would now be living and preaching the kingdom through the lives of his followers.

This kingdom worldview—the Way of Jesus—may be spiritual in nature, but it affects every area of life. Jesus' worldview unlocks a very specific way of life, a way of knowing what is really true, a picture of being what God meant us to be, and the power to live that out based on our relationship with God.

When we see and live by God's spiritual worldview, it combats darkness, injustice, and evil within the world. And that in turn brings resolution to the physical, economic, social, moral, ethical, and environmental problems of life. In fact, God's new world order, which Jesus spiritually imparts to his followers today, will someday be a permanent and all-pervasive world order established in a new heaven and a new earth where there is no more sin, pain, sorrow, or death. But until the final and permanent kingdom of heaven envelops the kingdom of earth, we are to be his witnesses, the combatants against the spirit of darkness, and the messengers of Jesus' worldview, which is to be lived out for all to see.

Therefore:

> *We believe the truth that Jesus' kingdom-of-God life and message forms our biblical worldview. It is this biblical worldview that not only provides us an accurate view of God, human history, life, relationships, death, and the world to come, but also a supernatural way to be and live in this present world.*

Over the past nine chapters we have begun to unlock the truths of a biblical worldview that we are to believe and live out. And while these truths are primarily spiritual in nature, they have a direct bearing on how we live and relate socially and culturally. Therefore, a kingdom-of-God worldview ought to be visibly influencing the world around us in a positive manner. And it has.

EVIDENCE THAT GOD'S KINGDOM HAS POSITIVELY INFLUENCED THE WORLD

"Religion poisons everything."[3] That is what contemporary atheist Christopher Hitchens has stated. Friedrich Nietzsche, a nineteenth-century atheist and author of *The Antichrist* wrote:

I *condemn* Christianity...It is, to me, the greatest of all imaginable corruptions; it seeks to work the ultimate corruption, nothing untouched by its depravity; it had turned every value into worthlessness, and every truth into a lie, and every integrity into baseness of the soul.[4]

To some, Christianity is the evil emperor imposing its will on the masses and threatening to suppress the free expressions of humanity. Although there are those past and present who, under the banner of Christianity, have waged war, enslaved people, and brought disgrace on the name of Christ, this is only a small, sad corner of the whole picture. It can be demonstrated that it is Jesus' kingdom worldview that has fostered more good and provided more positive contributions to society than any other force in history. If we were to highlight just a few of the positive influences of a biblical worldview they would include:

- the high value for human life
- care for the sick in creating hospitals
- literacy and education for the masses
- abolition of slavery in the Western world
- the elevation of women
- high standards of justice and civil liberties
- benevolence and charity work
- development of art and music
- the motivation and basis for modern science

Atheists and other detractors of Christianity fail to point out that it is the human propensity to be self-centered that has brought such misery and suffering upon the masses. Christianity is actually the antidote to this propensity, for it is the message and power of Christ that addresses the core problem of self-centeredness.

SELF-CENTEREDNESS VS. A
COMPASSIONATE HEART FOR OTHERS

Greed, corruption, abuse of power, and a basic disregard for others all spring from self-centeredness. Left unchecked, human nature will always revert to self-serving ways that seek to gain at another's expense. On the opposite side of the equation, making the interest and care of others as important as your own creates goodwill and harmony and meets human need. This is at the center of Jesus' teaching—it represents the very heart of God. Jesus said, "Do for others what you would like them to do for you. This is a summary of all that is taught in the law and the prophets" (Matthew 7:12).

Looking out for the interests of others, especially those in need, is the primary core value of Jesus' worldview. The expression used most often to describe Jesus' heart of love was that he was "moved with compassion." When he saw the two blind men...when he saw the leper...when he saw the sick and the hungry...he was "moved with compassion" (see Matthew 9:36; 14:14; 15:32; 20:34; Mark 1:41; 6:34; 8:2). And it is that Christlike heart that has empowered his followers to change the world for good.

Compassion toward others is a radical message now, and it was certainly so during the time of Christ. Within the Roman Empire during the first century, enslaving others was commonplace. Abortion was rampant. Parents abandoned virtually all babies that were deformed. Women had few rights and were considered the property of their husbands. Yet during this time James, a disciple of Jesus, stated: "Pure and lasting religion in the sight of God our Father means that we must care for orphans and widows in their troubles, and refuse to let the world corrupt us" (James 2:27).

These early Christians rejected the cultural practice of allowing abandoned babies and orphaned children to die on the streets. Instead, they would literally pick them up and adopt them into their own homes. What caused them to do this? It was the "moved with compassion" heart of their Lord being lived out in their lives. Early Christians believed everyone—including the poor, the homeless, the handicapped, the sick—was made in the image of God and had infinite value, dignity, and worth. By the third and fourth century this influence of Jesus' worldview was widespread. Sherwood Wirt, author of *The Social Conscience of the Evangelical,* documents what took place under the influence of Christianity by AD 500:

> Many permanent legal reforms were set in motion by Emperors Constantine (280-337) and Justinian (483-565) that can be laid to the influence of Christianity. Licentious and cruel sports were checked; new legislation was ordered to protect the slave, the prisoner, the mutilated man, the outcast woman. Children were granted important legal rights. Infant exposure was abolished. Women were raised from a status of degradation to that of legal protection. Hospitals and orphanages were created to take care of foundlings. Personal feuds and private wars were put under restraint...Branding of slaves was halted.[5]

It was Christians who cared for people society had largely forgotten. It was Christians who reached out to the blind, the lame, the elderly, the mentally handicapped, and those less fortunate when no one else would. And those efforts have continued until this day.

Often great works of compassion and charity are birthed by the dedication and sacrifice of a single follower of Jesus.

Basil of Caesarea was a fourth-century bishop in Asia Minor. He wrote, "I had wasted much time on follies and spent nearly all my youth in vain labors... Suddenly, I awoke as out of a deep sleep. I beheld the wonderful light of the Gospel truth, and recognized the nothingness of the wisdom of the princes of this world."[6] With a kingdom worldview, Basil championed the cause of the outcasts of society, working with the poor, the sick, and the prostitutes. He eventually built a large complex just outside of Caesarea called the Basiliad, which included a poorhouse, hospice, and hospital. Basil's compassionate heart of Christ and work with the needy was regarded at the time as one of the great wonders of the world.

William Booth came to the slums of East London in 1865 as an itinerant evangelist. At that time there were tens of thousands living on the streets, sleeping wherever they could find shelter. Food was scarce, and some 80,000 young women were prostituting themselves to survive.[7] William and Catherine

Booth mobilized an army (the Salvation Army) "to transform the living hell of the homeless into communities of self-helping, self-sustaining families."[8] Today the Salvation Army is one of the largest social aid providers in the world. The Christlike compassion of one couple over 150 years ago has been translated into a force of millions of volunteers aiding those in need.[9]

Jean-Henri Dunant was born in Geneva, Switzerland, in 1828 and raised by devout Christian parents. As a child he would accompany his mother on her visits to care for the poor and sick in Geneva's suburbs. In 1859 he was in Italy during the Battle of Solferino, where he witnessed nearly 40,000 wounded men begging for help on the battlefield. Moved with a Christlike compassion he persuaded the military leaders to release all captive medical personnel so they could tend to the wounded, friend and foe. Churches and private homes were transformed into makeshift hospitals. Dunant set about discussing formal procedures with the military for neutral medical aid during conflict for the alleviation of the suffering of the wounded.

His efforts resulted in the creation of a national Red Cross organization and the establishment of the Geneva Convention, which addressed how fighting armies would treat wounded soldiers. Today the International Federation of Red Cross is one of the world's largest humanitarian organizations providing disaster relief and emergency assistance.[10]

Jesus was "moved with compassion," and for centuries he has moved his followers with compassion to alleviate the suffering of the wounded and dying.

Beyond any shadow of a doubt Christianity has been a powerful redemptive force for good in our world. It is Jesus' kingdom worldview that has led his followers to establish protection for infants and the unborn, child labor laws, separation of church and state, liberty and justice, care for those in need, abolition of slavery in the Western world, and modern science. They have built universities and hospitals and brought about musical innovations and the advancement of the written word.[11]

And while the accomplishments of the Basils, William Booths, and Jean-Henri Dunants have been spectacular, these biblical worldview hall-of-famers represent only a fraction of the world-changing agents who have played a positive role. Currently, ministries such as Samaritan's Purse, World Vision International, and Compassion International are reaching out to bring hope and healing to many. I (Sean) have seen the positive impact of thousands of compassionate hearts reaching out to the former Soviet Union through Operation Carelift. This was an effort founded by my dad (Josh) to offer medical assistance and humanitarian aid to those in need. Today that simple effort has become an international relief agency called Unto.

It is Christ's kingdom worldview lived out in your everyday life and ours that is making a difference. As each of us embraces Jesus and lives out his ways, he is able to minister through us powerfully to make his prayer a reality:

> Our Father in heaven,
> may your name be honored.
> May your kingdom come soon.
> May your will be done here on earth,
> just as it is in heaven (Matthew 6:9-10).

DETERMINING YOUR KINGDOM WORLDVIEW

"I can't believe the gall of that guy," Mark said in a low tone as he sipped from his cup at an office coffee break.

"What guy?" Chris asked.

"Oh—Eric, the brilliant new VP of marketing." Mark's words dripped sarcasm. "He's out of his mind if he thinks he's going to get away with this."

"What's going on?" Chris asked impatiently.

"Well, he asked me last week to get him all my ideas for the upcoming product line," Mark began. "He knew I had spent a ton of time putting together some really great ideas. And I just found out this morning that he presented my ideas to the top brass and took all the credit for them."

"That's so wrong!" Chris responded.

"Don't think he's going to get away with it," retorted Mark. "I'm making it my personal mission to see that he goes down in flames!"

We've all been treated unjustly at some point in our lives. People take unfair advantage of others every day. And it's natural to want to see justice done. But the kingdom of this world has a means of obtaining justice that's quite different from that of the kingdom of heaven. In fact, the kingdom of this world sees and acts differently on every level than Jesus' kingdom. Jesus prayed these words to his Father concerning his followers:

> They do not belong to the world, just as I do not. I'm not asking you to take them out of the world, but to keep them safe from the evil one. They are not part of this world any more than I am (John 17:14-16).

Jesus prayed we would live in this world but not be a part of the way it thinks and lives. To do that requires we first have a relational transformation. We are to relate no longer to the beliefs and values of this world, but to Christ himself. And in that redeemed relationship we believe what he says and embrace his values. From Christ's new set of values we then act in a new set of ways. Instead of, for example, setting out to get even, we are to act as Christ did when he went to the cross. "He did not retaliate when he was insulted. When he suffered, he did not threaten to get even. He left his case in the hands of God, who always judges fairly" (1 Peter 2:23).

How Mark and the rest of us act in any given situation is based on a set of basic assumptions about how life works. And these assumptions define our worldview.

WHY YOUR WORLDVIEW MATTERS

We all have a worldview whether we know what it is or not—because everything we think and do is filtered through our assumption of how life works. We build those assumptions through a series of stages, and they finally emerge as actions.

First, all that you have learned and everything you know, even *how* you learned it, comes out of a relationship with someone or something, whether in person or online. You are a relational being, so much of what you are today is a direct result of who you've related to and how. Then, out of those relationships you establish what you believe. Relationships are the fertile ground in which beliefs grow. Then your beliefs shape what you value, and your values drive your actions (see diagram).

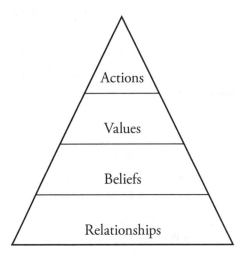

Let's look at Mark again. He grew up in an abusive home. His father wasn't around much, but when he was there, he was mean to Mark. At the age of 16, Mark fought back. He wasn't going to take it anymore. He moved in with his grandparents and finished high school. Now married and with a good job, he visits his parents now and again, but he's not close to them.

Every attitude we have and every behavior we exhibit comes from this developmental process of relationships, beliefs, and values.

Out of an unhealthy relationship with his father, Mark formed some beliefs about how the world works. He developed a belief that said people care only about themselves, and they will hurt you if you get in the way. From that belief came his values, which are to place great importance on your own turf and your own accomplishments and use them to further yourself. From that value came his mode of action, which was essentially self-protection. So Mark dealt with bullies and abusers with a "get smart, get even" course of action.

Most theologians and apologists would agree that our worldview comes out of our relationships, beliefs, and values. But that really doesn't define what a worldview is. Philosopher and theologian Dr. James Sire gave a clear definition from his book *The Universe Next Door.* He stated that a worldview is "a commitment, a fundamental orientation of the heart, that can be expressed as a story or in a set of presuppositions (assumptions which may be true, partially true, or entirely false) that we hold (consciously or subconsciously, consistently or inconsistently) about the basic constitution of reality, and that provides the foundation on which we live and have our being."[12]

Most of us arrive at our worldview without even knowing it. Yet Dr. Sire pointed out there are at least eight basic issues or questions that determine the assumptions we hold. You and I have probably already consciously or subconsciously answered those questions. If you have embraced the truths we have covered so far in this book, here is how you would answer the eight questions that define your worldview. These answers are stated in the first person as if you were answering them yourself.

1. *What is reality?* In other words, what do I consider to be ultimately real? When I stop to consider what makes anything in life real, I conclude it is God. Reality reflects the nature and character of a relational God who has created me as a relational being, and he defines my reality.

2. *How does the world exist?* I believe the personal Almighty God spoke into existence all that exists. He is the Creator God who formed the world around me and the reality in which I exist.

3. *What is a human being?* Humans are the personal creation of the relational God, made in his likeness and image with dignity and worth. Because God is three persons with infinite love in perfect relationship, I was created to live in loving relationship with God, myself, other humans, and the physical world I inhabit.

4. *Why is it possible to know anything?* An all-knowing God has given me, his creation, the capacity to know and be known. He is the source of all knowledge. All of eternity will not be enough for me to discover the infinite knowledge of God and his creation. I will only be able to scratch the surface.

5. *How do I know right from wrong?* Everything good and right and holy flows from God's character and nature, and only from them. To determine what is moral and ethical I must measure it by God and his Word as my universal standard of right and wrong.

6. *What happens to me at death?* First, I must die because sin has entered the human race and separated me from God, the life-giver. But because God is love and because he is merciful, he has provided a way for me to be brought back into relationship with him. Therefore, because I have accepted his provision (Christ's death on the cross), when I die physically I will live eternally with him in a new heaven and earth. Otherwise, I would be separated from him in an eternal aloneness—hell.

7. *What is the meaning of human history?* History is a meaningful sequence of events with which God interacts to move the human saga from a beginning, through a middle, and to an end. God created time, by which human history could be chronicled, and at the beginning of time he created the world and all there is. During the sequence of history since the fall of man, God is in the process of restoring all things to his original design. Sin and death will be done away with, and redeemed humans will forever live to glorify God in perfect relationship with him. The meaning of human history is ultimately the working out of God's purpose on the earth, which includes a purpose for my life culminating in eternity with him.

8. *What core commitments are consistent with my worldview?* I am committed to love and worship God with all my heart, soul, and mind and love my neighbor as myself. This means I am committed to seek to know God intimately; to love my first neighbor (my family), those within Christ's body, and those in the world around me; and to engage in Christ's mission to redeem the lost until his kingdom comes.

We propose that this biblical view of life makes sense out of all the confusion, chaos, and tragedies of this world. By adopting and affirming these truths, you have just defined your worldview. Next, we will discover how that biblical worldview defines you.

HOW YOUR WORLDVIEW DEFINES YOU

Can you live in Rome and not do as the Romans do? Can you walk among sinners and not walk in sin? Can you live in the world and not be part of it?

You can, just as faithful followers of Christ have done for centuries before you, when your thinking and behavior flow out of your intimate *relationship* with God. That relationship provides you, as God's child, solid *beliefs* about him, about yourself, and about the world around us. Those beliefs create certain *values* you then embrace. Those values reflect themselves in all your *attitudes and actions.*

When we embrace all 12 of the crucial truths highlighted in this book and strive to live them out, we are adopting and following a biblical worldview. While we cannot live out these truths perfectly, God is still at work in us perfecting his will in our lives. We experience his pleasure and joy because living out a biblical worldview ultimately provides the only satisfying answers to the three deepest questions of life.

ANSWERS THAT SATISFY

Who Are You?

You are a human being created in the image and likeness of a relational God. But you have lost your sense of identity because of your sin, which brought death to your Father-child relationship with your Creator. God took the initiative to bring you back into relationship with him, and because you have trusted in his solution (his Son dying in your stead) *you have regained your identity as a transformed, born-again child of God.* You have regained your family connection to your Father God.

Why Are You Here?

Made alive to God because of Christ, you enjoy a Father-child relationship that is continually conforming you to the image of God's Son. *Your purpose is to bring glory and honor to your God* by living to please him. You bring him pleasure; he brings you joy.

Where Are You Going?

Sin and death, pain and suffering, still exist. Yet God is on a mission to restore all things to his original design. You have joined his mission to proclaim the good news of God's kingdom to come. One day sin and death will be brought to an end. *Your destiny is to live eternally with God and your loved ones in a new heaven and a new earth.*

SUMMARY

Your biblical worldview gives you a clear sense of your identity, purpose, and destiny in life. As God empowers you to live out your worldview, he completes you, gives you a sense of meaning, and provides you an expectant hope of an eternal future. No other worldview provides so much joy. No other worldview provides such overwhelming evidence that it is true. No other worldview provides for such a glorious future and meaningful mission. These are the truths we will explore in our final two chapters.

THE CHURCH IS ALIVE AND ON A MISSION

As a kid, going to church just didn't make sense to me (Josh). About the most I got out of it was putting 50 cents in the offering basket and taking a dollar out. To me, the sermons were boring. Sitting for 45 minutes or so listening to a preacher saying things that didn't much relate to me seemed like a waste of time.

A lot of people today feel like that about church. Of course, if Jesus were literally the pastor of the church, it would make a big difference. I suppose he would be healing people left and right, feeding the hungry, and launching his eternal kingdom on earth to bring peace and joy to the whole world. Who wouldn't want to be part of that kind of a church?

Well, that is what Jesus' disciples thought too.

LAUNCHING JESUS' "KINGDOM CENTRAL"?

It had been a great month. The crowds were bigger than ever. The Messiah was displaying his power, and the sick were being healed instantly. "The crowd was amazed! Those who hadn't been able to speak were talking, the crippled were made well, the lame were walking around, and those who had been blind could see again!" (Matthew 15:31)

Four thousand men, not counting women and children, had been Jesus' outdoor congregation for three days, and they were getting hungry. Jesus asked how much food the disciples had. They told him they had seven loaves and a few small fish. So again, Jesus did the seemingly impossible. He prayed over the seven loaves and the few fish and told his disciples to distribute them to the crowd. After everyone ate all they wanted, the disciples gathered up the leftovers—seven large baskets full!

Jesus sent the masses home with full bellies and continued with his ministry of healing and spreading the kingdom message. When he had his small band of disciples alone he asked, "Who do people say that the Son of Man is?" (Matthew 16:13). They told him some thought he was Elijah; others thought he was Jeremiah or one of the other prophets. Then came the penetrating question—the question that really mattered: "'Who do you say I am?' Simon Peter answered, 'You are the Messiah, the Son of the living God.' Jesus replied, 'You are blessed, Simon son of John, because my Father in heaven has revealed this to you...Now I say to you that you are Peter [which means "rock"], and upon this rock I will build my church, and all the powers of hell will not conquer it'" (verses 15-18).

There it was! The declaration the disciples were looking for. Jesus said, "I will build my church." Now he would really launch his kingdom. With him healing the sick and feeding the people, the disciples would be guaranteed a megachurch in their first week of operation. This had to be great news to them. In fact, six days later Jesus took Peter, James, and John on an excursion up a mountain that further reinforced this church notion. Suddenly "Jesus' appearance was transformed so that his face shone like the sun, and his clothes became as white as light" (Matthew 17:2). And to their amazement Moses and Elijah appeared and started talking with Jesus.

This had to be it. Jesus would be the kingdom pastor of the great church on the mountain and Moses and Elijah would be his associate pastors. This would be the perfect location for "Kingdom Central"! So Peter blurted out, "Lord, it's wonderful for us to be here! If you want, I'll make three shelters as memorials—one for you, one for Moses, and one for Elijah" (verse 4).

But no sooner did Peter get his great idea out of his mouth than a bright light flashed and a voice came booming down from a cloud, "This is my dearly loved Son, who brings me great joy. Listen to him" (verse 5). The disciples were so shocked that they fell face down on the ground. Jesus came over and told them not to be afraid. When they looked up, Moses and Elijah were gone. And to top it off Jesus told them they must not tell anyone what they had seen until "the Son of Man has been raised from the dead" (verse 9).

This had to be confusing and frustrating to Peter, James, and John. Even if Jesus wasn't going to defeat the Romans and rule the nation politically, he could at least stick around after his resurrection and be pastor of the Kingdom Church on the Mount. What better way to spread the kingdom worldview than having King Jesus preach every week? And when new technologies were created he could be televised globally, launch the Jesus Facebook, and answer all questions and solve all problems online.

But there was, and is, a better way.

WHAT DOES THE CHURCH LOOK LIKE?

Jesus' idea of the church wasn't about a building that would serve as "Kingdom Central." Yes, Jesus told Peter he would build the church on the declaration that he was the Messiah, the true Son of God. But when he said "church," his word choice was *ekklesia,* which meant a gathering of people. In the culture of that time the word *ekklesia* was clearly understood to mean a public assembly of citizens. Its Hebrew counterpart meant an assembly before the Lord. Whether in Greek or Hebrew, *church* meant "the people of God," not a building.

Once the Holy Spirit filled the disciples and apostles after Pentecost, they understood the concept—the church was God's people. The church was Christ's agent to spread the kingdom message. The church was the visible representation of Christ himself.

When Jesus told his disciples to "go and make disciples of all the nations" (Matthew 28:19) he was delivering that command to his people, the church that would shortly be established. That church was given a mission, which was part of a greater mission of redemption and restoration of all things. Christ's initial step in that mission was to give his life as a ransom. He completed that through his death on the cross, but he would accomplish the rest of his mission through another means. With Jesus as head of his church, the kingdom would go viral—through the power of the Holy Spirit lived out in the community of his followers—and eventually every corner of the earth would be reached.

Jesus' new church wouldn't be a static organization, but a living organism. It wouldn't be about building an institution or a memorial, but about spreading a message and transforming the hearts of people. The New Testament uses at least six images to describe the church, none of which are about organizations, institutions, or physical buildings.

1. *The church is the new people of God.* The apostle Paul explained to the churches of Galatia that it didn't matter any longer whether the Jewish law of circumcision was performed. "What counts," Paul said, "is whether we really have been changed into new and different people. May God's mercy and peace be upon all those who live by this principle. They are the new people of God" (Galatians 6:15-16). God had named the Jewish nation of people as his chosen people in the past, but as Paul said to the churches at Ephesus, now "Jews and Gentiles are joined together in his church. This was his plan from all eternity, and it has now been carried out through Christ Jesus our Lord" (Ephesians 3:10-11). Jesus launched his church as a community of hope for all the nations of the world.

2. *The church is God's family.* Paul explained that Gentiles are no longer strangers. He said, "You are citizens along with all of God's holy people. You are members of God's family. We are his house, built on the foundation of the apostles and the prophets. And the cornerstone is Jesus Christ himself" (Ephesians 2:19-20). As Christians we are adopted into God's family, his church. We become his children—sons and daughters of God (see Romans 8:14-17).

3. *The church is the body of Christ.* "The church is his body; it is filled by Christ, who fills everything everywhere with his presence" (Ephesians 2:23). "Just as our bodies have many parts and each part has a special function, so it is with Christ's body...And since we are all

one body in Christ, we belong to each other, and each of us needs all the others" (Romans 12:4-5).

4. *The church is a holy temple where God lives.* "We who believe," Paul stated, "are carefully joined together, becoming a holy temple for the Lord. Through him you Gentiles are also joined together as part of this dwelling where God lives by his Spirit" (Ephesians 2:21-22). "Don't you realize that all of you together are the temple of God and that the Spirit of God lives in you?" (1 Corinthians 3:16).

5. *The church is Christ's pure bride.* Paul tells husbands to love their wives as Christ loves the church. "He gave up his life for her to make her holy and clean…He did this to present her to himself as a glorious church without a spot or wrinkle or any other blemish" (Ephesians 5:25-27).

6. *The church is Christ's agent to fulfill his mission to redeem the lost.* The apostle Peter said, "You are a kingdom of priests, God's holy nation, his very own possession. This is so you can show others the goodness of God" (1 Peter 2:9). Paul told the church in Corinth and the Christians throughout Greece that "God has given us the task of reconciling people to him…We are Christ's ambassadors, and God is using us to speak to you" (2 Corinthians 5:18, 20).

Therefore:

> *We believe the truth that the church is Christ's visible representation on earth, in which each transformed follower of Jesus is made part of his living body to individually and collectively fulfill God's redemptive purpose.*

When you become a transformed follower of Jesus you do not receive a personal, private relationship between just "Jesus and you." Each of us is made part of a community of Jesus-followers—the family, Christ's body, a holy temple where the Spirit of God lives, the bride of Christ, and the agency through which Christ is reaching out to the lost world. We the church "have the same Spirit, and we have all been called to the same glorious future. There is only one Lord, one faith, one baptism, and there is only one God and Father, who is over us all and in us all and living through us all" (Ephesians 4:4-6). We are a part of his church, and that church is still alive and well in the twenty-first century.

EVIDENCE GOD'S AUTHENTIC CHURCH IS ALIVE AND WELL

The church on the corner of Pershing and Maple is a white New England–style structure with a towering steeple. The church off State Road and Portage Trail is dome-shaped and seats over 5000. The church with an exit sign off the freeway glistens in the sunlight and seems to be made of crystal. There is definitely no shortage of churches in North America. In fact, there are hundreds of thousands of church buildings in the world attended by millions of people every week. So it's not difficult to believe churches exist. Yet visible buildings with people attending services don't necessarily constitute Christ's true church.

The real church is where God lives and moves and accomplishes his purpose.

The church is a community of believers where Christ, the head, is "over us all and in us all and living through us all" (Ephesians 4:6). Jesus said, "I tell you that if two of you on earth agree about anything you ask for, it will be done for you by my Father in heaven. For where two or three come together in my name, there am I with them" (Matthew 18:19-20 NIV). In other words, the *real* church is where God lives and moves and accomplishes his purpose. But what evidence is there that Christ is at work through his church in the twenty-first century?

During the Passover supper Jesus told his disciples, "I am giving you a new commandment: Love each other. Just as I have loved you, you should love each other. Your love for one another will prove to the world that you are my disciples [my church]" (John 13:34-35). This is what Jesus said would characterize the church—his love living in and through his followers. He said this love-filled community would be "the salt of the earth" and "the light of the world" so that the church's "good deeds [would] shine out for all to see, so that everyone will praise [their] heavenly Father" (Matthew 5:13-16).

The authentic church is this loving community that acts as "salt and light" and impacts the culture around it. That is what the early church was all about. Some, however, have pointed out the twenty-first-century church has largely lost its mission, and many churches are only a slight reflection of the invisible God. The late author and Christian historian Dr. Robert Webber passed along this startling quote:

- The church started as a missionary movement in Jerusalem.

- It moved to Rome and became an institution.

- It traveled to Europe and became a culture.

- It crossed the Atlantic to America and became a big business.[1]

It's true "church" organizations and institutions disappoint, and many may have lost their way as God's visible expression of himself. But if you look, you can find the church active and involved in the world. In his book *Transformation,* pastor Bob Roberts Jr. relates this story of seeing the church firsthand:

> I didn't even realize how lost I was until I saw what the church was really supposed to look like. At first, I didn't even recognize it; then I wanted to rationalize it. I had to go halfway around the world to find it—in the persecuted underground house church in Asia. I had heard the stories and statistics, but I had never met anyone face to face. They were nothing like me. They were nothing like any believers I had ever met. Not just culturally, but spiritually they blew me away. Sure, their theology is fuzzy. Some don't even

have whole parts of the Bible, only perhaps an entire book or a few passages. But they know God at a depth I never had nor knew anyone else who had.

Worship takes on a completely new expression on the other side of the world. No sound systems, no calculated transitions, just sweaty believers crammed together into small rooms, weeping as the Holy Spirit oozes out among them...No one is getting rich, and no one is fighting for control or position. If there is a favored position, it is the privilege of being the first to die. Living on the edge as they do leaves little room for insincerity or self-promotion. These people are living what I grew up hearing the church should be.

Through small, indigenous, underground house church networks, these churches are transforming lives and their cultures. They cannot be stopped. There are too many of them, and they are spreading everywhere, every day. Here's a shocker: Laypeople start these movements, not just those "called" to full-time vocational ministry. Their church planting is the result of transformed lives and not the result of a grand strategy, even though the strategy is grand.[2]

THE ACTIVE EXPRESSION OF THE CHURCH

Jesus' church exists today as it did in the first century. The process of its expansion is the same. Lives are transformed by Christ's saving power, those lives form a community of hope, love, and care, and they by nature become Jesus' ambassadors to proclaim his kingdom message of love and redemption to the world.

Much has been said and written on the purpose and role of the church.* While the following list is not exhaustive, it provides an outline of the active expression of the church as described by Scripture.

The church embodies what a community of redeemed people looks like. Jesus said we are to love one another as he loved us. The early church "met together

---

* Robert Webber, for one, has done an extensive study of the early church, how they fulfilled God's mission and how we can do the same today. Dr. Webber's book titled *Journey to Jesus* is a valuable resource in understanding what the authentic church looks like and how Christ intends it to express itself.

constantly and shared everything they had" (Acts 2:44). As Christ's body today, his followers need one another, serve one another, and live in harmony together. "If one part suffers, all the parts suffer with it, and if one part is honored, all the parts are glad" (1 Corinthians 12:26). That's what love does.

When the world looks at Jesus' church they see a holy people (2 Peter 3:14), a people in unity (1 Corinthians 12:25), a people depending on one another (Romans 12:5), and a people caring for one another (Romans 12:15).

The church is a reflection of the triune Godhead, who is the ultimate model of infinite love in perfect relationship. The church is the visible representation of the invisible God.

The church is a compassionate and healing presence to those in need. The church members in the book of Acts literally "sold their possessions and shared the proceeds with those in need" (2:45). Like its head, Jesus, the church is there to feed the hungry, clothe the naked, care for the sick, and bring healing to those who are suffering (see Matthew 25:31-46).

Steve Baughan is the former director of a ministry in Branson, Missouri, that specifically reaches out to addicts and the homeless. During his tenure there, he was sometimes criticized by Christians because he didn't necessarily preach the gospel to those in desperate need before he fed them, clothed them, and helped get a roof over their heads. Listen to Steve's response:

> Proclaiming a Christian message isn't only about quoting Scripture passages to people or walking someone through a gospel booklet. Some people have issues so intense that quoting a few selected Bible passages just doesn't cut it...
>
> Deeply hurting people simply can't hear your words over the roar of their lives going up in flames. What they need is a hose that gushes forth hope, love, and compassion in action. That might look like a hot meal, a place to sleep, and a commitment to hang in there with them, preferably from someone who has walked in their shoes...
>
> The message of Jesus that we offer says that your solution can begin in a relationship with me—I'm your friend. I am here to

remove your aloneness, I'll comfort you, help carry your burden. I'll connect with you as a person of value—I'll feed you, care for you, and take you in as family. That's what Jesus did with the Samaritan woman, the tax collector, the woman caught in adultery. And that is what he does with each of us. When we are Jesus to those who are hungry for wholeness, they will taste the salt of transformation in action—they will see the attractive light of our message. The gospel message isn't just about words of truth; it's about living that truth out in specific acts of love and compassion toward others.[3]

The church is also God's reconciling agent and ambassador to spread the gospel—the kingdom message. Jesus said, "You will be my witnesses in Jerusalem, and in all Judea and Samaria, and to the ends of the earth" (Acts 1:8 NIV). The church is God's means to reconcile a lost world to him (see 2 Corinthians 5:16-21). The heartbeat of the church is that of the relational heart of God, who wants to redeem and restore those who are alone and separated from him. Evangelism isn't about church-growth numbers or building an organization, it's about leading people into relationship with God.

The church is an equipping agent to make disciples who make disciples. Before Jesus ascended into heaven he gave his followers what has been referred to as the Great Commission: "Go and make disciples of all the nations" (Matthew 28:19). But that command didn't say, "Go out and start churches." Pastor Bob Roberts Jr. pointed out the misconception of the goal of starting churches in his book *The Multiplying Church*:

> I have a vision and a dream. Let's start a thousand churches over the next ten years, each one running a minimum of two thousand members, and in just ten years we will turn America upside-down with the gospel! That would work, right? Wrong—that scenario just happened over the past ten years [Roberts was writing in 2008], and there are fewer people in church today than ever before. How can that be? How could we have spent billions to start two thousand megachurches and yet have fewer people in church and a society that largely feels the church is antagonistic?

The answer is, in part, that it's not enough just to start churches for the sake of evangelism that will end when "conversion" takes place. Books on starting churches generally operate on the premise that we need to start churches because it is the best evangelistic method that exists. That is a true statement—but an insufficient reason for starting churches.[4]

Starting and building up church attendance isn't the "Great Commission" goal. Jesus said "make disciples" and the process would birth churches naturally.

The apostle Paul said that the church leadership's "responsibility is to equip God's people to do his [Christ's] work and build up the church, the body of Christ, until...we will be mature and full grown in the Lord, measuring up to the full stature of Christ" (Ephesians 4:12-13). Making disciples is a process of reproduction. As Christ's disciples are formed and equipped spiritually, they begin exercising their spiritual gifts and reproduction happens: New converts are born.

Paul told Timothy how this spiritual reproduction works when he said, "The things you have heard me say...entrust to reliable men who will also be qualified to teach others" (2 Timothy 2:2 NIV). This is not unlike our physical reproduction process. The loving and intimate relationship of a married couple results in the conception and birth of a newborn child. Through the physical and emotional nurturing and formation process, that child matures to adulthood, marries, and produces offspring as well. And the process continues generation after generation.

The early church grew naturally through a spiritual-formation process of discipleship that reproduced new believers generation after generation. This was not an addition strategy of professional preachers drawing new attendees to a building; it was a multiplication process of laypeople who, as disciples, reproduced other disciples that reproduced other disciples, and so on.

As Robert Webber observed, "Discipleship is not a vocation prescribed only for ministers and other full-time staff members in the church. Discipleship is the full-time spiritual vocation of *all* God's people."[5]

The church is responsible for equipping believers until they are formed spiritually to maturity (see Ephesians 4:11-16). For centuries the church has accomplished this as mature believers have journeyed together with new believers to know and live...

- a life of faith

- a life of worship

- a life of prayer

- a life of being conformed to the image of Christ in all relationships

- a life that continually resists the sin nature (also referred to as spiritual warfare)

- a life of making godly choices

- a life of spiritual reproduction

This is the church's model for making disciples today. It is a highly relational journey that is actually a two-way street. An older generation becomes models of godliness that invest their lives into a new generation. And a new generation is trained to seek the value of receiving from an older generation. The older, more mature believers give of their experience to the younger believers, and the younger believers seek after the wisdom of the mentors. Together the church equips people to become disciples who make disciples.

When you see a group of transformed followers of Jesus who 1) embody what the redeemed community of believers look like; 2) are meeting the needs of the hurting around them; 3) are reconciling the lost to God; and 4) are equipping its saints to reproduce themselves spiritually, you are seeing Jesus' church alive and well. You are seeing an expression of Christ living through his people.

The church is the new people of God, Christ's body, God's family—a place where God lives in his people, who are Christ's bride and his agent to fulfill his mission. That is Christ's church, and it is very much alive and visible all across the globe, bringing hope, love, healing, and salvation to a lost and needy world.

THE PRIORITY OF THE CHURCH

Growing up, church did not mean much to me (Josh) largely because what it offered didn't relate to my life. At least I didn't think it did. I was popular, so I felt accepted. I was good at sports, so I got lots of praise. I had many friends, so I felt appreciated. And since I wasn't religious, I didn't figure I needed church in my life.

But in reality I was a lonely person. Oh, I would make you think everyone was my best friend and I didn't have a care in the world. And while my many friends could be spread a mile wide, the friendships were really only an inch deep. On the inside I felt alone. What I didn't realize was that Jesus and his body, the church, were there to lead me to God and remove my human and spiritual aloneness.

Feeling alone isn't really an indication of sin in our lives or a mark that we are relationally inept. Aloneness is the God-given warning signal that tells us we need to experience a relationship with him and relationships with others, including his church. It is as if God placed within each of us a homing device that seeks out relationships when we begin to feel alone. And while sin does hinder us from developing the kind of relationship that removes our aloneness, sin is not the *cause* of our aloneness.

Remember, Adam lived in a perfect world without sin when God declared, "It is not good for the man to be alone" (Genesis 2:18). Obviously, God was there with perfect love for his human creation. Yet he knew Adam needed relational connections with his own kind. Therefore, God created another person to join the cycle of love relationship between Father, Son, Holy Spirit, and Adam. God could have said he was all Adam needed, but he didn't. He created a woman to help remove Adam's aloneness.

As we can see, God's intent was to prevent human aloneness by means of relationship both with himself and with a human family. He has gone on to design another means as well. He has given his devoted people, the church, the privilege and responsibility of entering into deep relationships with each other. Therefore, with God's three provisions for relationship—family, the church, and himself—we don't have to feel alone.

Yet some people resist the idea that we have a need for anyone but God. The idea of needing others is a little humiliating to them. God is all-powerful and the source of all there is in heaven and earth, so how could anyone possibly think he or she needs anything else? To support their position, they point to the apostle Paul, who supposedly declared all his sufficiency was in

Christ alone when he said, "I can do everything through him who gives me strength" (Philippians 4:13 NIV). This passage, they say, implies we are spiritually weak if we need anything other than God.

But notice what he says immediately after verse 13: "Yet it was good of you to share in my troubles…you sent me aid again and again when I was in need" (Philippians 4:14, 16 NIV). Paul's message was "I do everything through Christ and he is pleased to involve you in that process." We clearly need God, and God makes it clear we need one another.

TOGETHER FOR A GRAND PURPOSE

Scripture says, "We are all parts of his one body, and each of us has different work to do. And since we are all one body in Christ, we belong to each other, and each of us needs all the others" (Romans 12:5). God designed us to need one another when he created us in his image. He placed within each of us relational needs that cry out to be met in him and in one another. When these needs are met we feel joy and a sense of completeness. When they are not met we feel alone.

But there is much more to our need for God and one another than just getting our relational needs met. There is a lost world out there, and it's our task to preach and live the gospel and point that world to God. The means by which God has chosen to draw people to him is this same "homing device" that reaches out to remove aloneness: relationships.

When Jesus' church is joined in unity and love for one another, Christ is lifted up and people are relationally attracted to him. Jesus said, "Your love for one another will prove to the world that you are my disciples" (John 13:35). He went on to pray for that loving oneness of his body. "My prayer for all of them," Jesus said, "is that they will be one, just as you and I are one, Father… I in them and you in me, all being perfected into one. Then the world will know that you sent me and will understand that you love them as much as you love me" (17:21, 23).

The church becomes the true "salt of the earth" and "the light of the world" when believers are loving each other as Christ has loved each of them. The church's greatest platform for proclaiming the truth of Jesus Christ is living a life of love among one another and a life of integrity before the world. Paul said, "We try to live in such a way that no one will be hindered from finding the Lord by the way we act, and so no one can find fault with our ministry" (2 Corinthians 6:3).

In sin, alienated from God, people feel alone. The church is Christ's powerful presence on earth, calling out with open arms, "Come to me, all of you who are weary and carry heavy burdens, and I will give you rest" (Matthew 11:28). The church is the visible reflection of the invisible Christ. And when his body lives in relational unity with God and one another, God accomplishes his grand purpose of redeeming the lost.

THE PRIORITY: MEETING SPIRITUAL NEEDS OR HUMAN NEEDS?

While Scripture makes it clear that in relationship with God and one another we meet each other's needs, just what is it that we most deeply need?

Our needs can be placed largely in two broad categories: human needs and spiritual needs. Human needs include our emotional, physical, mental/educational, economic needs—and more. Spiritual needs include the need to be redeemed and justified by grace through faith in Jesus, the need for the Holy Spirit, the need to be consistently renewed through prayer, God's Word, and so on.

Which of these two needs—human or spiritual—do you think is the most important? Before you jump to what you may think is the obvious conclusion, consider the following story adapted from former pastor and church specialist David Ferguson's book entitled *The Never Alone Church*.

Your pastor is barely two minutes into his sermon when the side door near the front of the auditorium bursts open. Every head swivels to see two men enter, one a bedraggled "street person," and the other a thin, hollow-eyed man staggering and unsteady on his feet. Following the men, a poorly dressed young woman with two small children enters. All of them walk to the front row and sit down. The street person's matted hair and beard seem to hide his face like a mask. The other man can hardly sit up straight, and the young woman has trouble getting her children to quiet down and remain seated.

The eyes of the congregation flit nervously between your pastor and these surprise visitors. The air is thick with unasked questions: Who are these people and what do they want? How did they get past the ushers in the foyer? Are they drunk or stoned on drugs? Are they going to make a disturbance in the service? Has someone thought to call the police? Yet everyone sits motionless.

Your pastor steps off the platform and walks up to the street person and says, "What's your story?" The man stands, turns toward the congregation, and says, "I've been out of work for two years. I'm homeless, and I beg or steal whatever I can to keep alive."

The pastor looks at the next man and says, "And what's your story?" The sickly man makes it to his feet with some difficulty and states in a raspy voice: "I'm heavily medicated right now. I'm in the latter stages of AIDS. As a homosexual I've had multiple partners, and it's finally caught up to me."

Finally, your pastor turns to the young lady and poses the same question: "So what's your story?" The woman stands, turns toward the congregation, and says, "I'm an unmarried mother who's out of work and depending on the welfare system to make it. I don't know exactly who is the father to my children. It could be any number of men."

As the young woman sits down, your pastor looks at you and all those seated in the auditorium and asks: "What are the real needs represented in these stories and how are we to meet them?"[6]

How would you answer this question? How would your church answer it? Some people would say, "They need God first and foremost. They have a spiritual need to confess their sins. The lady needs to quit milking the welfare system, and they all need to straighten up their lives." Yet another group of people might say, "Before anything else, we need to offer these people hope. They all need unconditional acceptance, comfort, and immediate support. One needs shelter and food, two of them need an advocate to help them get back on their feet, and one needs care and comfort in his final days of life. They have human needs, and we need to meet them." So the real question here is this: Should the church love these people by primarily focusing first on their spiritual needs, or should they first focus on their human needs?

Is It a Question of Priority?

This question probably wouldn't even be asked if something hadn't happened shortly after the turn of the twentieth century. For decades the church had been at the forefront of social reforms and movements to address the human needs of people without neglecting their spiritual needs. However, some leaders who began rejecting certain foundational doctrines of the church also began interpreting Christianity solely in terms of a social gospel, neglecting or ignoring the spiritual dimension. Conservatives saw this involvement in social action to the neglect of spiritual concern as a substitution for truth.

As so often happens, a reaction to one extreme tends to breed an opposite error. After 1925, large numbers of conservative churches largely withdrew from social issues in an effort to reject liberal theology and take a stand for truth. In his book *The Younger Evangelical,* Robert Webber describes this shift as "The Great Reversal."[7] The aftereffects of this shift still linger, as even today many conservative churches see a clear separation between meeting human needs and spiritual needs and have opted to focus primarily on the spiritual side. It's clear that if the church addressed only human needs and never focused on spiritual needs, there would be an imbalance. But the Great Reversal has led to an imbalance in the opposite direction.

So what is the biblical priority? Should the church focus only on the spiritual needs of people and neglect human needs? Or does the church make spiritual needs the first priority and *then* address human needs? Or does it meet human needs first and hope the person somehow gets his spiritual needs met? Or does it meet human needs as a method of reaching a person spiritually?

Jesus Answers the Question

Christ, the head of the church, gives us the answer. The truth is, Jesus didn't make a clear distinction between human needs and spiritual needs. Jesus told his disciples: "'You must love the Lord your God with all your heart, all your soul, and all your mind.' This is the first and greatest commandment. A second is equally important: 'Love your neighbor as yourself.' All the other commandments and all the demands of the prophets are based on these two commandments" (Matthew 22:37-40).

Jesus was saying we are to love God with all that we are—spiritually, emotionally, mentally, physically, economically, and so on. And we are to love others for all that they are—spiritually, emotionally, mentally, physically, economically, and so on. He didn't put human needs ahead of spiritual needs or spiritual needs ahead of human needs.

Jesus actually met people at the point of their need of the moment, whether it was a spiritual or human need.

He did say, however, to love and worship him above all else, and he would in turn supply all our needs, both human and spiritual (see Matthew 6:19-34 and Philippians 4:18-20). But Jesus didn't separate out human and spiritual needs and say, "I'll meet this one first, this one second, this one third…" Jesus actually met people at the point of their need of the moment, whether it was a spiritual or human need.

Jesus didn't say to the blind man, "If you don't believe in me as your savior, then I'm not going to heal you." Nor did he say to the lame man, "I'll make you a deal: I'll repair your legs to wholeness if you have a relationship with me." Jesus was moved with compassion for the human and spiritual needs of these people and set out to meet them both.

Scripture describes an encounter between Jesus and a man named Zacchaeus. Although this man was Jewish, he was an agent of the hated Roman government, a tax collector. The Jewish people resented paying Roman taxes and resented even more those Jews that did the bidding of the Romans. Often these tax collectors extorted money from the people to pad their own pockets. So Zacchaeus no doubt felt rejected and criticized by his neighbors and perhaps was even fearful of reprisal. He certainly felt alone. So as a sinner he had a spiritual need to be forgiven. And being rejected by his fellow Jews, he had a human need to feel accepted.

So what did Jesus say to this rejected, cheating sinner? Zacchaeus was perched in a tree to get a better view of this Jesus of Nazareth as he walked by. When Jesus looked up at him the first thing he said was: "Quick, come down! For I must be a guest in your home today" (Luke 19:5).

Jesus couldn't have said anything more definitive to demonstrate his unconditional acceptance of this rejected tax collector. Eating with someone at his home in that day was the ultimate in communicating acceptance. Scripture says that "Zacchaeus quickly climbed down and took Jesus to his house in great excitement and joy. But the crowds were displeased. 'He has gone to be the guest of a notorious sinner,' they grumbled" (verses 6-7).

By eating with this sinner, Jesus didn't compromise the truth. He still held that cheating and stealing are wrong. But the Master obviously didn't think Zacchaeus needed a sermon on the evils of being a cheating tax collector at his first encounter. What Jesus did was to meet Zacchaeus at the point of his need for acceptance, and the tax collector responded to him in repentance by saying: "I will give half my wealth to the poor, Lord, and if I have overcharged people on their taxes, I will give them back four times as much" (verse 8). Jesus' relational approach addressed both Zacchaeus' human need and his spiritual need. That is a clear characteristic of Jesus.

Jesus' Great Commandment to love God and to love our neighbors is inseparably linked to his Great Commission to "make disciples of all the nations" (Matthew 28:19). Disciples are to be born out of our love for God and our neighbors. In other words, our human and spiritual needs are met by a love that says, "I care about you, and my love will take action to meet you at the point of your physical, emotional, spiritual, economic, and all other needs." It is a love that loves the whole person. The apostle John was talking about that kind of love when he said, "Let us stop just saying we love each other; let us really show it by our actions. It is by our actions that we know we are living in the truth" (1 John 3:18-19).

HOW THE CHURCH MEETS HUMAN AND SPIRITUAL NEEDS

Do you have a need for acceptance? Do you long for approval? Are you looking for praise? If you have a pulse you have these needs. Even your dog, if you have one, has these needs. But do our desires for acceptance, approval, praise, and so on represent human needs or spiritual needs?

The fact is, they represent both. When Jesus met Zacchaeus at the point of his need for acceptance, he actually met both a human and a spiritual need. As the Master Rabbi, his unconditional acceptance produced "great excitement and joy" in Zacchaeus. He felt valued by a fellow Jew. Perhaps for the first time since taking on his job with the Roman government, he felt he was worth something as a human being. But Zacchaeus needed more than just simple acceptance by one of his own. He needed his guilt over cheating removed. And as the Son of God, Jesus had the power to remove his guilt. Jesus' unconditional acceptance did elicit repentance from Zacchaeus, and Jesus met his spiritual need for forgiveness.

Both our human and spiritual needs can actually be categorized under the single umbrella of relational needs. We have a relational need to feel accepted by God, which is a spiritual need, as well as to be accepted by others, which is a human need. We have a relational need to feel the approval of God, a spiritual need, and to feel the approval of others, a human need. We also have a relational longing for a sense of security, for praise, for attention, and so on. And each of these needs has both a spiritual and human dimension. So when we begin to meet people at the point of their relational needs, God is pleased to actually involve us in addressing both their human and spiritual needs without necessarily assigning those needs a priority.

And the exciting thing is, God has brought his church together to meet all our relational needs, both spiritual and human. Listen to Paul as he describes the church:

> God has put the body together in such a way that extra honor and care are given to those parts that have less dignity. This makes for harmony among the members, so that all the members care for each other equally. If one part suffers, all the parts suffer with it, and if one part is honored, all the parts are glad (1 Corinthians 12:24-26).

This passage makes it clear that members of the church are to care for one another lovingly, comforting each other in suffering and rejoicing with each other in good fortune. This makes us feel cared for. It also creates unity among God's people both spiritually and on the human level.

Paul also said, "We who believe are carefully joined together, becoming a holy temple for the Lord" (Ephesians 2:21). This is a unity that goes beyond avoiding dissention and division. It is a unity that harmoniously fits your spiritual gift together with a different but complementary spiritual gift of a fellow believer. And this is done in such a way that your strengths are maximized and your weaknesses are made irrelevant. So by locking arms with those who are strong where you are weak, your weakness becomes strong. This meets your need for respect, support, and approval, and you gain a sense of completeness and competence you would never experience alone.

When members of Christ's body are fitted together in this fashion, God accomplishes great things through them. As the spiritual gift of exhortation is combined with the spiritual gift of teaching, then in turn combined with the gift of hospitality, and then with the gift of administration with the gift of evangelism, and so on, we all experience the power of God at work in a mighty way. And when each of us acts upon our need for one another, it keeps a person from stepping out front and declaring, "I'm really the important one here" or "I'm the one who's really making everything happen." Accepting that each of us is made complete within Christ's body keeps us from focusing on ourselves so we can focus on the one who is really deserving—Christ.

LOVING THE WHOLE PERSON

We have already identified a number of relational needs that represent both spiritual and human needs, such as acceptance, comfort, support, respect, and approval. There are many such needs identified in Scripture. David Ferguson has identified over 50 relational needs in Scripture. We will touch on ten that he covers extensively in his book *The Never Alone Church*. The better we understand these relational needs, the better we can understand how God wants to love others through us to meet the human and spiritual needs of those around us. It is through this love of the whole person that God is pleased to make the church truly relevant in the lives of others. It is "your love for one another," Jesus said, that "will prove to the world that you are my disciples [my church]" (John 13:35).

Love Meets the Need for Comfort

Love gives comfort by giving hope; easing grief or pain; consoling; and hurting with a person.

"He [God] is the source of every mercy and the God who comforts us. He comforts us in all our troubles so that we can comfort others" (2 Corinthians 1:3-4).

Love Meets the Need for Attention (Care)

Love shows care or attention by taking thought of another, conveying interest and concern, entering another's world.

"All the members [of the church] care for each other equally" (1 Corinthians 12:25).

Love Meets the Need for Acceptance

Love offers acceptance without conditions by loving others for who they are.

"Accept each other just as Christ has accepted you; then God will be glorified" (Romans 15:7).

Love Meets the Need for Appreciation

Love expresses appreciation by praising another and communicating gratefulness through words and deeds.

"I praise you for remembering me in everything" (1 Corinthians 11:2 NIV).

Love Meets the Need for Support

Love provides support by coming alongside another to lift a load and help carry a problem.

"Carry each other's burdens, and in this way you will fulfill the law of Christ" (Galatians 6:2 NIV).

Love Meets the Need for Encouragement

Love offers encouragement by inspiring with courage and urging another forward to a positive goal.

"Encourage each other and build each other up" (1 Thessalonians 5:11).

Love Meets the Need for Affection

Love shows affection that communicates care and closeness by offering endearing words and appropriate physical touch.

"Love each other with genuine affection" (Romans 12:10).

Love Meets the Need for Approval

Love gives approval by expressing satisfaction with a person, demonstrating that he or she has pleased another.

"If you serve Christ with this attitude, you will please God. And other people will approve of you, too" (Romans 14:18).

Love Meets the Need for Security

Love provides security by eliminating danger and removing the fear of loss, want, and broken relationships.

"Perfect love expels all fear" (1 John 4:18).

Love Meets the Need for Respect

Love shows respect by valuing a person highly and communicating to that person that he or she is of great worth.

"Show respect for everyone" (1 Peter 2:17).

WE NEVER HAVE TO BE ALONE

Christ has given us his body, the church, so we can be equipped for service and minister his love to others to meet the human and spiritual needs of those around us. As a part of such a church, we never have to be alone. Christ is present in our lives through the indwelling presence of God's Holy Spirit, and the members of his body are there to be with us through thick or thin.

God's church is alive and well today to offer hope as a living embodiment of Jesus' love that, among other things, says to you and a needy world:

- There is *comfort* to ease your physical hurts, to provide a shoulder to cry on, and to produce inner healing.

- There is *attention* (care) that communicates you are so important to God that he died to have a relationship with you, and his church is here to help address all your human and spiritual needs.

- There is *acceptance* that says you are loved for who you are, no matter what.

- There is *appreciation* that gives praise to you for who you are and what you've done.

- There is *support* when you need a helping hand or a shoulder to help you carry a heavy load.

- There is *encouragement* when you are struggling with disappointments, failure, or difficulty.

- There is *affection* to help you know that through it all, you are truly loved.

- There is *approval* that says, "I am pleased with you."

- There is *security* in times of danger to remove your fear of the future.

- There is *respect* that honors you for what you think and values you for the contribution you bring.

The church, Christ's body, is alive and well in order to

equip God's people to do his work and build up the church. This will continue until we come to such unity in our faith and knowledge of God's Son that we will be mature and full grown in the Lord, measuring up to the full stature of Christ. Then we will no longer be like children, forever changing our minds about what we believe because someone has told us something different or because someone has cleverly lied to us and made the lie sound like the truth. Instead, we will hold to the truth in love, becoming more and more in every way like Christ, who is the head of his body, the church (Ephesians 4:12-15).

CHRIST WILL RETURN

The shingles were half blown off the barn. Some of the windows were broken. The siding on one side was almost gone, and what little paint remained on the trim was faded and peeling. The barn door was sagging, indicating the entire foundation of the place was of questionable stability. Weeds of every kind overgrew the ground, which was caked with layers of dead leaves and windblown trash accumulated over the years.

I (Sean) stood there looking at the old place as my dad (Josh) swept his arm toward it and told my sisters and me that this was the 120-acre dairy farm he had called home when he was growing up just outside Union City, Michigan. I looked at the dilapidated barn, the precariously leaning corncrib, and the overgrown fields and tried to imagine what the place must have looked like in the early 1940s.

Dad could remember when his older sister would come home to visit and how he'd help make homemade ice cream on the back porch of the house. He said his mother made the best root beer in all of Michigan, and he had guzzled all the root-beer floats his parents would let him drink. Josh clearly saw more in this acreage than my sisters and I did. We saw a place in ruins; through the enhancing lens of memory he saw it as it once was.

As we walked toward the corncrib, Josh's entire demeanor changed. Pleasant thoughts of homemade ice cream and root beer quickly faded. The reality was that happy childhood memories for my father were few and far between. We were just a few feet from the old leaning shed when he abruptly stopped.

As he stared at the weather-beaten structure, tears began to trickle down his face. Within seconds he was overwhelmed with emotion. He seemed paralyzed by the memories of that terrible day of shame and abandonment so many years ago. As if re-running an old movie, he seemed to see that 11-year-old boy, frightened and alone, buried inside up to his neck in corn, hiding from the humiliating scene of a drunken father out of control. It was more than he could bear, and he wept openly. My sisters and I wrapped our arms around our dad and wept with him.

I saw my dad differently that day. This old farm, now in ruins, had been his childhood home. He had so much wanted it to be a place of peace and safety, joy and happiness. But home had been far from that for Josh. And on that day I understood in a deeper way just how painful his childhood had been—a ruined childhood that could never be restored to what it should have been.

JESUS IS COMING AGAIN TO RESTORE WHAT IS IN RUINS

Two thousand years ago God saw through human eyes an entire world in ruins. What had once been a paradise of peace and safety, joy and happiness, was now a world of pain and suffering, murder and destruction. The Son of God stood before the city filled with people who were rejecting him and grieved. "O Jerusalem, Jerusalem, the city that kills the prophets and stones God's messengers! How often I have wanted to gather your children together as a hen protects her chicks beneath her wings, but you wouldn't let me. And now look, your house is left to you, empty and desolate. For I tell you this, you will never see me again until you say, 'Bless the one who comes in the name of the Lord!'" (Matthew 23:37-39).

I (Josh) didn't have the means to restore the old McDowell dairy farm to what it once was. And even if I could have repaired the old place, I couldn't bring back my mother and father, run back the clock, and make my childhood home into a happy and loving family; that was all in the unchangeable past.

But unlike us, God can restore what has been ruined, both the physical creation and our broken relationships. As Matthew writes, "Bless the one who comes in the name of the Lord!" (23:39). For Christ will return and take this physical "house" and our earthly home that is now "empty and desolate" and completely restore it.

God has promised to renew each of his children to his
original design and restore this earth to what it once was.

The apostle Paul tells us "all creation anticipates the day when it will join God's children in glorious freedom from death and decay. For we know that all creation has been groaning as in pains of childbirth right up to the present time" (Romans 8:21-22). The old McDowell farm along with every other place on earth is going to be restored to a home that will surpass the Garden of Eden.

And what about our painful memories and disappointments in life? Paul goes on to say we all "groan to be released from pain and suffering. We, too, wait anxiously for that day when God will give us our full rights as his children, including the new bodies he has promised us" (Romans 8:23).

God will do more than just restore the earth to its pristine and perfect condition; he will restore us as well. Whether it's pain of the past or suffering in the present, God has promised to renew each of his children to his original design and restore this earth to what it once was.

Jesus Will Return to Restore the Earth

The psalmist David declares, "The earth is the LORD's, and everything in it, the world, and all who live in it" (Psalm 24:1 NIV). God made the heavens and the earth and called them "very good," and he hasn't surrendered his title and right to them. They may be in ruins now, but he has definite plans to restore them to a perfect world for us to live in.

Jesus told his disciples he was going away to prepare a place for them and for all of us. And he gave this promise: "I will come again and receive you to Myself, that where I am, there you may be also" (John 14:3 NASB). After Pentecost, Peter preached this same message to the people of Jerusalem: that Jesus "must remain in heaven until the time for the final restoration of all things, as God promised long ago through his prophets" (Acts 3:21). And what had the prophets said about God's restoration plans?

Look! I am creating new heavens and a new earth—so wonderful that no one will even think about the old ones anymore (Isaiah 65:17).

The time will come when all the earth will be filled, as the waters fill the sea, with an awareness of the glory of the LORD (Habakkuk 2:14).

"As the new heavens and the new earth that I make will endure before me," declares the LORD, "so will your name and descendants endure" (Isaiah 66:22 NIV).

These promises God declared were directed to the children of Israel, but they also include us as beneficiaries. When Peter asked what was in store for the disciples that followed Jesus, he said, "At the renewal of all things, when the Son of Man sits on his glorious throne, you who have followed me will also sit on twelve thrones, judging the twelve tribes of Israel" (Matthew 19:28 NIV). Peter later wrote, "In keeping with his promise we are looking forward to a new heaven and a new earth, the home of righteousness" (2 Peter 3:13 NIV). Jesus also told us that "when the Son of Man comes in his glory," he "will say to those on his right; 'Come, you who are blessed by my Father; take your inheritance, the kingdom prepared for you since the creation of the world'" (Matthew 25:31, 34 NIV).

God has not given up on his original plan. He has neither abandoned the idea of a perfect earth, nor has he laid aside his plan for his children to live in a perfect place forever. He has no intention of taking us away to some distant heaven and then destroying this earth he designed to be our home. After his resurrection, Jesus ascended into heaven with a promise to return. He will return and restore this earth to his original design. God's perfect plan is "to bring all things in heaven and on earth together under one head, even Christ" (Ephesians 1:10 NIV).

Notice in the verse above Paul tells us the earth, as well as heaven, will be under one head. If we who now live on the earth were to be taken into heaven, what would be left on the earth to be brought together under one head? Heaven is God's home. The earth is our home, not only now, but forever, just as God originally intended. And it is Jesus who will eternally bring us together with God and connect his home with ours. In John's revelation he saw the holy city, the New Jerusalem, coming down from God out of heaven and said, "Look, the home of God is now among his people! He will live with them, and they will be his people. God himself will be with them" (Revelation 21:3).

Theologian Randy Alcorn puts it this way in his book *Heaven*:

> There will be one cosmos, one universe united under one Lord— forever. This is the unstoppable plan of God. This is where history is headed. When God walked with Adam and Eve in the Garden, Earth was Heaven's backyard. The New Earth will even be more than that—it will be Heaven itself. And those who know Jesus will have the privilege of living there.[1]

When God's restoration project is complete, we will experience a renewed earth in the perfection of the Garden of Eden. "No longer will anything be cursed" (Revelation 22:3). No more thorns or thistles to prick our bodies. No more difficulty in getting things to grow. No more "survival of the fittest" among the animals, for they will all be at peace with one another. In fact, there will be no discord or fighting or evil anywhere, because "nothing evil will be allowed to enter—no one who practices shameful idolatry and dishonesty—but only those whose names are written in the Lamb's Book of Life" (Revelation 21:27).

Jesus Will Return to Restore Our Bodies

When Christ returns he will fulfill the promise he made through Isaiah the prophet long ago: "In that day he [God] will remove the cloud of gloom, the shadow of death that hangs over the earth. He will swallow up death forever! The Sovereign LORD will wipe away all tears. He will remove forever all insults and mockery against his land and people" (Isaiah 25:7-8).

As his redeemed children, we will live forever on this perfect earth where "there will be no more death or sorrow or crying or pain. For the old world and its evils are gone forever" (Revelation 21:4). Our earthly bodies will be "transformed into heavenly bodies that will never die. When this happens... then at last the Scriptures will come true: 'Death is swallowed up in victory'" (1 Corinthians 15:53-54).

And all this, the restoration of our bodies and a new world, is dependent upon Jesus Christ returning to destroy death and, of course, his archenemy, the devil. Jesus first had to die as an atonement for our sin. And he did. He then had to conquer death through his resurrection to become our High Priest. And he did. And upon his second coming he will destroy death and the evil one to renew and restore all things.

> Only as a human being could he [Jesus] die, and only by dying could he break the power of the Devil, who had the power of death (Hebrews 2:14).

> Christ was raised first; then when Christ comes back, all his people will be raised. After that the end will come, when he will turn the Kingdom over to God the Father, having put down all enemies of every kind. For Christ must reign until he humbles all his enemies beneath his feet. And the last enemy to be destroyed is death (1 Corinthians 15:23-26).

> The Son of God appeared for this purpose, to destroy the works of the devil (1 John 3:8 NASB).

> When he has conquered all things, the Son will present himself to God, so that God, who gave his Son authority over all things, will be utterly supreme over everything everywhere (1 Corinthians 15:28).

Therefore:

> *We believe the truth that Jesus will return to resurrect our lifeless bodies into everlasting bodies, abolish sin, and restore the earth to a perfect world where he will live with us forever and forever.*

Jesus conquered death through his resurrection and will one day return to earth and exercise his power to cast the devil, death, and the grave into the lake of fire, known as the second death (see Revelation 20:10-15). Christ's resurrection is a prerequisite to his return and the entire restoration plan to give us new bodies and a new earth. Christ has promised to return and do this for us. And we can rest in his promise. As the writer of Hebrews said, "It is impossible for God to lie" (6:18).

EVIDENCE FOR LIFE AFTER DEATH

If you are looking forward to enjoying a perfectly restored earth where you will live forever with a new body, that says something very positive about your faith. Clearly you believe there is life after death. In this book, and no doubt in many other places, you have encountered strong evidence to strengthen your faith.

But you may not know there is further evidence that you have an eternal soul that will live on after this life. In fact, there are many evidences underscoring the belief there is life after death. Numerous books have been written on the subject, notably *Beyond Death* by J.P. Moreland and Gary Habermas. You might also enjoy two YouTube interviews I (Sean) conducted, one about the evidence for the soul and one about the evidence for near-death experiences.[2]

These and other resources provide solid evidence for life after death. We will highlight just four in this chapter.

1. ETERNITY PLANTED IN THE HUMAN HEART

Several years ago one of my (Sean's) former students relayed to me a conversation she had on the first day of her college English class. The teacher began by reading an article by a science-fiction writer who believed computers and technology would produce superhumans who would take over the world within the next few decades. This teacher was hoping these superhumans would be environmentalists so they would want to preserve our lesser-evolved selves. My former student raised her hand and asked, "How can a purely material thing spawn consciousness?" The teacher simply laughed and said, "Oh, I suppose you believe in the soul too?" And the whole class laughed as well.

A good number of educators and scientists today believe the physical world is the only reality and the human soul and an afterlife simply do not exist. Yet this view has not been the universal conclusion throughout history. In fact, virtually every culture from the very dawning of civilization has believed in a life beyond the grave in which some type of soul survives death of the body.

It is amazing, when you stop to think about it, that a universal belief in the afterlife has dominated historical thinking in spite of little empirical evidence to justify it. Of course, people do have reason to believe some things they have not experienced. They believe there is a Mount Everest even if they haven't climbed its rugged heights. They believe in the Great Barrier Reef off the coast of Australia even though they have never swum the depth of the Coral Sea. It is universally accepted that hundreds of swallows travel like clockwork in a 12,000-mile round-trip from Argentina to San Juan Capistrano each year, even though most people haven't witnessed the event firsthand.

In spite of the fact that most people have neither seen nor experienced these sights or events directly, they can be empirically observed and have been for many years—some for centuries. People record physical encounters and experiences such as these in writings, pictures, TV specials, and nature documentaries. So it's natural for others to accept them as fact because it's clear they can be physically proven.

But it is another matter when all cultures in history up to the present affirm their belief in something that seems impossible to record or experience and live to tell about it. Why is the belief that there is life after death affirmed almost unanimously among every culture in history without empirical evidence? It seems clear that the "sense" there is a life after death has been implanted deeply within the heart of humans. Wise King Solomon said that God "has planted eternity in the human heart, but even so, people cannot see the whole scope of God's work from beginning to end" (Ecclesiastes 3:11). Though humans cannot see into the next life, the vast majority believe it's there, and they have believed that since the dawn of time.

2. FREE WILL OF THE SOUL

In chapter 8 of my (Sean's) book on the "new atheism," *Is God Just a Human Invention?*, I deal with the fact that if we didn't have a soul we would not have the capacity to choose freely. Following is an adaptation from that chapter.

In 1996, American culture critic Tom Wolfe wrote a short essay titled "Sorry, but Your Soul Just Died." He discussed a new imaging technique that enabled neuroscientists to study the brain of a patient during a thought or emotion. He said, "Since consciousness and thought are entirely physical products of your brain and nervous system—and since your brain arrived fully imprinted at birth—what makes you think you have free will? Where is it going to come from?"[3] We agree with this much of the conclusion of Wolfe's argument. If there is no soul, then free will does not exist.

If materialism is true, then a human being is simply a body. If *you* are solely a material system, then you have no inner *self* that has the capacity to choose freely between options. You have no center of consciousness to make reasoned decisions. What seems to you to be a self capable of making choices is then merely a phantom projected by the mechanical processes of your brain, which is controlled solely by material processes reacting to external stimuli. Your physical systems operate completely by external programming, not by inner decision-making. Thus, if materialism is true, you do not have any genuine ability to choose your actions. What would seem to be a choice is actually predetermined by mechanical neural processes operating according to the way nature programmed your brain.

But this seems to contradict how we experience the world. We operate as if our minds freely make decisions that are carried out by the circuitry of our brains. For instance, if a stranger stops to open the door for us, we would likely describe his thought process by saying, "The polite man made up his *mind* to stay a moment longer and hold the door open for us." We would not say, "The circuitry in his brain caused him to turn around and hold the door open." We assume he *freely* chose to open the door, which is why we would likely express our thanks. Expressing thanks for an act of kindness would make no sense if we were both simply mechanical machines acting according to the inescapable programming of our brain circuitry.

The experience of making free choices seems so authentic that people cannot act as though that sense of choosing is counterfeit. Philosopher John Searle reminds us that if a waiter presents us with a choice of either pork or veal, we cannot rightly say, "Look, I'm a determinist. I'll just have to wait and see what order happens!"[4]

Denying free will comes at a high price, for it raises troubling questions: How is love meaningful if not *freely* chosen? How can we hold people morally accountable for their actions if they could not have done otherwise? What's the point of punishment? For that matter, what's the point of reward? Our capacity for free will clearly points to the reality of the human soul.[5]

3. NEAR-DEATH EXPERIENCES

Pam Reynolds had little option left. She had an aneurysm on her brain stem that could not be removed through conventional medical procedures. So she chose an experimental procedure called "cardiac standstill." Surgeons put her under general anesthesia to get her brain into a nonresponsive state. Then they lowered her body temperature to 60 degrees, stopped her heart to prevent blood flow to her brain, and put her into a "clinically dead" state.

With blood drained from Pam's brain, surgeons quickly removed the aneurysm and brought her back from the brink of death. *USA Today* featured the story in an article titled "The God Choice."[6] It quoted Pam as saying she consciously left her body and witnessed the entire operation from above the surgeons. She was able to describe intimate details of the operating room procedure, including how many surgeons and attendants were involved. She described the Midas Rex bone saw used to cut open her skull, the drill bits, blade containers, and so on. She was also able to relay specific detailed conversations between the surgeons she overheard. All the details were confirmed from the official hospital records. The doctors had no scientific explanation for Pam's "out of body" experience.

Thousands of references to near-death experiences (NDEs) reach back as far as the writings of Plato, three hundred years before Christ. In more recent times, the academic community has begun studying and taking note of the force of these accounts. In 2017, for example, the University of Missouri Press published a book based on a series of editorials and articles appearing in *Missouri Medicine: The Journal of the Missouri State Medical Association* from 2013 to 2015. They were written only by physicians who were and are esteemed in the field of near-death experiences *and* who personally had an NDE. They estimate between nine and 20 million people in the U.S. alone have experienced an NDE. Dr. Dean Radin, PhD, one of the foremost experts in using evidence and laboratory-based science to study NDEs, comes to this conclusion about the evidence: "Over a century of laboratory studies have investigated whether it is possible in principle for the mind to transcend the physical boundaries of the brain. The cumulative experimental database strongly indicates that it can."[7]

The power of near-death experiences is not so much in the lurid details related to heaven or hell that someone may report. Rather, it's that people somehow obtain information they simply could not obtain while being medically dead. These experiences demonstrate that consciousness continues after the body ceases to function. This doesn't prove life continues *forever* after death, but they do show consciousness is not tied simply to the physical body.

Atheists, who make up most of the critics of near-death experiences, point out that these phenomena are not valid proofs for life after death because the people involved weren't permanently dead. Technically that may be so, in that the people were not dead for numerous days and then rose from the grave to give their stories. But because someone isn't permanently dead doesn't mean they can't be temporarily dead. Some of these patients met the criteria of being medically dead but nonetheless were able to be revived. The real point of these reports is to gather information about what comes after death. And since we are lacking access to experiences from those who are permanently dead, the next best thing is to get information from those who have been very close to death or temporarily dead.

Yet we agree that while near-death experiences may refute the position held by some who say "nothing exists after death," they still do not provide empirical evidence the soul is immortal or indicate what the afterlife is really like. Some would contend, like the apostle Thomas after the resurrection, that they will not believe until they see better proof. Fair enough. Now let's consider the historical evidence that life continues after the grave.

4. REALITY OF THE UNSEEN WORLD

The apostle Paul wrote, "We are not fighting against people made of flesh and blood, but against the evil rulers and authorities of the unseen world...and against wicked spirits in the heavenly realms" (Ephesians 6:12). Paul speaks here of a world or a dimension that is real yet unseen to us as humans.

After Jesus died and rose from the grave, he demonstrated his ability to pass from the "seen world" into this "unseen world" at will. Remember when two of Jesus' disciples were walking to the village of Emmaus? Jesus came along and spoke with them, but they didn't recognize him. As they arrived home they invited this "stranger" to spend the evening with them. And as they were preparing to eat, they recognized the "stranger" was actually Jesus. "And at that moment he disappeared!" (Luke 24:31). Where did he go? He had a real body, yet he vanished into an "unseen world."

When these two disciples related their experiences to the rest of the disciples, Jesus again appeared before them. They were frightened and thought they were seeing a ghost. "'Why are you frightened?' he asked. 'Why do you doubt who I am? Look at my hands. Look at my feet. You can see that it's really me. Touch me and make sure that I am not a ghost, because ghosts don't have bodies, as you see that I do" (Luke 24:38-39).

Jesus had a real body that could move from the physical dimension in which we exist into an unseen physical dimension—the "unseen world" and "the heavenly realms" that Paul referred to. The Scriptures reliably document what the disciples saw and what Jesus did and said after he rose from the dead.

Here's why this is important: A few years ago, I (Sean) was speaking on a university campus in Southern California. One of the students asked how we could know if there is life after death. My response was to say, "The best way to know if there is life after death is to talk with someone who has died, come back, and can tell us about it." We have already seen the accounts from near-death experiences that strongly indicate life continues after physical death. But these accounts involve *near*-death experiences. With Jesus, we have the account of someone who died and rose on the third day. Jesus even said he was going to go prepare a place for his disciples with his Father (John 14:3).

So if the resurrection is true, as we saw in chapter 6, then we have reason to believe there is life after death. And if there is life after death, then the unseen world is real. While there is a range of evidences for the existence of the supernatural realm, including the evidence for the demonic, the ultimate proof comes from the resurrection of Jesus.[8] If Jesus has risen, then he is God. If Jesus has risen, then there is life after death. If Jesus has risen, then the unseen realm is real.

So there is solid evidence for life after death. The Jesus of history lived and died and rose again, making a way for us to live after death. We all sense a living soul existing within us, just as every society has in the earth's history. Our capacity for free will confirms the existence of an immaterial soul. Near-death experiences reveal that people experience consciousness and sensation beyond their physical bodies. Although much more evidence than we have explored here exists, these evidences add up to an intelligent, reasonable faith. We are able to see with spiritual eyes what Jesus promised we will experience with our new bodies on a new earth for all eternity. Jesus said, "Don't be troubled. You trust God, now trust in me. There are many rooms in my Father's home, and I am going to prepare a place for you. If this were not so, I would tell you plainly. When everything is ready, I will come and get you, so that you will always be with me where I am" (John 14:1-3).

EXPERIENCING ETERNAL JOY

Our new home was great. The smell of fresh paint was still in the air. There wasn't a single stain on the carpet. The apartment was brand-new, and Stephanie and I (Sean) were eager to move in. We did move, and while I enjoyed our new home for its freshness, its beauty, and its newness, I still reached out for the familiar. Certain things just fit who I am and how I function, and even with all the excitement and glamour of a new home, I didn't want those things to change. I wanted my desk placed in a similar position as in our last home. I liked the fact that our old, comfortable living room furniture was in our new place. I liked the newness, but I also loved and appreciated the familiar.

The home God has planned for you for all eternity will be a pristine, glorious new home, yet it will retain the comfortable familiarity you love. God is not creating a strange place for you that will require you to completely readjust your tastes and change who you are. Rather, he is restoring the old—getting rid of the scars, damage, and malfunctions inflicted by the fall. You will enjoy the restored beauty of the earth with its lush forests, majestic mountains, sparkling water, and an animal kingdom with the multitude of species no longer at odds with each other.

There will be no curse upon the New Earth, and the perfection God originally intended will emerge unsullied in all its wonder and glory. While everything will be fresh and new, you will see it as a place of complete familiarity. You will realize that this is where you were meant to be all along—in a place where you fit so perfectly that it's clear it was designed expressly to your innermost tastes. In fact, this will be exactly what God has done (see Isaiah 65; Revelation 21–22).

But more than that, your future home will be a place where you will be with your loved ones, a place where the word *family* takes on a whole new meaning. Our earthly families and friends can be great. We talk together, play together, eat together; we are there for one another. But Uncle Joe can become irritating, and Aunt Sarah can talk and talk and talk. We can tire at times of being with family and friends. Yet in our new home these relational imperfections will be removed along with the imperfections of the environment. People will relate to each other exactly as they should have related all along. Indeed, there will be nothing but bliss in every aspect of our lives because we will be entering into the pure joy of God himself.

Jesus gave an illustration of what it will be like to enter into the kingdom of heaven. He said the Master would pay us the greatest of compliments by saying, "Well done, my good and faithful servants." But there would be even more. He will go on to add, "You were faithful with a few things, I will put you in charge of many things; enter into the joy of your master" (Matthew 25:23 NASB). Our entry into the kingdom of heaven is so much more than just a reward; it is our initiation into a whole new realm of meaning and significance for our lives.

LIVING IN THE JOY OF GOD

Jesus told his followers to remain in his love, and then he said, "I have told you this so that my joy may be in you and that your joy may be complete"

(John 15:11 NIV). In our new eternal home we will enter into God's joy in a literal sense. What does this entering into God's joy look like? We get a hint of it in our experiences with our own children.

Several years ago Stephanie and I (Sean) took our family to a gigantic water park. It had twisty slides, wave machines, multicolored water caverns—the works. And I have to tell you, the little kid inside me came out. Stephanie and I played with Scottie in the wave pool, and it was a huge thrill to see our little boy having such fun. But Scottie was reluctant to play on all the elaborate enhancements to this "swimming pool." So I tried the twisty slide and the "shoot the rapids" slide first and explored the multicolored caverns on my own. Stephanie and Scottie watched me from the shallow side of this water world of joy.

Then I came up to Scottie and said, "Son, you've got to try this stuff—it's so much fun. Let me show you what a blast this is." He was still reluctant, but he saw something in my face and heard something in my voice that said, "Come on, do this with me, please." He sensed I was saying, "Enter into the joy of your father." And when he joined me on those slides, he had a blast—or should I say, a splash. As Scottie's loving father, it really did thrill me that he had so much fun.

This is a small sample of what it must mean when God says to us, "Enter into the joy of your Master." He is thrilled that we get to experience so much joy. Our first joy will be to see him face-to-face. The apostle John describes his own face-to-face encounter with the God-man in all his glory, saying, "His face was as bright as the sun in all its brilliance. When I saw him, I fell at his feet as dead" (Revelation 1:16-17). Of course, without a new and transformed body we couldn't even look fully into the face of God and live (see Exodus 33:20; 1 Timothy 6:16). But with new glorified bodies we will be able to see God's glorious face. And the first thing we will undoubtedly see is his expression of pure joy. To be in the presence of our God and Savior and to see him face-to-face will, in itself, be the greatest experience we will ever have.

But some readers may wonder why simply gazing into the face of God would be such a magnificent experience. We know we cannot fully explain why this will be such a joy, but it's such an important aspect of our life in God's restored kingdom that we must give it a shot.

No doubt every male reader of this book has seen the face of a beautiful woman that stopped him in his tracks. And every female has seen the face of a man who almost made her swoon. We recognize this awe in the presence of extreme beauty by using the term "stunning" to describe such faces. Now, add to this experience the factor of relationship—of love. Have you ever been in the presence of that special person—say, gazing across the table at him or her during a candlelight dinner—and thought you had never seen anything so glorious? Your breath came deeper and your heart beat faster, just to think you actually had a relationship with such a glorious creature.

Now take these experiences one step further. Think for a moment about the look of a young bride in all her radiant glory, waiting in the foyer of the church for the first chords of the "Wedding March" as she anticipates meeting her lover at the altar. She can hardly wait. Consider the gaze of a bridegroom, standing nervously with his best man as he expectantly looks down the aisle toward that door where she will soon appear. Then imagine his knees weakening with unbearable ecstasy as the music begins and that radiant face appears and approaches, filled with love and joy meant only for him. He is enraptured, transported, lifted into a realm of joy he has never imagined. This beautiful creature loves him so much she has chosen to spend her entire life devoted to him. It is the experience one never forgets, an experience that shapes one's entire life.

As when a father receives a prodigal son back home from a life on a pig farm, you will experience the thrilling ecstasy of hearing God say, "Enter into the joy of your Master."

The beauty of the most beautiful woman or the most handsome man in the world is merely a shadow of the beauty of the face of God, who is the source of all beauty. The love in the face of the most devoted bride or groom is merely a shadow of the love of God, who is the source and perfection of all love. To go far beyond the images of beauty and love that so overwhelm us even in this fallen world and behold the face that is the fountain of all beauty and love will simply be the greatest single moment we will ever experience.

It's an experience we can presently imagine only by comparison to the weaker manifestations of love and beauty we experience on this sin-damaged earth.

The inexpressible joy you will see on God's face at your arrival home has partly to do with his sense of completion. When God created a perfect world, he "saw that it was good." But of course it was ruined by sin. So after thousands of years of watching his beloved creation endure pain and suffering, he will soon experience the joy of seeing you as one of his redeemed children entering into what he originally designed—a paradise without sin where you will enjoy him and he will enjoy you forever. As when a father receives a prodigal son back home from life on a pig farm, you will experience the thrilling ecstasy of hearing God say, "Enter into the joy of your Master."

Experiencing God's Relational Joy

When God invites you to enter into his joy, he is allowing you to share a relational experience that has previously been beyond your emotional ability to comprehend. Just as I knew Scottie would be thrilled with the giant waterslide, God knows full well what his infinite love in perfect relationship will mean to you, even though you cannot presently comprehend it. Adam and Eve got a taste of it for but a fleeting moment. After Christ's return God will lead you into a relational glory and goodness with him that mere mortal minds and emotions cannot comprehend. But with a new body and a full eternity at your disposal, you will have all of forever to absorb it.

Just what is this relational joy of God? It is being invited to participate in the Source of love who fills the universe. The Father has eternally loved the Son. The Son has eternally loved the Father. The Holy Spirit has eternally loved the Father and the Son. The Triune Godhead has been in perfect relationship with each other for all eternity. Yet God is inviting us into their perfect circle of relationship.

A blissful eternal life is all about knowing God. Jesus prayed to his Father and said, "This is the way to have eternal life—to know you, the only true God, and Jesus Christ, the one you sent to earth" (John 17:3). Our firsthand experience of knowing God will grow throughout eternity, and our love of him will expand to contain it. As we come to know God's nature of unconditional acceptance, we will experience a secure love beyond measure. As we learn of his infinite grace, we will capture the strength and unity of his love. As we explore the humility and servanthood of God's heart, we will come to understand his true greatness. As we come to know the true essence of the Triune God with all his infinite devotion, faithfulness, goodness, and holiness, our capacity to love and grow to be like God will produce an ever-increasing enjoyment of his infinite joy and satisfaction throughout the ages of eternity. It will be as if God says to each of us, "My infinite joy as the Father, Son, and Holy Spirit is now in you because you are in us, and your joy is being made complete throughout time without end." That will become your reality when Christ returns and restores all things.

Experiencing God's Creative Joy

My little Scottie saw the joy in my face when he agreed to go down the waterslide with me. But he also experienced the thrill of actually going down the waterslide. While we will experience God's relational joy, we will also thrill at literally experiencing the New Earth God is preparing for us.

Imagine Jesus showing you around some of the sights of the new earth and saying, "Oh, you've got to try this fruit. This tastes so good I want you to enjoy it with me." Or think of him saying, "I love this mountain view; come stand here with me and enjoy the magnificent splendor of this vista I've restored for you." You have a God who is excited for you. He wants you to enjoy him and all that he has created for you.

It may be hard to grasp that God desires us to really enjoy our new home with him. But he does. Paul told Timothy to tell others not to put their hope in earthly wealth "but to put their hope in God, who richly provides us with everything for our enjoyment" (1 Timothy 6:17 NIV). He created this earth for our enjoyment, but sin ruined it all. In our new home sin will be eliminated, and we will enter into the joy of God's restored creation forever.

But God's invitation to enjoy his restored creation does not mean he intends us to be mere spectators. We will not be placed in an eternal rocking chair to passively enjoy the beauty of God's handiwork. Remember in Jesus' illustration the Master said, "You were faithful with a few things, I will put you in charge of many things" (Matthew 25:23 NASB). There will be things to do, projects we will be "in charge of."

Randy Alcorn quotes theologian Dallas Willard, who comments on Matthew 25:23:

> A place in God's creation order has been reserved for each one of us from before the beginning of cosmic existence. His plan is for us to develop, as apprentices to Jesus, to the point where we can take our place in the ongoing creativity of the universe.

Alcorn then goes on to say:

> God is grooming us for leadership. He's watching to see how we demonstrate our faithfulness. He does that through his apprenticeship program, one that prepares us for Heaven. Christ is not simply preparing a place for us; he is preparing us for that place.[9]

After God created the original earth he told Adam and Eve, "Be fruitful and increase in number; fill the earth and subdue it. Rule over the fish of the sea and the birds of the air and over every living creature that moves on the ground" (Genesis 1:28 NIV). God had a responsibility in mind for his original created family of humans, and he has a responsibility for his future redeemed children. In his vision John saw those who were washed in the blood of the Lamb given a place at "the throne of God," where they will "serve him day and night" (Revelation 7:15 NIV). So our present faithfulness to God is rewarded with future responsibilities in our new home.

At first glance, this promise may not immediately appeal to you. You might think, *I'm stressed out with all the responsibilities piled on me here. I was hoping heaven would free me from all that.* Randy Alcorn answers this fear with an insightful perspective:

> Service is a reward, not a punishment. This idea is foreign to people who dislike their work and only put up with it until retirement. We think that faithful work should be rewarded by a vacation for the rest of our lives. But God offers us something very different: more work, more responsibilities, increased opportunities, along

with greater abilities, resources, wisdom, and empowerment. We will have sharp minds, strong bodies, clear purpose, and unabated joy. The more we serve Christ now, the greater our capacity will be to serve him in Heaven.[10]

There are many things we may not know about the new heaven and new earth. What exactly we can expect to be doing for all eternity is still veiled in mystery. It is a great secret yet to be revealed. But we do know this: Whatever task he has planned for you will fit you exactly. When you receive your assignment, you will suddenly understand just what your particular talents were meant to accomplish. It will be your dream job—the path to fulfillment of all your deepest ambitions.

The place we live in now is only our temporary world. God is preparing for us a new place that will be our "dream home" because we will enter into God's relational and creative joy forever. John "heard a loud shout from the throne saying, 'Look, the home of God is now among his people! He will live with them, and they will be his people. God himself will be with them. He will remove all of their sorrows, and there will be no more death or sorrow or crying or pain. For the old world and its evils are gone forever'" (Revelation 21:3-4). Our future home will be everything we ever dreamed of and much more.

FULFILLING YOUR DESTINY

Have you ever seen the bumper sticker that reads: "Don't Follow Me, I'm Lost"? Some people live their lives wandering about with little sense of direction or sense of mission in life. But if there was ever a person with a focused mission in life, it was Jesus. And he has passed that mission on to each of us.

Jesus came to earth to lay down his life as a sacrifice to redeem us and bring us back to God and establish his kingdom. Jesus' message was all about this new kingdom to come. He "began to preach, 'Turn from your sins and turn to God, because the Kingdom of Heaven is near'" and from that point on "Jesus traveled throughout Galilee teaching in the synagogues, preaching everywhere the Good News about the Kingdom" (Matthew 4:17, 23).

Practically everything Jesus said and did was an effort to contrast the two kingdoms—the kingdom of heaven and the kingdom of this world. He said to his Father that his followers "do not belong to the world" and "are not part of this world any more than I am" (John 17:14, 16). Our real home isn't here. Jesus doesn't want us to get comfortable living here; that is why he said, "Don't store up treasures here on earth, where they can be eaten by moths and get rusty" (Matthew 6:19). He wants us to see this life and our temporal world from his perspective—an eternal perspective.

The apostle Paul warned us about those whose "god is their appetite"— their craving for earthly pleasures—"and all they think about is this life here on earth. But we are citizens of heaven," Paul said, "where the Lord Jesus Christ lives. And we are eagerly waiting for him to return as our Savior" (Philippians 3:19-20). Living as "citizens of heaven" while residing on this earth isn't easy, especially when we face life's trials, discouragements, and difficulties.

Living in this world but not being of this world, of course, does not insulate us from its pain and heartache. We may experience the joy of Christ in our hearts while suffering the physical pain of a disease, the financial loss of unemployment, or the emotional loss of a disrupted or destroyed relationship or the death of a loved one.

We may believe Christ's mission will be complete one day when he returns to destroy sin and death and restore us to a new heaven and earth, but that belief can sometimes grow weak in the face of tragedy. Jesus tried to prepare his own disciples for the impending tragedy of his death when he said, "Truly, you will weep and mourn over what is going to happen to me, but the world will rejoice. You will grieve, but your grief will suddenly turn to wonderful joy when you see me again...I have told you all this so that you may have peace in me. Here on earth you will have many trials and sorrows. But take heart, because I have overcome the world" (John 16:20, 33).

Jesus was not caught off guard on that frightful day on Calvary. He knew that day was coming; he knew exactly what he was doing; and he was masterfully in control. That's why he told his disciples, "Don't be troubled. You trust God, now trust in me" (John 14:1). Yes, he knew he was about to die, but he also knew death would have no power over him. He was appealing to his followers to rest in him and commit their troubles to him. "Have peace in me," he said. It was as if he were saying, "Trust me no matter what, for I'm going to work things out for your good and my glory. What will seem like a disaster with my death is really for your good, because through it all I will redeem you and restore everything back to what I originally planned. I am the God of Redemption, *and* I am also the God of Restoration."

WHERE AM I GOING?

It's not hard to see now, after the fact, that Christ was in control of the situation of his death. His resurrection from the grave proves it. We can see how he took his torturous death and transformed it into the means of salvation for the human race.

We could chide the disciples for not trusting in Christ enough and for not believing he knew what he was doing. But as we said, it's not so easy to exhibit that kind of trust in the midst of trials or tragedy. It's hard to have a spirit of gratitude, courage, and optimism unless, of course, we view this temporal world with all its trials from God's eternal perspective.

In Romans 8, the apostle Paul gives us several eternal insights. He first says, "Even we Christians, although we have the Holy Spirit within us as a foretaste of future glory, also groan to be released from pain and suffering" (verse 23). This passage makes it clear that optimism doesn't come from denying our present pain. Paul goes on to say that "the Holy Spirit helps us in our distress…And we know that God causes everything to work together for the good of those who love God and are called according to his purpose for them" (verses 26, 28). Paul had the answer: We can place our trust in God because he is sovereign and obviously knows what he's doing. When we do this, the Holy Spirit, who lives inside each individual Christian, will cause everything to work together for good.

This does not mean everything will work together for our comfort, or everything will work together to spare us difficulties, pain, or trials. It is not a belief that says everything that happens to God's people in this death-cursed world is somehow good. Sickness is not good. Death is not good. Pain is not good. Sorrow, sadness, and suffering are not good. However, by trusting in God, not only as our Savior but also as our sovereign Lord who does all things well, we can be confident he will cause all things—even the bad things that happen to us—to work together for our good and his glory. Our confidence in and conviction about a God who loves us beyond words and causes all things, even tragedies, to work together for good can produce within us a spirit of gratitude, courage, and optimism in the face of life—and death.

It is faith in a sovereign God that moves us beyond a human perspective on life to an eternal perspective. The apostle Paul was a living example of this eternal mind-set. Listen to his heart of gratitude as he shares his God-inspired letter to the church at Corinth. Read the words carefully. Note how his faith in the resurrected Christ provided him with a sense of courage and optimism, even in the most difficult of times:

> We are pressed on every side by troubles, but we are not crushed and broken. We are perplexed, but we don't give up and quit. We are hunted down, but God never abandons us. We get knocked down, but we get up again and keep going…We know that the same God who raised our Lord Jesus will also raise us with Jesus and present us to himself along with you. All of these things are for your benefit…

> That is why we never give up. Though our bodies are dying, our spirits are being renewed every day. For our present troubles are quite small and won't last very long. Yet they produce for us an immeasurably great glory that will last forever! So we don't look at the troubles we can see right now; rather, we look forward to what we have not yet seen. For the troubles we see will soon be over, but the joys to come will last forever (2 Corinthians 4:8-9, 14-18).

What an amazing approach to life's problems! Paul didn't run from difficulties in order to avoid pain, nor did he try to deny that difficulties existed in his life. He acknowledged his suffering and viewed the trials of life from an eternal perspective, knowing that the God of all comfort was there to ease his pain (see 1 Corinthians 2:3-4). He trusted in a sovereign God who would cause everything to work together for good. Paul's faith in a God who had everything under control enabled him to see the difficulties of this life as producing "an immeasurably great glory that will last forever!"

Because of the resurrection, we are destined to live forever in new bodies on a new earth, an existence that will be so enjoyable anything "we suffer now is nothing compared to the glory [God] will give us later." For we "wait anxiously for that day when God will give us our full rights as his children, including the new bodies he has promised us" (Romans 8:18, 23).

God's kingdom defines where we are going. For we are destined to have our struggles, suffering, and death transformed into blessings, joy, and a life at home with God for all eternity.

Our "priceless inheritance" is a state of being in which we will be given "full rights" to reign with Christ in the new kingdom of heaven on a new earth. It is a kingdom "pure and undefiled, beyond the reach of change and decay" (1 Peter 1:4). This kingdom that will completely encompass the new earth is our destiny. God's kingdom defines where we are going. For we are destined to have our struggles, suffering, and death transformed into blessings, joy, and a life at home with God for all eternity. We will inherit a new heaven and a new earth as our eternal home. This is our destiny.

Christ is saying to us, "Trust me. I am alive and in control of every situation. I will take your struggles and change them into blessings. I will take your suffering and turn it into joy. And as your inheritance I will give you a new heaven and a new earth as your eternal home. How can I do that? I'm the sovereign, almighty King of the universe, who can do all things and who causes everything to work together for the good of those who love me and are called according to my purpose. So trust in me, no matter what."[11]

OUR MISSION

Our destiny may be eternal life at home with God, but we aren't there yet. "So be truly glad!" the apostle Peter said. "There is wonderful joy ahead, even though it is necessary for you to endure many trials for a while" (1 Peter 1:6). And Peter made it clear why God is keeping us here. He has a mission for us to accomplish.

"We are looking forward to the new heavens and new earth he has promised," Peter said, "a world where everyone is right with God. And so, dear friends, while you are waiting for these things to happen, make every effort to live a pure and blameless life. And be at peace with God. And remember, the Lord is waiting so that people have time to be saved" (2 Peter 3:13-15). We may be waiting to live on the new earth, but it's not time yet. The Lord appears to be waiting to usher in that final day so those around us still have time to trust in him. Our task here is to participate in God's mission to reach these people by living pure and blameless lives that reflect his nature and draw others to him.

During the years of Jesus' life on earth, "God was in Christ, reconciling the world to himself" (2 Corinthians 5:19). Now, Christ is in us, and Paul says that God "has committed to us the message of reconciliation. We are therefore Christ's ambassadors, as though God were making his appeal through us" (verses 19-20 NIV). He wants to involve us in his mission of drawing people to him by the attitudes we have, the things we say, and the way we act— especially in times of adversity and trouble.

God did not cause any of the suffering or difficulties you may be going through right now. But God is not caught off guard or blindsided by your suffering. He knows that in this fallen world, suffering is inevitable. Yet your sovereign God causes all your circumstances—both the good and the bad— to work together for good. As you make Christ more and more at home in your life, the gracious, long-suffering Spirit of God can be seen in your suffering. And in those circumstances, people clearly see Christ.

We often seem to fulfill Christ's mission to reach others most effectively when we are enduring times of crisis, suffering, or persecution. Nearly all of us can exhibit love, joy, peace, patience, and so on when the wind is at our back and we're sailing high. But how many people display gratitude, courage, and optimism in the midst of a storm? Displaying these attributes in such times is what causes people to sit up and take notice: when tragedy strikes, when you're hurting, when you're mistreated.

Think of the trials, struggles, or suffering you may be going through right now. It's not a sin to feel discouraged or frustrated with the tests of life. But can you sense how God wants to be there for you with his love, support, and comfort? What gives him pleasure is to fill you so completely with an abundance of his joy and blessing during your difficulties that you actually become grateful for the trials you're experiencing. And when people see how courageous and optimistic you are during your troubled times, they will be drawn to Christ.

When we fully submit ourselves to God, we can be especially encouraged when trouble strikes or problems come our way. It is during these times that we can become aware we have been assigned a mission, if we are willing to accept it—a mission to exhibit a Christlike spirit and share the love of Christ with those around us. Far from being a cause for complaint or self-pity, we should see such instances as great compliments. God trusts us enough to bestow on us the great honor of reflecting his glory in circumstances that might discourage those who do not trust him.

As you can see, sharing Christ with others doesn't have to be thought of as a chore or obligation. Rather, it is an opportunity to reveal Christ through our lives to others. It does require, however, a basic understanding of what to say and how to share a simple presentation of the gospel as we explained in chapter 7. But once that is learned, it's a matter of developing a lifestyle that makes you a walking example of Christ. As people recognize you as a person who lives in a temporal world with an eternal perspective, they too will catch a glimpse of your King and his kingdom, the King who has prepared you "an eternal house in heaven, not built by human hands" (2 Corinthians 5:1 NIV).[12]

NOTES

INTRODUCTION: THE REAL MEANING OF TRUTH

1. Adapted from Josh McDowell, Bob Hostetler, and David H. Bellis, *Beyond Belief to Convictions* (Wheaton, IL: Tyndale House Publishers, 2002), 52-53.

2. "Hardwired to Connect: The New Scientific Case for Authoritative Communities," The Commission on Children at Risk, 2003.

3. As quoted by Sean McDowell, *Apologetics for a New Generation* (Eugene, OR: Harvest House Publishers, 2009), 142.

4. J.P. Moreland, *Love Your God with All Your Mind* (Colorado Springs, CO: NavPress, 1997), 25.

TRUTH ONE: GOD EXISTS

1. Pat Brennan, "Our Milky Way Galaxy: How Big Is Space?" April 2, 2019, NASA EXOPLANET EXPLORATION, https://exoplanets.nasa.gov/blog/1563/our-milky-way-galaxy-how-big-is-space/.

2. Joe S. McIlhaney, Jr. and Freda McKissic Bush, *Hooked: The Brain Science on How Casual Sex Affects Human Development* (Chicago, IL: Northfield, 2008, updated 2019), 26.

3. Wikipedia, article: "Age and Size of the Universe" at www.en.wikipedia.org/wiki/universe, 2009.

4. Sean McDowell and Jonathan Morrow, *Is God Just a Human Invention? And Seventeen Other Questions Raised by the New Atheists* (Grand Rapids, MI: Kregel, 2010), 74-76.

5. William Lane Craig interviewed by Lee Strobel, *The Case for a Creator* (Grand Rapids, MI: Zondervan, 2004), 109.

6. William A. Dembski and Sean McDowell, *Understanding Intelligent Design* (Eugene, OR: Harvest House Publishers, 2008), 122-123.

7. Here is the calculation for these estimates: 2 meters of DNA / cell 30,000,000,000,000 cells / person = 60,000,000,000,000 meters of DNA / person. 60,000,000,000,000 meters DNA / person / 294,320,000,000 meters / round trip to the sun = 203.8 round trips of DNA to the sun / person.

8. Hill Roberts and Mark Whorton, *Holman QuickSource Guide to Understanding Creation* (Nashville, TN: B & H Publishing, 2008), 109-110.

9. Ibid., 133-134.

10. Sean McDowell, *Ethix* (Nashville, TN: Broadman & Holman Publishers, 2006), 49-50; embedded citation from Fyodor Dostoyevsky, *The Brothers Karamazov* (New York, NY: Bantam Books, 1970), 95.

11. Bertrand Russell, *Why I Am Not a Christian* (New York, NY: Simon & Schuster, 1957), 107.

12. Adapted from Josh McDowell and Thomas Williams, *In Search of Certainty* (Wheaton, IL: Tyndale House Publishers, 2003), 66.

13. Charles W. Colson, *The Faith* (Grand Rapids, MI: Zondervan, 2008), 171.

TRUTH TWO: GOD'S WORD CAN BE TRUSTED

1. Adapted from Josh McDowell, Bob Hostetler, and David H. Bellis, *Beyond Belief to Convictions* (Wheaton, IL: Tyndale House Publishers, 2002), 157-158, 163-165; and www.seanmcdowell.org.

2. Ibid., 166-178.

3. Josh McDowell and Sean McDowell, *Evidence That Demands a Verdict* (Nashville, TN: Nelson, 2017), 98.

4. Ibid., 102.

5. Josh McDowell, *The New Evidence That Demands a Verdict* (Nashville, TN: Nelson, 1999), 79.

6. Adapted from McDowell, *Evidence*, chart, 56.

7. Ibid., 47-48.

8. Daniel B. Wallace, editor, *Revisiting the Corruption of the New Testament: Manuscript, Patristic, and Apocryphal Evidence* (Grand Rapids, MI: Kregel Publications, 2011), 28-29.

9. We are not saying that differences in the manuscripts never touch on important theological issues. But no theological issue hangs on a single textually unclear segment of the Bible. Our theology is constructed from a web of data across the Bible. For instance, a claim to Jesus' deity has some textual ambiguity in John 1:18, but there is plenty of other clear manuscript support for Jesus' deity elsewhere.

10. Adapted from McDowell, Hostetler, and Bellis, 167-169, 176-179.

11. Titus Kennedy, *Unearthing the Bible* (Eugene, OR: Harvest House Publishers, 2020), 28-29. Used with permission.

12. Ibid., 48-49.

13. Ibid., 74-75.

14. Ibid., 94-95.

15. Ibid., 98-99.

16. Ibid., 130-131.

17. Ibid., 160-161.

18. This chapter is adapted from chapters 6 and 7 of Josh McDowell and Bob Hostetler, *Right from Wrong* (Nashville, TN: Word Publishing, 1994).

19. S.I. McMillen, *None of These Diseases* (Westwood, NJ: Spire Books, 1968), from the Preface.

20. This chapter is adapted from chapters 10 and 11 of Josh McDowell and Bob Hostetler, *Right from Wrong* (Nashville, TN: Word Publishing, 1994).

21. "Ex-Porn Star Becomes a Pastor: The Story of Joshua Broome," YouTube, https://www.youtube.com/watch?v=WqPglqhDXBQ&t=3s.

22. Rob Palkovitz, "Gendered Parenting and Children's Well-Being," in *Gender and Parenthood: Biological and Scientific Perspectives*, ed., by Bradford Wilcox and Kathleen Kover Kline (New York: Columbia University Press, 2013), 223.

23. Palkovitz, "Gendered," 226.

24. Palkovitz, "Gendered," entire paragraph, 226-227.

TRUTH THREE: ALL HAVE SINNED

1. Adapted from Josh McDowell and Thomas Williams, *The Relational Word* (Holiday, FL: Green Key Books, 2006), 21-24.

2. Aldous Huxley, "Confessions of a Professed Atheist," *Report: Perspective on the News*, vol. 3 (June 1966), 19.

3. The State of Theology, https://thestateoftheology.com/.

4. Clay Jones, "We Don't Take Human Evil Seriously, so We Don't Understand Why We Suffer." Used with permission.

5. Langdon Gilkey, *Shantung Compound: The Story of Men and Women Under Pressure* (San Francisco: Harper, 1966), 92. Gilkey continues, "What is unique about human existence 'on the margin' is not that people's characters change for better or worse, for they do not. It is that the importance and so the 'emotional voltage' of every issue is increased greatly. Now much more vulnerable than before, we are more inclined to be aware of our own interests, more frightened if they are threatened, and thus much more determined to protect them. A marginal existence neither improves men nor makes them wicked; it places a premium on every action, and in doing so reveals the actual inward character that every man has always possessed."

6. Gilkey, *Shantung Compound*, 92.

7. This paragraph and the two immediately above it were adapted and include quoted material from Clay Jones, "We Don't Take Human Evil Seriously, so We Don't Understand Why We Suffer." Used with permission.

8. Adapted from Josh McDowell and Thomas Williams, *The Relational Word* (Holiday, FL: Green Key Books, 2006), 24-25.

TRUTH FOUR: GOD BECAME HUMAN

1. C.S. Lewis, *Mere Christianity* (New York, NY: Macmillan, 1960), 40-41.

2. Diagram drawn from Josh McDowell, *Evidence That Demands a Verdict* (Nashville, TN: Thomas Nelson Publishers, 2017), 197.

3. Dr. Jeff Myers, *Truth Changes Everything* (Grand Rapids, MI: Baker Books, 2022).

4. Gary R. Collins, quoted in Lee Strobel, *The Case for Christ* (Grand Rapids, MI: Zondervan, 1998), 147.

5. Drawn from Josh McDowell and Sean McDowell, *More Than a Carpenter* (Wheaton, IL: Tyndale House Publishers, 2009), 30-39.

6. Adapted from chapter 4 of Josh McDowell, Bob Hostetler, and David H. Bellis, *Beyond Belief to Convictions* (Wheaton, IL: Tyndale House Publishers, 2002), 68-71.

7. Drawn from chapter 5 of Josh McDowell, Bob Hostetler, and David H. Bellis, *Beyond Belief to Convictions* (Wheaton, IL: Tyndale House Publishers, 2002), 92-93.

8. Drawn from David and Teresa Ferguson, *Never Alone* (Wheaton, IL: Tyndale House Publishers, 2001), 87-88.

9. Drawn from Josh McDowell, Bob Hostetler, and David H. Bellis, *Beyond Belief to Convictions* (Wheaton, IL: Tyndale House Publishers, 2002), 147-149.

TRUTH FIVE: JESUS WAS GOD'S PERFECT SACRIFICE

1. Charles Wesley (1707–1788), Robert K. Brown and Mark R. Norton, compilers, *The One Year Book of Hymns* (Wheaton, IL: Tyndale House Publishers, 1995), March 29.

2. Max Lucado, *3:16: The Numbers of Hope* (Nashville, TN: Thomas Nelson Publishers, 2007), 42.

3. Charles W. Colson, *The Faith* (Grand Rapids, MI: Zondervan, 2008), 164-165.

4. Jeff Myers, *Handoff* (Dayton, TN: Legacy Worldwide, 2008), 128.

TRUTH SIX: JESUS ROSE FROM THE DEAD

1. Gerd Lüdemann, *What Really Happened to Jesus: A Historical Approach to the Resurrection*, tr. John Bowden (Louisville, KY: Westminster John Knox Press, 1995), 1.

2. Stephen T. Davis, *Risen Indeed* (Grand Rapids, MI: Eerdmans, 1993), 79-80.

3. George Hanson, *The Resurrection and the Life* (London, England: William Clowes & Son, 1911), 24.

4. John Dominic Crossan, *Jesus: A Revolutionary Biography* (San Francisco, CA: Harper Collins, 1991), 145.

5. David Friedrich Strauss, *The Life of Jesus for People*, 2nd ed., vol. 1 (London, England: William & Norgate, 1879), 412.

6. Adapted from Josh McDowell, Bob Hostetler, and David H. Bellis, *Beyond Belief to Convictions* (Wheaton, IL: Tyndale House Publishers, 2002), 261-270.

7. Dr. Sean McDowell, "Debunking the Hallucination Hypothesis: Leading Doctors Speak on Jesus," YouTube video, 58:00, https://www.youtube.com/watch?v=iT12FnjJLKI.

8. Drawn from McDowell, Hostetler, Bellis, *Beyond Belief to Convictions*, 271-273.

9. Dan Cohn-Sherbok, "The Resurrection of Jesus: A Jewish View," in *Resurrection Reconsidered*, Gavin D'Costa, gen. ed. (Oxford, UK: Oneworld Publications, 1996), 200.

10. N.T. Wright, "Christian Origins and the Resurrection of Jesus: The Resurrection as a Historical Problem," *Sewanee Theological Review*, vol. 41:2 (Easter 1998), 111, emphasis added.

11. N.T. Wright, "The Transforming Reality of the Bodily Resurrection," in *The Meaning of Jesus: Two Visions* by N.T. Wright and Marcus Borg (New York, NY: HarperCollins Publishers, 1999), 115.

12. Michael Licona, "Paul on the Nature of the Resurrection Body," in *Buried Hope or Risen Savior: The Search for the Jesus Tomb*, ed. Charles L. Quarles (Nashville, TN: B&H Academic, 2008), 177-198.

13. Stephen T. Davis, *Risen Indeed* (Grand Rapids, MI: Eerdmans, 1993), 56.

14. Norman I. Geisler, *Baker Encyclopedia of Christian Apologetics* (Grand Rapids, MI: Baker Books, 1999), 662.

15. Drawn from McDowell and McDowell, *Evidence for the Resurrection*, 204-206.

16. Paul Rhodes Eddy and Gregory A. Boyd, *The Jesus Legend* (Grand Rapids, MI: Baker Books, 2007), 142.

17. McDowell and McDowell, *Evidence for the Resurrection*, 232-233.

18. Drawn from Josh McDowell and Sean McDowell, *Evidence for the Resurrection* (Ventura, CA: Regal Publishing, 2009), 57-58.

19. Drawn from McDowell and McDowell, *Evidence for the Resurrection*, 64-66.

20. C.S. Lewis, *Mere Christianity* (New York, NY: Collier Books, 1960), 118.

21. Max Lucado, *When God Whispers Your Name* (Dallas, TX: Word Publishing, 1994), 101.

22. Calvin Miller, *Into the Depths of God* (Minneapolis, MN: Bethany House Publishers, 2000), 15.

TRUTH SEVEN: WE ARE JUSTIFIED THROUGH FAITH

1. Drawn from Bascom Palmer Eye Institute, "Cataracts," www.bpei.med.miami.edu/site/disease/disease_cataracts.asp (2009).

2. Drawn from Josh McDowell, Bob Hostetler, and David H. Bellis, *Beyond Belief to Convictions* (Wheaton, IL: Tyndale House Publishers, 2002), 71-76.

3. Adapted from Josh McDowell and Sean McDowell, *More Than a Carpenter* (Wheaton, IL: Tyndale House Publishers, 2005), 160-165.

TRUTH EIGHT: CHRISTIANS ARE A TRANSFORMED PEOPLE

1. Adapted from Wikipedia, article "Caterpillar," www.wikipedia.org/wiki/caterpillar#behavior.

2. Drawn from Jeffrey A. Bogue, *Living Naked* (Akron, OH: Living Naked Press, 2009), 123-126.

3. Drawn from Francis Collins, *The Language of God* (New York, NY: Free Press, 2006), 19-20.

4. Drawn from Jeffrey A. Bogue, *Living Naked* (Akron, OH: Living Naked Press, 2009), 42-44, 45-48.

5. Adapted from Josh McDowell, *See Yourself as God Sees You* (Wheaton, IL: Tyndale House Publishers, 1999), 110-120.

TRUTH NINE: WE WORSHIP ONE GOD IN THREE PERSONS

1. Alan Hirsch, *The Forgotten Ways* (Grand Rapids, MI: Brazos Press, 2006), 18.

2. Adapted from Sean McDowell, *Ethix* (Nashville, TN: Broadman & Holman Publishers, 2006), 15.

3. Bill Bright, *Have You Made the Wonderful Discovery of the Spirit-Filled Life?* (Peachtree City, GA: New Life Resources of Campus Crusade for Christ International, 1966, 1995, 2000, 2008). *Have You Made the Wonderful Discovery of the Spirit-Filled Life?* written by Bill Bright © 1966–2010 Bright Media Foundation (BMF) and Campus Crusade for Christ International (CCCI). All rights reserved. www.campus crusade.com. Included with permission.

TRUTH TEN: GOD'S KINGDOM IS AT HAND

1. This section is based on material that appears in a self-published work by Dave Bellis, et al., *God Is Up to Something* (Hamilton, OH: The WordsWorth Group, 2008), 1-2. Used with permission.

2. C.S. Lewis, *Mere Christianity* (New York, NY: Macmillan, 1943), 36.

3. Christopher Hitchens, *God Is Not Great: How Religion Poisons Everything* (New York, NY: Twelve Books, 2007), 13.

4. F.W. Nietzsche, *The Antichrist*, tr. H.L. Mencken (Torrance, CA: The Noontide Press, 1980), 180.

5. Sherwood Eliot Wirt, *The Social Conscience of the Evangelical* (New York, NY: Harper and Row, 1968), 31.

6. "Basil of Caesarea," http://en.wikipedia.org/wiki/St_Basil.

7. Charles W. Colson, *The Faith* (Grand Rapids, MI: Zondervan, 2008), 169.

8. Trevor Yaxley with Carolyn Vanderwal, *William and Catherine: The Legacy of the Booths, Founders of the Salvation Army* (Bloomington, MN: Bethany House Publishers, 2003), 221.

9. Wikipedia, article: "The Salvation Army," http://en.wikipedia.org/wiki/The_Salvation_Army, 2009.

10. www.answers.com/topic/henry-dunant.

11. See the writings of Jonathan Hill, *What Has Christianity Ever Done for Us?: How It Shaped the Modern World* (Downers Grove, IL: InterVarsity Press, 2005); Rodney Stark, *For the Glory of God: How Monotheism Led to Reformations, Science, Witch-Hunts, and the End of Slavery* (Princeton, NJ: Princeton University Press, 2003); Rodney Stark, *The Victory of Reason: How Christianity Led to Freedom, Capitalism, and Western Success* (New York, NY: Random House, 2005); and Vincent Carroll and Dave Shiflett, *Christianity on Trial: Arguments against Anti-Religious Bigotry* (San Francisco, CA: Encounter Books, 2002).

12. James W. Sire, *The Universe Next Door* (Downers Grove, IL IVP Academic; Sixth Edition, 2020), 6.

TRUTH ELEVEN: THE CHURCH IS ALIVE AND ON A MISSION

1. Robert Webber, *Listening to the Beliefs of Emerging Churches* (Grand Rapids, MI: Zondervan, 2007), 9.

2. Bob Roberts Jr., *Transformation* (Grand Rapids, MI: Zondervan, 2006), 19-20.

3. Dave Bellis, et al., *God Is Up to Something* (Hamilton, OH: The WordsWorth Group, 2008), 22-23.

4. Bob Roberts Jr., *The Multiplying Church* (Grand Rapids, MI: Zondervan, 2008), 25.

5. Robert Webber, *Journey to Jesus* (Nashville, TN: Abingdon Press, 2001), 102-103.

6. Story adapted from David Ferguson, *The Never Alone Church* (Wheaton, IL: Tyndale House Publishers, 1998), 77-78.

7. Robert Webber, *The Younger Evangelical* (Grand Rapids, MI: Baker Books, 2002), 29.

TRUTH TWELVE: CHRIST WILL RETURN

1. Randy Alcorn, *Heaven* (Wheaton, IL: Tyndale House Publishers, 2004), 101.

2. Dr. Sean McDowell, "Evidence for the Soul: A Conversation with J.P. Moreland," YouTube, https://www.youtube.com/watch?v=oD7OCHl1odA; Dr. Sean McDowell, "Near-Death Experiences: The Evidence," YouTube, https://www.youtube.com/watch?v=fhqLc6GPu-U.

3. Tom Wolfe, "Sorry, but Your Soul Just Died," originally published in *Forbes ASAP* (1996). Reprinted with permission at http://orthodoxytoday.org/articles/Wolfe-Sorry-But-Your-Soul-Just-Died.php.

4. John Searle, *Freedom and Neurobiology* (New York, NY: Columbia University Press, 2007).

5. Sean McDowell and Jonathan Morrow, *Is God Just a Human Invention?: And Seventeen Other Questions Raised by the New Atheists* (Grand Rapids, MI: Kregel, 2010), chapter 8.

6. Barbara Bradley Hagerty, "The God Choice," USA Today, June 22, 2009, 9a.

7. Dean Radin, "Out of One's Mind or Beyond the Brain? The Challenge of Interpreting Near-Death Experiences," in *The Science of Near-Death Experiences*, ed. by John C. Hagan III (Columbia, MO: University of Missouri Press, 2017), 29.

8. Billy Hallowell, *Playing with Fire: A Modern Investigation into Demons, Exorcism, and Ghosts* (Nashville, TN: Emanate Books, 2020).

9. Randy Alcorn, *Heaven* (Wheaton, IL: Tyndale House Publishers, 2004), 215.

10. Ibid., 226.

11. Drawn from Josh McDowell, Bob Hostetler, and David H. Bellis, *Beyond Belief to Convictions* (Wheaton, IL: Tyndale House Publishers, 2002), 246-252.

12. Ibid., 279-280.

ABOUT THE AUTHORS

As a young man, **Josh McDowell** was a skeptic of Christianity. However, while attending Kellogg College in Michigan, he was challenged by a group of Christian students to intellectually examine the claims of Jesus Christ. Josh accepted the challenge. Then in a museum library in London, England, where he was studying ancient biblical artifacts, he experienced a breakthrough moment. The words "It's true!" have resonated throughout his ministry ever since. For more than 60 years, Josh has shared both his testimony and the evidence that God is real and relevant to our everyday lives with the world.

Through his work with Cru and the global outreach of Josh McDowell Ministry, millions of people in 139 countries have been exposed to the love of Christ. Josh is the author or coauthor of more than 150 books, including such classics as *More Than a Carpenter* and *Evidence That Demands a Verdict.*

Josh and his wife, Dottie, have been married for more than 50 years and have four grown children and 11 grandchildren.

Sean McDowell, PhD, is a professor of apologetics at Talbot School of Theology, Biola University. He is the author, editor, or coauthor of more than 20 books. Sean is also active on social media, using a range of platforms to equip Christians to live out their faith with confidence and boldness and to provide them with tools to disciple the next generation of young people. He is also a popular YouTuber, discussing apologetics, worldview, and other "hot" topics from a biblical perspective.

Sean and his wife, Stephanie, have been married for more than two decades and have three children. They live in Southern California.

Serving others until the whole world hears about Jesus.

Josh McDowell
A CRU MINISTRY

Sharing Truth With
A New Generation

SeanMcDowell.org

🐦 Sean_McDowell
🎵 Sean_McDowell
📷 SeanMcDowell
▶️ Dr. Sean McDowell
Podcast: The Think Biblically Podcast

To learn more about Harvest House books and
to read sample chapters, visit our website:

www.HarvestHousePublishers.com

HARVEST HOUSE PUBLISHERS
EUGENE, OREGON